**Also by Sammy Franco**

Combat Pressure Points
Cane Fighting
Double End Bag Training
The Heavy Bag Bible
The Widow Maker Compendium
Invincible: Mental Toughness Techniques for Peak Performance
Unleash Hell: A Step-by-Step Guide to Devastating Widow Maker Combinations
Feral Fighting: Advanced Widow Maker Fighting Techniques
The Widow Maker Program: Extreme Self-Defense for Deadly Force Situations
Savage Street Fighting: Tactical Savagery as a Last Resort
Heavy Bag Combinations
Heavy Bag Training
The Complete Body Opponent Bag Book
Stand and Deliver: A Street Warrior's Guide to Tactical Combat Stances
Maximum Damage: Hidden Secrets Behind Brutal Fighting Combinations
First Strike: End a Fight in Ten Seconds or Less
The Bigger They Are, The Harder They Fall
Self-Defense Tips and Tricks
Kubotan Power: Quick & Simple Steps to Mastering the Kubotan Keychain
Gun Safety: For Home Defense and Concealed Carry
Out of the Cage: A Guide to Beating a Mixed Martial Artist on the Street
Warrior Wisdom: Inspiring Ideas from the World's Greatest Warriors
War Machine: How to Transform Yourself Into a Vicious Street Fighter
When Seconds Count: Self-Defense for the Real World
Killer Instinct: Unarmed Combat for Street Survival
Street Lethal: Unarmed Urban Combat

**1001 Street Fighting Secrets**
Copyright © 2023 by Sammy Franco
ISBN: 978-1-941845-77-6
Printed in the United States of America
Visit online at: ContemporaryFightingArts.com

All rights reserved. Except for use in a review, no portion of this book may be reproduced in any form without the express written permission of the author.

*For Jack*

1001 STREET FIGHTING SECRETS

# Contents

| | |
|---|---|
| **About This Book** | xi |
| **Introduction** <br> Contemporary Fighting Arts | 1 |
| **Chapter One** <br> Street Fighting Fundamentals | 15 |
| **Chapter Two** <br> Training and Conditioning | 75 |
| **Chapter Three** <br> Attributes of Combat | 131 |
| **Chapter Four** <br> Tactics and Strategy | 165 |
| **Chapter Five** <br> Grappling and Ground Fighting | 231 |
| **Chapter Six** <br> Bludgeons and Stick Fighting | 271 |
| **Chapter Seven** <br> Knife Defense and Knife Fighting | 293 |
| **Chapter Eight** <br> Firearms and Combat Shooting | 327 |
| **Chapter Nine** <br> Philosophy | 379 |
| **Glossary** | 393 |
| **Suggested Reading & Viewing** | 433 |
| **About Sammy Franco** | 437 |

*"To know that one has a secret is to know half the secret itself."*

– Henry Ward Beecher

# Disclaimer

The author, publisher, and distributors of this book will accept no responsibility, nor are they liable to any person or entity whatsoever for any injury, damage, or loss of any sort that may arise out of practicing, teaching, or disseminating of any techniques or ideas contained herein.

You assume full responsibility for the use of the information in this book and agree that the author, distributor and contributors hold no liability to you for claims, damages, costs and expenses, legal fees, or any other costs incurred due to or in any way related to your reliance on anything derived from this book or its contents.

Additionally, it is the reader's responsibility to research and comply with all local, state, and federal laws and regulations pertaining to the possession, carry, and use of self-defense weapons. This book is for educational reference information only!

Before you begin any exercise or activity, including those suggested in this book, it is important to check with your physician to see if you have any condition that might be aggravated by strenuous training. The information contained in this book is not designed to diagnose, treat, or manage any physical health conditions.

# The Final Secret

You'll notice that the last secret in this book is replaced with a question mark. You, the reader, must find the final secret. Here's a clue: this book was written with some secrets placed in a unique order. When you discover this unique formation or pattern, you'll be one step closer to finding the final secret to this book. This task, however, is not easy and is reserved for only the most inquisitive and analytical reader.

Good luck!

1001 STREET FIGHTING SECRETS

x

# About This Book

*1,001 Street Fighting Secrets* is an exhaustive compilation of principles and techniques of my unique system of combat, Contemporary Fighting Arts (CFA). This book is my magnum opus, and will hopefully prove to be the most in-depth, detailed, and complete collection of fighting techniques ever compiled.

Chapter One covers all the foundational elements of street fighting. Topics include stances, offensive skills, natural body weapons, defensive skills and techniques, breathing, common errors, centerline theory, weight distributions, range specialization, stabilizer and mover theory, characteristics of fighting, energy transfer, power generators, combative subtleties, footwork skills, target zones, and ranges of combat.

Chapter Two covers training and conditioning for the rigors of both armed and unarmed combat. You will learn the importance of combat conditioning, training zones, stretching, diet and nutrition, visualization, impact tolerance, sparring drills, training routines, compound attack development, somatotype training, training dos and don'ts, and shadow fighting.

Chapter Three introduces you to the attributes of both armed and unarmed fighting. Some include decisiveness, agility, distancing, explosiveness, pain tolerance, viciousness, speed, power, balance, timing, finesse, accuracy, target recognition, offensive reaction time, evasiveness, confidence, awareness, range proficiency, relaxation, combative uniformity, deceptiveness, the "killer instinct," telegraphic cognizance, histrionics, and adaptability.

Chapter Four teaches you a plethora of street fighting tactics and strategies, including ambush zone avoidance, low-line kicking techniques, methods of attack, combative assumptions, first-strike principle, assessment skills, de-escalation skills, multiple assailant combat, legal considerations, street smart tactics, barroom etiquette, the neutral zone, strategic positioning, environmental exploitation, makeshift weaponry, offensive and defensive range manipulation, and the pitfalls of dependency.

Chapter Five covers grappling and ground fighting. Besides teaching you myriad submission holds, this chapter will teach you ground fighting positions, pummeling skills, the dangers of positional asphyxia, sprawling methods, hand grips, ground fighting with weapons, nuclear and conventional ground fighting tactics, grappling planes, escapes, and reversals.

Chapter Six acquaints you with bludgeons and stick fighting, including: the limitations of zoning, stick grips, deflections, blocks, stick fighting ranges, retention skills, training drills, long arc deficiencies, footwork, stick strangles, swing stages, bludgeon characteristics, disarming techniques, and reverberation paths.

Chapter Seven launches you into the sobering world of edged weapons. In this chapter you will learn about knife defense stances, knife grips, training drills, footwork, secondary weapons, retention skills, the V-grip, knife fighting tactics, survival principles, drawing skills, cutting angles, withdrawing skills, strategic leaning, insertion points, and knife-palming methods.

Chapter Eight introduces you to the ultimate force option—firearms. In this chapter you will learn about semiautomatics, revolvers, firearm fundamentals, firearm safety rules, center mass selection, the double-tap principle, one-hand reloading, entry tactics, drawing and retention skills, disarming techniques, shooting positions, cover vs. concealment, ammunition criteria, speed loading, muzzle flash, contact shooting, cartridge malfunctions, ammunition storage, immediate action drills, and the fatal funnel.

Finally, Chapter Nine bridges the gap between the

technical and philosophical aspects of combat. In this chapter, you will acquire a greater appreciation of Contemporary Fighting Arts, and a better understanding of the man who created it. This chapter will touch upon the following intellectual themes: pacifism, courage, fear, loyalty, honor, logic, conceptualization, perfectionism, laws of reality, diplomacy, ego, good vs. evil, myth vs. reality, and the belief in a higher power.

When reading this text you'll notice that some secrets overlap or replicate others. Don't be alarmed. This is expected since most principles of combat are consanguineous. Like pieces of a jigsaw puzzle, they all possess related elements.

One final note to the reader: If you find a particular secret that you'd like to explore further, please refer to the suggested reading & viewing section in the back of this book.

Walk in peace.

Sammy Franco
Founder
ContemporaryFightingArts.com

1001 STREET FIGHTING SECRETS

# INTRODUCTION
## Contemporary Fighting Arts

1001 STREET FIGHTING SECRETS

# Exploring Contemporary Fighting Arts

Before diving head first into this book, I'd like to first introduce you to my unique system of fighting, Contemporary Fighting Arts (CFA). I hope it will give you a greater understanding and appreciation of the material covered in this book. And for those of you who are already familiar with CFA, you can skip to chapter one.

Contemporary Fighting Arts® (CFA), is a state-of-the-art combat system that was introduced to the world in 1983. This sophisticated and practical system of self-defense is designed specifically to provide efficient and effective methods to avoid, defuse, confront, and neutralize both armed and unarmed assailants in a variety of deadly situations and circumstances.

Unlike karate, kung-fu, mixed martial arts and the like, CFA is the first offensive-based American martial art that is specifically designed for the violence that plagues our cruel city streets. CFA dispenses with the extraneous and the impractical and focuses on real-life street fighting.

Every technique and tactic found within the CFA system must meet three essential criteria for fighting: efficiency, effectiveness, and safety. Efficiency means that the techniques permit you to reach your combative objective quickly and economically. Effectiveness means that the elements of the system will produce the desired effect. Finally, Safety means that the combative elements provide the least amount of danger and risk for you - the fighter.

CFA is not about tournaments or senseless competition. It doesn't require you to waste time and energy practicing forms (katas) or other impractical rituals. There are no theatrical kicks or exotic techniques. Finally, CFA doesn't adhere blindly to tradition for tradition's sake. Simply put, it's a scientific yet pragmatic approach to staying alive on the streets.

CFA has been taught to people of all walks of life. Some include the U.S. Border Patrol, police officers, deputy sheriffs, security guards, military personnel, private investigators, surgeons, lawyers, college professors, airline pilots, as well as black belts, boxers, and kick boxers. CFA's broad appeal results from its ability to teach people how to really fight.

## It's All In The Name

Before discussing the components that make up Contemporary Fighting Arts, it is important to understand how CFA acquired its unique name. To begin, the first word, "Contemporary," was selected because it refers to the system's modern, up-to-date orientation. Unlike traditional martial arts, CFA is specifically designed to meet the challenges of our modern world.

The second term, "Fighting," was chosen because it accurately describes the system's combat orientation. After all, why not just call it Contemporary Martial Arts? There are two reasons for this. First, the word "martial" conjures up images of traditional and impractical martial art forms that are antithetical to the system. Second, why dilute a perfectly functional name when the word "fighting" defines the system so succinctly? Contemporary Fighting Arts is about teaching people how to really fight.

Let's look at the last word, "Arts." In the subjective sense, "art" refers to the combat skills that are acquired through arduous study, practice, and observation. The bottom line is that effective street fighting skills will require consistent practice and attention. Take, for example, something as seemingly basic as an elbow strike, which will actually require hundreds of hours of practice to perfect.

The pluralization of the word "Art" reflects CFA's protean instruction. The various components of CFA's training (i.e., firearms training, stick fighting, ground fighting, natural body weapon mastery, and so on) have all truly earned their status as individual art forms and, as such, require years of consistent study and practice to perfect.

To acquire a greater understanding of CFA, here is an overview of the system's three vital components: the physical, the mental, and the spiritual.

## The Physical Component

The physical component of CFA focuses on the physical development of a fighter, including physical fitness, weapon and technique mastery, and self-defense attributes.

### Physical Fitness

If you are going to prevail in a street fight, you must be physically fit. It's that simple. In fact, you will never master the tools and skills of combat unless you're in excellent physical shape. On the average, you will have to spend more than an hour a day to achieve maximum fitness.

In CFA physical fitness comprises the following three broad components: cardiorespiratory conditioning, muscular/skeletal conditioning, and proper body composition.

The cardiorespiratory system includes the heart, lungs, and circulatory system, which undergo tremendous stress during the course of a street fight. So you're going to have to run, jog, bike, swim, or skip rope to develop sound cardiorespiratory conditioning. Each aerobic workout should last a minimum of 30 minutes and be performed at least four times per week.

The second component of physical fitness is muscular/skeletal conditioning. In the streets, the strong survive and the rest go to the morgue. To strengthen your bones and muscles to withstand the rigors of a real fight, your program must include progressive resistance (weight training) and calisthenics. You will also need a stretching program designed to loosen up every muscle group. You can't kick, punch, ground fight, or otherwise execute the necessary body mechanics if you're "tight" or inflexible. Stretching on a regular basis will also increase the muscles' range of motion, improve circulation, reduce the possibility of injury, and relieve daily stress.

The final component of physical fitness is proper body composition: simply, the ratio of fat to lean body tissue. Your diet and training regimen will affect your level or percentage of body fat significantly. A sensible and consistent exercise program accompanied by a healthy and balanced diet will facilitate proper body composition. Do not neglect this important aspect of physical fitness.

**Weapon and Technique Mastery**

You won't stand a chance against a vicious assailant if you don't master the techniques of fighting. In CFA, we teach our students both armed and unarmed methods of combat. Unarmed fighting requires that you master a complete arsenal of natural body weapons and techniques. In conjunction, you must also learn the various stances, hand positioning, footwork, body mechanics, defensive structure, locks, chokes,

# INTRODUCTION

and various holds. Keep in mind that something as simple as a basic punch will actually require hundreds of hours to perfect.

Range proficiency is another important aspect of weapon and technique mastery. Briefly, range proficiency is the ability to fight effectively in all three ranges of unarmed fighting. Although punching range tools are emphasized in CFA, kicking and grappling ranges cannot be neglected. Our kicking range tools consist of deceptive and powerful low-line kicks. Grappling range tools include head-butts, elbows, knees, foot stomps, biting, tearing, gouging, and crushing tactics.

Although CFA focuses on striking, we also teach our students a myriad of chokes, locks, and holds that can be used in a ground fight. While such grappling range submission techniques are not the most preferred methods of dealing with a ground fighting situation, they must be developed.

Defensive tools and skills are also taught. Our defensive structure is efficient, uncomplicated, and impenetrable. It provides the fighter maximum protection while allowing complete freedom of choice for acquiring offensive control. Our defensive structure is based on distance, parrying, blocking, evading, mobility, and stance structure. Simplicity is always the key.

Students are also instructed in specific methods of armed

fighting. For example, CFA provides instruction about firearms for personal and household protection. We provide specific guidelines for handgun purchasing, operation, nomenclature, proper caliber, shooting fundamentals, cleaning, and safe storage. Our firearm program also focuses on owner responsibility and the legal ramifications regarding the use of deadly force.

CFA's weapons program also consists of natural body weapons, knives and edged weapons, single and double stick, makeshift weaponry, the side-handle baton, and oleoresin capsicum (OC) spray.

**Combat Attributes**

Your offensive and defensive tools are useless unless they are used strategically. For any tool or technique to be effective in a real fight, it must be accompanied by specific attributes. Attributes are qualities that enhance a particular tool, technique, or maneuver. Some examples include speed, power, timing, coordination, accuracy, non-telegraphic movement, balance, and target orientation.

CFA also has a wide variety of training drills and methodologies designed to develop and sharpen these combat attributes. For example, our students learn to ground fight while blindfolded, spar with one arm tied down, and fight while handcuffed.

Reality is the key. For example, in class students participate in full-contact drills against fully padded assailants, and real weapon disarms are rehearsed and analyzed in a variety of dangerous scenarios. Students also train with a large variety of equipment, including heavy bags, double-end bags, uppercut bags, pummel bags, focus mitts, striking shields, mirrors, rattan sticks, training bats, kicking pads, knife drones, trigger-sensitive (mock) guns, full-body armor, and numerous environmental props.

There are more than two hundred unique training

# INTRODUCTION

methodologies used in Contemporary Fighting Arts. Each one is scientifically designed to prepare students for the hard-core realities of real world combat. There are also three specific training methodologies used to develop and sharpen the fundamental attributes and skills of armed and unarmed fighting, including proficiency training, conditioning training, and street training.

Proficiency training can be used for both armed and unarmed skills. When conducted properly, proficiency training develops speed, power, accuracy, non-telegraphic movement, balance, and general psychomotor skill. The training objective is to sharpen one specific body weapon, maneuver, or technique at a time by executing it over and over for a prescribed number of repetitions. Each time the technique or maneuver is executed with "clean" form at various speeds. Movements are also performed with the eyes closed to develop a kinesthetic "feel" for the action. Proficiency training can be accomplished through the use of various types of equipment, including the heavy bag, double-end bag, focus mitts, training knives, real and mock pistols, striking shields, shin and knee guards, foam and plastic bats, mannequin heads, and so on.

Conditioning training develops endurance, fluidity, rhythm, distancing, timing, speed, footwork, and balance. In most cases, this type of training requires the student to deliver a variety of fighting combinations for three- or four-minute rounds separated by 30-second breaks. Like proficiency training, this type of training can also be performed at various speeds. A good workout consists of at least five rounds. Conditioning training can be performed on the bags with full-contact sparring gear, rubber training knives, focus mitts, kicking shields, and shin guards, or against imaginary assailants in shadow fighting.

Conditioning training is not necessarily limited to just three- or four-minute rounds. For example, CFA's ground fighting training can last as long as 30 minutes. The bottom line is that it all depends on what you are training for.

Street training is the final preparation for the real thing. Since many violent altercations are explosive, lasting an average of 20 seconds, you must prepare for this possible scenario. This means delivering explosive and powerful compound attacks with vicious intent for approximately 20 seconds, resting one minute, and then repeating the process.

Street training prepares you for the stress and immediate fatigue of a real fight. It also develops speed, power, explosiveness, target selection and recognition, timing, footwork, pacing, and breath control. You should practice this methodology in different lighting, on different terrains, and in different environmental settings. You can use different types of training equipment as well. For example, you can prepare yourself for multiple assailants by having your training partners attack you with focus mitts from a variety of angles, ranges, and target postures. For 20 seconds, go after them with low-line kicks, powerful punches, and devastating strikes.

When all is said and done, the physical component creates a fighter who is physically fit and armed with an arsenal of techniques that can be deployed with destructive results.

INTRODUCTION

## The Mental Component

The mental component of CFA focuses on the cerebral aspects of a fighter, developing killer instinct, strategic/tactical awareness, analysis and integration skills, philosophy, and cognitive skills.

### The Killer Instinct

Deep within each of us is a cold and deadly primal power known as the "killer instinct." The killer instinct is a vicious combat mentality that surges to your consciousness and turns you into a fierce fighter who is free of fear, anger, and apprehension. If you want to survive the horrifying dynamics of real criminal violence, you must cultivate and utilize this instinctive killer mentality.

Visualization and crisis rehearsal are just two techniques used to develop, refine, and channel this extraordinary source of strength and energy so that it can be used to its full potential.

### Strategic/Tactical Awareness

Strategy is the bedrock of preparedness. In CFA, there are three unique categories of strategic awareness that will diminish the likelihood of criminal victimization. They are criminal awareness, situational awareness, and self-awareness. When developed, these essential skills prepare you to assess a wide variety of threats instantaneously and accurately. Once you've made a proper threat assessment, you will be able to choose one of the following five self-defense options: comply, escape, de-escalate, assert, or fight back.

CFA also teaches students to assess a variety of other important factors, including the assailant's demeanor, intent, range, positioning and weapon capability, as well as such environmental issues as escape routes, barriers, terrain, and makeshift weaponry. In addition to assessment skills, CFA also teaches students how to enhance perception and observation skills.

## Analysis and Integration Skills

The analytical process is intricately linked to understanding how to defend yourself in any threatening situation. If you want to be the best, every aspect of fighting and personal protection must be dissected. Every strategy, tactic, movement, and concept must be broken down to its atomic parts. The three planes (physical, mental, spiritual) of self-defense must be unified scientifically through arduous practice and constant exploration.

CFA's most advanced practitioners have sound insight and understanding of a wide range of sciences and disciplines. They include human anatomy, kinesiology, criminal justice, sociology, kinesics, proxemics, combat physics, emergency medicine, crisis management, histrionics, police and military science, the psychology of aggression, and the role of archetypes.

Analytical exercises are also a regular part of CFA training. For example, we conduct problem-solving sessions involving particular assailants attacking in defined environments. We move hypothetical attackers through various ranges to provide insight into tactical solutions. We scrutinize different methods of attack for their general utility in combat. We also discuss the legal ramifications of self-defense on a frequent basis.

In addition to problem-solving sessions, students are slowly exposed to concepts of integration and modification. Oral and written examinations are given to measure intellectual accomplishment. Unlike systems, CFA does not use colored belts or sashes to identify the student's level of proficiency.

## Philosophy

Philosophical resolution is essential to a fighter's mental confidence and clarity. Anyone learning the art of war must find the ultimate answers to questions concerning the use of violence in defense of himself or others. To advance to the highest levels of combat awareness, you must find clear and lucid answers to such provocative questions as could you take the life of another, what are your fears, who are you, why are you interested in studying Contemporary Fighting Arts, why are you reading this book, and what is good and what is evil? If you haven't begun the quest to formulate these important questions and answers, then take a break. It's time to figure out just why you want to know the laws and rules of destruction.

**Cognitive Combat Skills**

Cognitive combat exercises are also important for improving one's fighting skills. CFA uses visualization and crisis rehearsal scenarios to improve general body mechanics, tools and techniques, and maneuvers, as well as tactic selection. Mental clarity, concentration, and emotional control are also developed to enhance one's ability to call upon the controlled killer instinct.

## The Spiritual Component

There are many tough fighters out there. In fact, they reside in every town in every country. However, most are nothing more than vicious animals that lack self-mastery. And self-mastery is what separates the true warrior from the eternal novice.

I am not referring to religious precepts or beliefs when I speak of CFA's spiritual component. Unlike most martial arts, CFA does not merge religion into its spiritual aspect. Religion is a very personal and private matter and should never, be incorporated into any fighting system. CFA's spiritual component is not something that is taught or studied. Rather, it is that which transcends the physical and mental aspects of being and reality. There is a deeper part of each of us that is a tremendous source of truth and accomplishment.

In CFA, the spiritual component is something that is slowly and progressively acquired. During the challenging quest of combat training, one begins to tap the higher qualities of human nature. Those elements of our being that inherently enable us to know right from wrong and good from evil. As we slowly develop this aspect of our total self, we begin to strengthen qualities profoundly important to the "truth." Such qualities are essential to your growth through the mastery of inner peace, the clarity of your "vision," and your recognition of universal truths.

One of the goals of my system is to promote virtue and moral responsibility in people who have extreme capacities for physical and mental destructiveness. The spiritual component of fighting is truly the most difficult aspect of personal growth. Yet, unlike the physical component, where the practitioner's abilities will be limited to some degree by genetics and other natural factors, the spiritual component of combat offers unlimited potential for growth and development. In the final analysis, CFA's spiritual component poses the greatest challenges for the student. It is an open-ended plane of unlimited advancement.

# CHAPTER ONE
## Street Fighting Fundamentals

*"Combat fundamentals are the stepping stones to victory."*

STREET FIGHTING FUNDAMENTALS

# THE BASICS

**1. DON'T BLINK.**

Avoid reflexive blinking when a punch or kick is thrown at you. A split-second blink could leave you vulnerable to another blow. Blinking is a natural reflex. As a matter of fact, the eye blinks every two to ten seconds. However, reflexive eye blinking can be eliminated with proper combat training. For example, during sparring and full-contact sessions, you must make a conscious effort to keep your head forward and your eyes open amid flying blows. Acquiring this skill, of course, will take time and, above all, courage.

**2. BREATHE.**

Breathing is one of the most important and often neglected aspects of fighting. Proper breathing promotes muscular relaxation and increases the speed and efficiency of your compound attack. The rate at which you breathe will also determine how quickly your cardiorespiratory system can recover from a violent encounter. NOTE: Always remember to exhale whenever you are executing a striking tool or technique.

**3. RELAX.**

Learn to relax and avoid tensing your muscles when fighting. Muscular tension will throw off your timing, retard the speed of your movements, and wear you out during a fight. Combative preparation is one of the best methods of preventing unnecessary muscular tension.

**4. BE EFFICIENT.**

Every tool, technique, or tactic that you employ in a street fight must be efficient. Efficiency means that the techniques are direct and can be deployed rapidly, allowing you to reach your objective quickly and economically. Efficient techniques are also easy to learn and maintain, and they can be retained under the severe stress of combat. Remember, a technique does not have to be complex to be sophisticated.

## 5. BE EFFECTIVE.

Be certain that the tools, techniques, and tactics that you employ in a self-defense situation are effective. Effectiveness means the weapons in your arsenal can produce the desired effects.

## 6. BE SAFE.

Never gamble with your life in a street fight. Taking undue or unnecessary risks in a fight is not only stupid, it's suicidal. Every technique and tactic that you employ in a fight must be safe. Safety means that the elements and mechanics of a particular movement present the least amount of danger and risk for you in combat. When you execute a tool or technique, it should offer minimal target openings and minimize your loss of balance.

## 7. USE LOW-MAINTENANCE TECHNIQUES.

Always employ low-maintenance tools in a fight. Such tools require the least amount of training to maintain their proficiency and generally require no preliminary stretching. The following are some low-maintenance tools: finger jabs, palm heels, head butts, thumb gouges, elbow and knee strikes, and hammer fists. Your combat arsenal must be free of high-maintenance tools that require preliminary warm-up or stretching movements. Remember, there is no time to warm up in a fight.

STREET FIGHTING FUNDAMENTALS

## 8. KNOW THE THREE TARGET ZONES.

The assailant's anatomical targets are located in one of three possible *target zones*. Zone One (head region) consists of targets related to the assailant's senses, including the eyes, temples, nose, chin, and back of neck. Zone Two (neck, torso, groin) consists of targets related to the assailant's breathing, including the throat, solar plexus, ribs, and groin. Zone Three (legs and feet) consists of anatomical targets related to the assailant's mobility, including the thighs, knees, shins, insteps, and toes.

ZONE 1

ZONE 2

ZONE 3

## 9. KNOW THE CHARACTERISTICS OF COMBAT.

The more you know about fighting, the less fearful and the better prepared you will be. The following are just a few characteristics of *real* combat: (1) combat is fast and explosive, (2) combat is unpredictable and spontaneous, (3) combat is ugly and brutal, (4) combat is extremely dangerous, (5)

19

unarmed combat often turns into a ground fight, (6) most unarmed combatants head hunt, (7) combat is intimate, (8) kicking is seldom used, (9) compound attacks usually end an unarmed encounter, (10) there are no rules, (11) spectators enjoy watching a fight and may likely join in, (12) combat is almost always unfair, (13) you will not be able to rest until your threat is neutralized, (14) your adversary will most likely be larger and stronger than you.

## 10. ACQUAINT YOURSELF WITH YOUR KILLER INSTINCT.

During a real fight, you must utilize a combat mentality to channel a destructiveness exceeding that of your attacker. This is the *killer instinct*. The killer instinct is a cold, primal mentality that surges to your conscious mind and turns you into a vicious combatant. Deep within every person is deadly primal power, a virtuous killer instinct that is cold, emotionless, and primed for destruction. The killer instinct is a reservoir of energy and strength. It can channel your destructiveness by producing a mental source of cold, destructive energy. If necessary, it fuels the determination to fight to the death.

Everyone has a killer instinct. That's just the way we're made. The following 14 factors integrate harmoniously to create the killer instinct: (1) clear thinking, (2) heightened situational awareness, (3) adrenaline surge, (4) physical mobilization, (5) psychomotor control, (6) absence of distractions, (7) unified mind (tunnel vision), (8) courage, (9) tactical implementation, (10) lack of emotion, (11) breath control, (12) pseudospeciation, (13) viciousness, and, finally, (14) pain tolerance.

STREET FIGHTING FUNDAMENTALS

## 11. MASTER NATURAL BODY WEAPONS.

*Body weapons* are simply the various body parts that can be used to disable, cripple, or kill an assailant. They include: (1) head - used for butting in the grappling range of combat; (2) teeth - used for biting tactics in close-quarter range; (3) voice - used for distracting/startling your assailant; (4) elbows - used as striking tools in the grappling range of combat; (5) fists - used for punching techniques in the punching range; (6) palms - used to deliver palm-heel strikes in the punching range; (7) fingers/nails - used for jabbing, gouging, and clawing the eyes and pulling, tearing, and crushing the throat and testicles; (8) edge of hands - used to deliver knife-hand strikes in both punching and grappling ranges; (9) knees - used to deliver debilitating strikes in the grappling range; (10) shins - used to strike the assailant's thigh, knee, or groin; (11) insteps - used to deliver strikes in the kicking range; (12) heels of feet - used for kicking and stomping techniques; and (13) balls of feet - used for kicking techniques.

## 12. KNOW THE RANGES OF UNARMED COMBAT.

There are three ranges or distances of unarmed combat, as follows: (1) kicking range - the farthest distance of unarmed combat, at which you would use your legs to strike your adversary; (2) punching range - the midrange of unarmed combat, at which distance you are able to strike your assailant effectively with your hands; and (3) grappling range - the third and final range of unarmed combat, which is divided into two different planes, vertical and horizontal. In the vertical plane, you can generally deliver impact techniques, some of which include elbow and knee strikes, head butts, gouging and crushing tactics, and biting and tearing techniques. In the horizontal plane, you are ground fighting with your adversary and can deliver all of the previously mentioned techniques, including various submission holds, locks, and chokes.

## 13. DON'T TELEGRAPH.

Successfully neutralizing your adversary requires that you do not forewarn your assailant of your intentions. Telegraphing means inadvertently making your intentions known to your assailant. There are many subtle forms of telegraphing that must be avoided in combat. Here are just a few: (1) cocking your arm back prior to punching or striking; (2) tensing your neck, shoulders, or arms prior to striking; (3) widening your eyes or raising your eyebrows; (4) shifting your shoulders; (5) grinning or opening your mouth; and (6) taking a sudden, deep breath.

One of the most effective ways to prevent telegraphing movement is to maintain a poker face prior to executing any combat movement. Actually you should avoid all facial expressions when faced with a threatening adversary. You can also study your techniques and movements in front of a full-length mirror or have a training partner videotape your movements. These training procedures will assist you in identifying and ultimately eliminating telegraphic movements.

## 14. BLADE YOUR BODY.

Never stand squarely in front of your assailant. Not only does this stance expose vital targets, it also diminishes your balance, inhibits efficient footwork, and minimizes your reach. Always try to maintain a 45-degree stance from your assailant. This position will help minimize target exposure, enhance your balance, promote mobility, and set up your natural body weapons.

## 15. ANGLE YOUR CHIN.

Always keep your chin angled slightly down when you assume any type of stance. This movement will make you a more elusive target and help minimize direct strikes to your eyes, nose, jaw, chin, and throat. However, avoid forcing your

## STREET FIGHTING FUNDAMENTALS

*Kicking Range.*

*Punching Range.*

*Grappling Range.*

*Grappling Range (horizontal plane).*

chin down too low. This will inhibit the mechanical fluidity of your tools and techniques and ultimately slow you down

## 16. PROTECT YOUR CENTERLINE.

Your *centerline* is an imaginary vertical line that divides your body in half. Located on this line are some of your most vital impact targets (eyes, nose, chin, throat, solar plexus, and groin). Your centerline plays a critical role in both armed and unarmed encounters and is best protected through strategic body angulation (stance) and effective mobility.

## 17. KEEP BOTH HANDS UP, ALWAYS.

When squared off with an assailant, avoid the natural tendency to lower your hand guard, which leaves you wide open to a possible counterattack. Remember, when executing a punch or strike, keep your other hand up to either defend against a counterattack or follow up with another strike.

## 18. MAINTAIN PROPER WEIGHT DISTRIBUTION.

When squared off with your assailant, try to maintain a 50% weight distribution. This noncommittal weight distribution will provide you with the ability to move in any direction quickly and efficiently, while also supplying the necessary stability defend against blows and strikes.

# STREET FIGHTING FUNDAMENTALS

## 19. PROTECT YOUR HEAD AT ALL COSTS.

Your head (this includes top, front, sides, and back) is the computer center that controls the functioning of your entire body. Since most of your vital senses (smell, sight, hearing, and equilibrium) are stored there, you must keep it out of harm's way. Applying the proper stance accomplishes this.

## 20. KEEP YOUR FEET SHOULDER-WIDTH APART.

When assuming any stance, the distance between your feet is a critical factor. If your feet are too close to each other you will lack the necessary balance to maintain an effective fighting structure. If your feet are too far apart you'll be rigid and static, thus restricting your ability to move quickly. However, by keeping your feet approximately shoulder-width apart, you will provide your stance with sufficient balance and stability without sacrificing mobility.

## 21. KEEP YOUR FEET PARALLEL.

When assuming a stance, keep both feet parallel and positioned at a 45-degree angle from the adversary. This position will improve your balance and stability when stationary and when moving.

## 22. KEEP YOUR FRONT FOOT TURNED INWARD.

When assuming a stance, be certain to keep your front foot turned inward at a 45-degree angle from your adversary. This strategic foot positioning is important for the following two reasons: (1) it protects your groin from a direct kick, and (2) it prevents a possible knee dislocation by allowing your lead knee to bend or flex when kicked by your adversary.

## 23. IDENTIFY YOUR STRONG SIDE.

It's important for you to know which side of your body is stronger for both armed and unarmed combat. The term *strong side* refers to the side of your body (hands, arms, and legs) that has the greater amount of strength and psychomotor skill. For example, a right-handed fighter will usually have a dominant right side, while a left-handed fighter will have a stronger left side. In combat (excluding firearms), always try to keep your stronger side forward to enhance the speed, power, and accuracy of your initiating blow. Keep in mind, however, that your ultimate objective in training is to develop and, ultimately, possess two strong sides.

## 24. PERFECT THE FIGHTING STANCE.

The *fighting stance* is a strategic and aggressive posture you assume when squared off with an assailant. In unarmed combat, the fighting stance is used for both offensive and defensive purposes. It stresses strategic soundness and simplicity over complexity and style. The fighting stance also facilitates maximum execution of body weapons while simultaneously protecting your vital anatomical body targets against possible counterstrikes.

When assuming a fighting stance, blade your feet and body at a 45-degree angle from your assailant. This moves your body targets back and away from direct strikes but still leaves you strategically positioned. Keep your stronger side forward, facing your adversary. Place your feet approximately shoulder-width apart. Keep both knees bent and flexible. Keep both of your hands up and align your lead hand in front of the rear hand. When holding up your guard in this position, make certain not to tighten your shoulders or arms. Stay relaxed and loose. Finally, keep your chin angled slightly down.

## 25. KEEP YOUR ARMS LOOSE.

When assuming a fighting stance, try to keep your arms loose, with your fingers curled and your wrists straight. This will help prevent muscular tension and increase the speed of your movements.

## 26. ELBOWS POINT DOWN.

When assuming the fighting stance, be sure to maintain a proper hand guard. Make certain that your lead arm is bent at approximately a 90-degree angle and that your rear arm is kept back by your chin. Avoid the tendency to let both your elbows flair out to the sides. This type of elbow positioning is dangerous for two key reasons: (1) it exposes your waist and ribs to a variety of possible strikes and edged-weapon attacks, (2) it places your hands out of proper body mechanic alignment, which diminishes power, and unnecessarily exposes your centerline.

## 27. ALIGN YOUR HANDS.

When assuming a fighting stance, try to align both your rear and lead hands. This will protect your centerline, temporarily negate the assailant's linear assault, and set up your body weapons. Never open your hands wide apart and expose your centerline in an attempt to draw your assailant's attack. You'll get hurt! The open-hand guard is only used for the bludgeon- defense stance.

## 28. STABILITY IS ESSENTIAL.

If your stability is compromised, then so is your stance. Here are four principles to keep in mind when trying to maintain stability in your stance: (1) keep your center of gravity directly over your feet, (2) the lower you drop your center of gravity to its support base, the greater stability you will have, (3) the wider your stance, the greater your stability, (4) the heavier the fighter, the greater his stability.

## 29. DON'T STEP FORWARD.

Stepping forward to assume a fighting stance is risky for the following reasons: (1) it moves you closer to your assailant before your protective structure is soundly established, (2) it dramatically reduces your defensive reaction time, and it also looks aggressive from a witness' perspective. Therefore, get into the habit of stepping back into a stance.

## 30. USE THE KNIFE-DEFENSE STANCE.

The *knife-defense stance* is a strategic posture that a fighter assumes when confronted by an attacker with a knife or edged weapon. To assume this protective stance, execute the following: (1) blade your feet and torso at approximately a 45-degree angle from the attacker; (2) slightly hunch your shoulders forward and let your stomach sink inward, which will move your vital targets farther away from the knife; (3) stay relaxed and vigilant; (4) keep your head back and away from random slashes or stabs; (5) keep your hands, arms, and elbows close to your body to diminish target opportunities to the assailant; (6) cup your hands with your palms facing you, which will turn soft tissue, veins, and arteries in the arms away from the blade; (6) keep your knees slightly bent and flexible with both legs approximately shoulder-width apart; (7) keep your body weight equally distributed on each leg; and (8) keep your chin angled slightly down.

## 31. PERFECT THE DE-ESCALATION STANCE.

Successfully de-escalating a hostile person requires that you maintain a nonaggressive physiology. It's imperative that you assume a stance that is strategically sound yet nonthreatening. The *de-escalation stance* (for kicking and punching ranges) can be acquired by following these steps: (1) blade your body at approximately a 45-degree angle from the adversary; (2) keep both of your feet approximately shoulder-width apart and bend your knees slightly with your weight evenly distributed; (3) keep both of your hands open, relaxed, and up to protect the upper-body targets; (4) be certain to keep your torso, pelvis, head, and back erect; (5) stay relaxed and alert - remain at ease and in total control of your emotions and body; and (6) avoid any muscular tension - don't tighten up!

## 32. SHOW YOUR PALMS.

When assuming the de-escalation stance, have both of your palms facing the assailant. This hand positioning is important for the following reasons: (1) it's congruent with the rest of your nonaggressive physiology; (2) it protects a greater area of your centerline; (3) it promotes muscular relaxation, thus enhancing the speed and delivery of both offensive and defensive techniques; (4) it aids in the prevention of onlooker intervention; (5) if you're in a situation that escalates into a fight and you are taken to court later, the judge or jury will look favorably upon the person who appeared nonthreatening prior to the fight; and (6) it's deceptive, allowing you to launch a first strike, if necessary.

## 33. PERFECT THE BLUDGEON-DEFENSE STANCE.

The *bludgeon-defense stance* is a strategic posture used when confronted by a bludgeon-wielding attacker. To assume this stance, execute the following: (1) keep your stronger side forward, facing your adversary; (2) blade your feet and torso at approximately a 45-degree angle to the attacker; (3) keep both of your hands up (beside each other); (4) keep your hands, arms, and elbows close to your body; (5) keep your head behind your hands and stay relaxed and vigilant; (6) keep your knees slightly bent and flexible with both legs approximately shoulder-width apart; (7) keep your body weight equally distributed on each leg; and (8) keep your chin angled slightly down. When assuming a bludgeon-defense stance, avoid tightening your shoulders or arms.

## 34. STAGES OF COMBAT DETERMINE STANCES.

Selecting the appropriate stance for a particular self-defense situation requires a solid understanding of the *two stages of combat*, and they include: (1) Pre-contact stage - refers to the moments before you're physically engaging with your assailant. During this stage, you're either *aware* or *unaware* of the threat that awaits you. During the awareness state of the pre-contact phase, you have time (perhaps a few seconds) to prepare yourself both mentally and physically for violence. In some cases, you might have the opportunity to engage in some dialogue with your adversary before shit hits the fan. Strategic stances like the de-escalation and natural stances are particularly useful, (2) Contact stage - essentially, the fight is on! Physical contact has occurred between you and the adversary. The fighting stance, among several other, will frequently come into play.

## 35. PERFECT THE NATURAL STANCE.

The *natural stance* is utilized when you're approached by a suspicious stranger. To assume the natural stance, apply the following: (1) angle your body 45 degrees from the suspicious individual; (2) keep both of your feet approximately shoulder-width apart and your knees slightly bent with your weight evenly distributed; (3) keep both of your hands in front of your body with some type of natural movement (e.g., rub your hands together, scratch your wrist or nose), which will help protect your upper gates from a possible attack; (4) make certain to keep your torso, pelvis, head, and back erect; and (5) stay relaxed but alert, avoiding any muscular tension in your shoulders, neck, arms, or thighs.

## 36. DON'T RELY ON A STANCE.

Although the fighting stance is the foundation of a fighting system, learn to fight your assailant without a combat stance. Practice and train yourself to execute your fighting techniques without any foundational structure. Remember, any stance is often a luxury in a fight.

# KICKING TECHNIQUES

**37. KICK HIM.**

*Kicking range* is the farthest distance of unarmed combat. There are many advantages to kicking in a fight. Here is a list of some: (1) surprise - since most strikes are delivered with the hands, kicking techniques can surprise an assailant; (2) power - since the legs are more powerful than the hands, kicking techniques can generate more force; (3) time - kicks can buy you some time by temporarily keeping multiple assailants at bay; (4) closing of the distance gap - kicks can be used to close the distance gap between you and the assailant safely; (5) entry into a range of combat - kicks can be utilized as an entry tool into a range of combat; (6) injury - kicks can be used as a tool to injure an assailant; (7) safety - compared to the other ranges of unarmed combat, kicking range is a safer distance from which to launch your attack. *WARNING: Kicking techniques should be used sparingly in combat.*

**38. ONLY KICK BELOW THE WAIST.**

If you are going to execute kicking techniques in a fight, always employ low-line kicks to targets below the assailant's waist. They are efficient, effective, deceptive, non telegraphic, and relatively safe. Low-line targets include the groin, quadriceps, common peroneal nerve (approximately 4 inches above the knee area), knee, and shin.

**39. KICK WITH YOUR LEAD LEG.**

Kicking techniques are an important component of your arsenal. Although most kicks can be delivered from both your lead and rear legs, it's vital to execute 90 percent of your kicks from your lead leg. This is important for several reasons, including the following: (1) it is closer to your assailant's anatomical targets, (2) it accelerates your offensive reaction time, (3) it dramatically reduces telegraphing, (4) it reduces your assailant's defensive reaction time, (5) it improves the accuracy of your strike, and (6) it is safer for you.

## 40. MASTER THE VERTICAL KICK.

The *vertical kick* is one of the fastest kicks used in combat. This kick is delivered off your lead leg and travels on a vertical path to the assailant's groin and, in some cases, his face. To execute the vertical kick, maintain your balance while quickly shifting your weight back to your rear leg and simultaneously raising your lead leg vertically into the assailant's groin. Once contact is made, quickly force your leg back to the ground. Keep your supporting leg bent for balance.

When delivering a vertical kick, be certain to make contact with your instep. The instep is a good impact tool because it increases the power of your kick, prevents broken toes, and also lengthens the surface area of your natural body weapon. Avoid the tendency to snap your knee as you deliver the kick. Vertical kicks can be delivered in three different directions— vertically, at a right angle, and at a left angle.

## 41. MASTER THE PUSH KICK.

The *push kick* is another efficient kick delivered from your lead leg. To deliver the kick, quickly shift your weight to your rear leg and simultaneously raise your lead leg. Thrust the ball of your foot into the assailant's groin, quadriceps, knee, or shin. Quickly drop your leg to the ground. Make certain to keep your supporting leg bent for balance.

When delivering a push kick into the assailant's quadriceps, it's very important to make contact with the ball of your foot. This action will maximize the penetration of the kick into the assailant's muscle and nerves. You can also quickly snap the ball of the foot into the assailant's shinbone to loosen front grabs. When striking the assailant with the ball of your foot, remember to pull your toes back to avoid jamming or breaking them.

*Here, Franco demonstrates the push kick.*

## 42. MASTER THE SIDE KICK.

The *side kick* is a powerful linear kick executed from the lead leg. Contact is made with the heel. To execute the kick, shift your weight back, pivot your rear foot, and simultaneously raise and thrust your lead hip and leg into the assailant. Remember that you must pivot your rear foot to facilitate proper skeletal alignment (shoulder, hip, and heel alignment). The side kick is targeted for either the assailant's hip, thigh, knee, or shinbone.

## 43. HIT WITH THE HEEL OF YOUR FOOT.

When delivering a side kick to either the assailant's knee or shin, make contact with your heel. This action will ensure maximum force by creating proper skeletal alignment. When fighting an assailant in the grappling range (vertical), you can use the heel of your foot to stomp down on his toes.

# STREET FIGHTING FUNDAMENTALS

*Pictured here, the side kick.*

## 44. MAINTAIN SKELETAL ALIGNMENT.

One of the most important considerations when executing a side kick is maintaining proper skeletal alignment. Skeletal alignment is the proper alignment of your body, which maximizes the structural integrity of your kick. Therefore, when executing a side kick, always make certain that the heel, knee, and hip of your kicking leg are properly aligned

## 45. KNOW THE SIDE KICK VARIATIONS.

There are three variations of a side kick that can be employed. Each one serves a unique purpose. They include: (1) Destroyer - used to destroy the assailant's targets, (2) Closer - used to safely close the distance gap between you and the assailant, and (3) Checker - used to keep multiple assailants away and buy you time to escape. The following chart illustrates significant characteristics of each kick. For example, the destroyer variation of the side kick requires a maximal chamber, delivers maximum power, generates minimal speed, and has a high potential for telegraphing.

| SIDE KICK | CHAMBER TYPE | POWER LEVEL | SPEED LEVEL | TELEGRAPHIC POTENTIAL |
|---|---|---|---|---|
| **Destroyer** | maximal | maximal | minimal | high |
| **Closer** | moderate | moderate | moderate | moderate |
| **Checker** | minimal | minimal | maximum | low |

## 46. AVOID THESE COMMON SIDE KICK ERRORS.

Here are two common mistakes that occur when executing a side kick: (1) Failure to chamber your leg - your kick will have no force. To remedy this, lift your leg to the bent-knee position (this is known as a moderate chamber position), (2) Your toes lead the extension - you will jam your toes and sprain your ankle. To remedy this, pull your toes back toward your knee. This will ensure that your kick is leading with the heel of your foot.

## 47. THE SIDE KICK HAS LIMITATIONS.

Since most combat stances are predicated on blading your body at a 45-degree angle from your assailant, the side kick does have limited applications. Remember, to execute a side kick properly, you will need to position your body at a 90-degree angle from your target. This obviously presents a problem when you're standing at a 45- degree angle. Executing a side kick from a 45-degree angle can be dangerous because you'll need to pivot your hips and body. This, of course, would telegraph your attack to your adversary.

## 48. MASTER THE HOOK KICK.

The *hook kick* is thrown from your rear leg. Contact is made with either your instep or shinbone. It's, by far, the most powerful kick you can deliver, because you are torquing your entire body into the target. To execute the hook kick, step at a 45-degree angle and simultaneously twist and drive your rear leg and hip into your target. Make certain to pivot your base foot and follow through your target. When executing the hook kick, either aim for your assailant's knee or drive your shin into the assailant's common peroneal nerve (approximately 4 inches above the knee). This will collapse and temporarily immobilize the assailant's leg. Keep in mind that if you strike the knee you can cause permanent damage to the cartilage, ligaments, and tendons. When executing a hook kick, always allow your kick to sink into your assailant's leg briefly. This will maximize the force and penetration of your kick.

*Here, Franco demonstrates the hook kick.*

## 49. HIT WITH YOUR SHIN.

Striking your adversary with your shinbone can quickly cripple him and bring him to his knees in agony. When kicking with your shin, remember to aim for soft tissue targets like the assailant's thigh (specifically, his common peroneal nerve), side of knee, or groin. Don't forget to follow through your target and land in a stable stance.

## 50. AVOID USING HIGH-LINE KICKS.

High-line kicks are kicking techniques directed to targets above the assailant's waist. Never execute a high-line kick in a fight. Here are just a few reasons why: (1) balance - even the great kickers agree that high-line kicks can cause them to lose their balance easily; (2) inefficiency - they are not an efficient method of striking your assailant at this range; (3) no power - the less gravitational pull you put into a kick, the less power you will have; (4) clothing - the clothing you are wearing can drastically limit your ability to execute a high-line kick; (5) terrain - you must have ideal terrain conditions to even consider throwing a high-line kick; (6) flexibility - exceptional flexibility is a prerequisite to execute a high-line kick properly; (7) appendage barriers - high-line kicks must generally be directed to the upper torso and head (why kick where the assailant's arms are?); (8) closest weapon to closest target violation - your legs are closer to the assailant's low-line targets, not his high-line targets; (9) interception - high-line kicks can be intercepted and grabbed by a well-seasoned fighter; (10) lacks speed - high-line kicks take longer to reach their target than low-line kicks; (11) telegraphing - due to the greater travel distance, high-line kicks have a greater tendency to be telegraphed; (12) distance from the ground - high-line kicks take your legs farther away from the ground, thus slowing down your overall compound attack; (13) energy expenditure - high-line kicks require more energy to execute than low-line kicks; (14) target exposure - high-line kicks expose several targets to the assailant during their delivery; (15) high profile - high-line kicks are closer to the assailant's field of vision and are thus easier to see and to defend against.

# STREET FIGHTING FUNDAMENTALS

### 51. AVOID KICKING COMBINATIONS.

Don't throw a kicking combination in a fight. What most people don't realize is that kicking techniques are a means to an end but not an end in themselves. Frankly, they're highly overrated!

### 52. AVOID USING FULL-CHAMBER KICKS.

Chambering a kick means raising or "cocking" the appendage to a maximum height prior to delivering the kick. Full-chambered kicks are dangerous and risky for the following reasons: (1) they are too telegraphic, (2) they are unnecessary for power, (3) they open you up for a counterattack, (4) they can throw you off balance, and (5) they reduce the delivery speed of your kick.

### 53. NEVER RECHAMBER.

After executing any kick, drop your extended leg to the ground and complete the rest of your compound attack immediately. Never rechamber your leg in a fight. This is dangerous for the following reasons: (1) it throws you off balance, (2) it exposes your anatomical targets unnecessarily, (3) it breaks your offensive flow, (4) it allows your adversary the opportunity to counterattack immediately, and (5) it prohibits the establishment of a sound fighting structure.

### 54. KEEP YOUR LEGS ON THE GROUND.

Although kicking techniques are an important part of your repertoire of self-defense techniques, the legs are best used for mobility. You should kick only if it's absolutely necessary in a fight.

## PUNCHING TECHNIQUES

### 55. MAKE A PROPER FIST.

It's ironic how some of the most experienced fighters don't know how to make a proper fist. Improper fist clenching can be disastrous for the following reasons: (1) you can jam, sprain, or break your fingers; (2) you will destroy your wrist alignment, resulting in a sprained or broken wrist; or (3) you'll lose significant power when striking. To make a proper fist, tightly clench the four fingers evenly in the palm of your hand. Make certain that your thumb is wrapped securely around your second and third knuckles and flexed down toward the wrist.

### 56. MASTER THE SIX PRINCIPLES OF STRIKING

For any strike to be considered effective, it must possess the following qualities: (1) it must be accurately delivered to the vulnerable targets on the assailant's body, (2) it must be delivered rapidly, (3) it must be delivered with debilitating power, (4) it must be delivered economically - devoid of body mechanic "energy leaks", (5) it must be delivered with minimum danger and risk for the practitioner, and (6) it must be delivered at the proper moment.

# STREET FIGHTING FUNDAMENTALS

### 57. MAXIMIZE ENERGY TRANSFER.

Since you may only get one opportunity to strike your adversary, it's important to maximize the force (impact) of your blow. When delivering your strike, allow the energy to transfer completely into your target. To maximize this energy transfer, you will need to allow your blow to sink into your target for a fraction of a second before your retract it. This is known as the "fluid shock principle." *WARNING: Avoid jabbing or flicking punches. Such movements are futile and will only open you up to a variety of possible counterstrikes.*

### 58. TIGHTEN ON IMPACT.

Remember to tighten your fists upon impact with your selected target. This action will allow your natural body weapon to travel with optimum speed and efficiency, and augment the impact power of your strike.

### 59. AVOID COMMON PUNCHING ERRORS.

Avoid these common punching errors: (1) cocking your arm - this will telegraph your blow to the assailant, (2) dropping your other hand down - your assailant could effectively counterstrike, (3) tensing up - this will slow you down considerably, (4) lifting up your chin - this will expose your chin and throat to a possible strike, (5) dropping your shoulder - this will also open you up to a possible counterstrike, and (6) collapsing your wrist - this will result in a severe wrist sprain.

### 60. KEEP YOUR WRISTS STRAIGHT.

When throwing punches (circular or linear), make certain your wrists are correctly aligned with your forearm or you'll either sprain or break it. A sprained or broken wrist will put you out of commission immediately in most fights. When used properly, the heavy bag will train and condition you to keep your wrists straight when delivering powerful punches.

### 61. CENTER KNUCKLE CONTACT.

Punching effectively is truly an art form, requiring considerable time and training to master. When punching, hit with your center knuckle. This will maximize the impact of your blow, it affords proper skeletal alignment, and prevent unnecessary wrist sprains. *CAUTION: Avoid striking your assailant with your first two knuckles. This impact area diffuses the weight transfer of the blow and can also cause a sprained or broken wrist.*

### 62. STABILIZE AND MOVE.

When delivering a blow from a stationary position, apply the "stabilizer and mover" theory. This means torquing one side of your body (the striking side) while simultaneously stabilizing the other side. Applying this theory of body mechanics maximizes the power of your blows and minimizes your loss of balance.

### 63. SNAP YOUR PUNCHES.

Punches should snap when they hit a target. Here are a few suggestions to ensure that your punches will snap on

# STREET FIGHTING FUNDAMENTALS

impact: (1) try to accurately time the delivery of your blow, (2) properly judge the distance of your impact target, (3) avoid excessive follow-through when striking your target, (4) focus on retracting your blow without sacrificing neutralizing power, (5) avoid fully extending your elbow when punching.

## 64. USE YOUR THREE POWER GENERATORS.

When executing hand techniques from a stationary position, there are three anatomical *power generators* that will allow you to torque your body maximally. They include the following: (1) shoulders, (2) hips, and (3) feet. Maximally torquing your body into the blow will increase both the force and penetration of the blow. However, there is a very fine line between power and speed in relation to the three anatomical power generators. Here's an analytical breakdown:

| GENERATOR TYPE | POWER LEVEL | SPEED LEVEL |
|---|---|---|
| SHOULDER | minimal | maximal |
| *HIPS | moderate | moderate |
| **FEET | maximal | minimal |

*The hips are used in conjunction with the shoulder.
**The feet are used in conjunction with the hips and shoulder.

Employ all three power generators in the following circumstances: (1) when first introduced to a punching or striking technique; this will help you acquire body mechanic mastery, and (2) when executing a "first strike" from a stationary position. In most street fighting situations, however, it's best to utilize the first two power generators (shoulders and hips) in conjunction with forward movement when delivering a compound attack from the vertical plane.

## 65. DON'T LOCK YOUR ELBOWS.

When throwing linear punches, be certain not to lock your elbows. Elbow locking is a common problem among novices. When delivering a linear blow, your arm should be extended toward the target until the elbow is not more than a couple inches short of full extension. After contact is made with the target, the fist is returned back to the guard position. If your elbow locks upon impact, it will have a pushing effect and rob you of critical power.

## 66. FOLLOW THE LINE.

When executing linear blows (lead straights, rear crosses, finger jabs, palm heels), remember that your line of initiation should always be your line of retraction. Avoid arcing or dropping your blow. Such sloppy body mechanics will throw you off balance, minimize your impact power, and open you up for a possible counterattack. Failure to maintain a straight-line trajectory is usually caused by the following: (1) your elbow not traveling behind your punch, (2) premature wrist torque.

## 67. MASTER THE FINGER JAB STRIKE.

The *finger jab* is a quick, non telegraphic strike executed from your lead arm. Contact is made with your fingertips. The strike is likened to that of a snakebite. To execute the finger jab properly, quickly shoot your arm out and back. Don't tense your muscles prior to the execution of the strike. Just relax and send it out.

Targets for the finger jab are the assailant's eyes. Don't forget that a finger jab strike can cause temporary or permanent blindness, severe pain, and shock. With the finger jab, you want speed, accuracy, and, above all, non telegraphic movement.

# STREET FIGHTING FUNDAMENTALS

*Here, Franco demonstrates the finger jab.*

## 68. MASTER THE LEAD STRAIGHT.

The *lead straight* is a linear punch thrown from your lead arm, and contact is made with the center knuckle. To execute the lead straight, quickly twist your lead leg, hip, and shoulder forward. Snap your blow into the target and return to the starting position. A common mistake is to throw the punch and let it deflect off to the side. Targets for the lead straight include the nose, chin, and solar plexus.

## 69. MASTER THE PALM HEEL STRIKE.

The *palm-heel* strike is a powerful, open-hand linear blow that can be delivered from either the lead or rear arm. Contact is made with the heel of your palm with the fingers pointing up. Targets include your assailant's nose and chin.

When delivering the blow, be certain to torque your shoulder, hips, and foot into the direction of the strike. Make certain that your arm extends straight and the heel of your palm makes contact with either the assailant's nose or chin, then return to the starting position. Remember to retract your arm along the same line in which you initiated the strike.

*The palm heel strike.*

## 70. AVOID THESE PALM-HEEL ERRORS.

There are two common errors associated with the palm-heel strike: (1) Leading with the fingertips and not the heel of the palm. This is dangerous because it can cause finger jamming and certainly negate the effectiveness of your strike. To remedy this error, make certain to hyperextend your wrist prior to target impact. (2) Splaying fingers and thumb apart. This problem can also cause finger jamming and rob you of critical impact power. To remedy it, concentrate on keeping your thumb tucked and your fingers pressed together.

## 71. MASTER THE REAR CROSS.

The *rear cross* is the most powerful linear tool in your unarmed arsenal. This punch travels in a straight line to your assailant's nose, chin, or solar plexus. Proper waist twisting and weight transfer are of paramount importance to the rear cross. You must shift your weight from your rear foot to your lead leg as you throw the punch. You can generate bone-crushing force by torquing your rear foot, hip, and shoulder into the direction of the blow. To maximize the impact of the punch, make certain that your fist is positioned horizontally. Avoid overextending the blow or exposing your chin during its execution.

*Here, Franco demonstrates the rear cross.*

## 72. MASTER THE HOOK PUNCH.

The *hook punch* is one of the most devastating blows in your arsenal that can be delivered from both the lead and rear sides. However, it's also one of the most difficult to master. To execute the hook punch properly, you must maintain the correct wrist, forearm, and shoulder alignment. When delivering the strike, be certain your arm is bent at least 90 degrees and that your wrist and forearm are kept straight throughout the movement.

To execute the hook punch, quickly and smoothly raise your elbow up so that your arm is parallel to the ground while simultaneously torquing your shoulder, hip, and foot in the direction of the blow. As you throw the punch, be certain that your fist is positioned vertically. Never position your fist horizontally when throwing a hook. This inferior hand placement can cause a sprained or broken wrist.

## 73. KNOW THESE HOOK PUNCH FACTS.

The hook punch (lead and rear) is considered the heavy artillery of punches. However, there are some important facts that you should know about this blow. They include the following: (1) because of its angle of attack, the hook punch should be used judiciously with minimal telegraphing. Only highly skilled fighters should use the hook punch as an initiation blow in a street fight, (2) the hook punch is most commonly used when the adversary has dropped his hand guard or when the assailant's facial centerline is being flooded with linear blows, (3) the hook punch is a fractal tool that can be applied in both punching and grappling range combat.

## 74. MASTER THE UPPERCUT.

The *uppercut* is a powerful blow that can be delivered in both the punching and grappling ranges. This fractal tool travels in a vertical direction to either the assailant's chin or body, and it can be delivered from either the lead or rear arm.

To execute the uppercut, quickly twist and lift your body in the direction of the blow. Make certain that the punch has a short arc and that you avoid any "winding up" motions.

## 75. MASTER THE SHOVEL-HOOK PUNCH.

The *shovel hook* is a powerful punch that travels diagonally into your assailant. Like the hook punch, this blow can be delivered from both the lead and rear sides. Here is a good way to remember the proper angle of this punch: if the hook punch is positioned at three o'clock and your uppercut is at six o'clock, then your shovel hook is positioned between three and six o'clock. To properly execute the rear shovel hook, dip your shoulder and simultaneously twist your rear leg and hip into your target and then drive your entire body into the assailant. Once again, keep balanced and follow through your selected target.

## 76. MASTER THE HAMMER FIST.

The *hammer fist* is a powerful strike that can be delivered vertically and horizontally to either the assailant's nose or neck. To deliver the vertical hammer fist, begin by raising your fist, keeping your elbow flexed. Drive your clenched fist down in a vertical line onto the back of your assailant's neck.

Be certain to bend at your hips and knees and follow through your target.

To deliver the horizontal hammer fist, begin from the on-guard position, then simultaneously torque your shoulder, hip, and leg horizontally into your assailant's nose. Remember to keep your elbow bent on impact and maintain your balance throughout execution. *CAUTION: Never deliver a hammer-fist with a straight arm. This will rob you of speed and power and possibly cause a severe elbow strain.*

## 77. WEB HIM.

*Webbing* is a multi-purpose technique that serves several functions in unarmed combat. Some include the following: (1) Entry Tool - in order to apply the *Razing* method of fighting, you'll need to safely close the distance gap between you and your adversary. Fortunately, webbing can be used as a safe and dependable entry tool to CQC range (the distance where *razing* techniques are applied).

(2) First Strike Weapon - webbing is a devastating "stand-alone" striking technique that's virtually undetectable when executed. When delivered correctly, the webbing strike is safe, efficient and extremely effective.

(3) Razing Set-Up - if your webbing strike doesn't knock-out your adversary, it will soften him up (physically and psychologically) for the second phase of attack - razing!

(4) Defensive Tool - webbing can actually be used as a defensive response against an attack, and it's particularly effective when used in conjunction with the de-escalation stance.

*Here, Franco demonstrates the Webbing strike.*

STREET FIGHTING FUNDAMENTALS

## 78. MASTER THE KNIFE-HAND STRIKE.

The *Horizontal knife-hand* strike is another fractal tool that can be delivered in both grappling and punching ranges. It can also be delivered from both the lead and rear hands. To deliver the strike, quickly whip your hips, shoulder, and edge of your hand across and into the adversary's throat. Be certain to follow through the target. *WARNING:* The *Horizontal knife-hand should only be used in life-and-death situations!* Be certain that it is legally justified.

## 79. DON'T JAB.

The boxer's jab is a common punch used to throw the assailant off balance, set him up for another blow, test his skill, and keep him from moving toward you. Although this punch might be appropriate for the boxing ring, it has no purpose in real combat. The jab is unsuitable for combat for the following reasons: (1) it lacks neutralizing power, (2) it can expose you to a counterstrike, (3) it agitates your assailant, and (4) it prolongs the fight and allows the assailant the opportunity to counter with viciousness.

## 80. DON'T BACK FIST.

The back fist is a very popular punch used by many martial artists. Nevertheless, never employ a back fist in a real fight. It lacks neutralizing power and opens you up to a possible counterattack. Also, you can easily smash the delicate bones in the back of your hand if you come in contact with the assailant's head. If you want to attack the assailant with an angular blow, use a hook punch instead.

## 81. DON'T PROBE.

Never use a kick or punch to probe, test, or feel your assailant. Combat is the last place you want to experiment with the assailant. You don't want to employ techniques that probe, test, or stun your assailant. You want powerful, neutralizing blows that end the fight quickly and efficiently.

## 82. DON'T USE SPINNING PUNCHES.

There is no question that spinning techniques can generate tremendous power from cranking the entire body behind the blow. However, such techniques are risky. Spinning punches and kicks are impractical for the following reasons: (1) they're inefficient, (2) they require you to take your eyes off the assailant, (3) they momentarily expose your back to a possible attack, (4) they telegraph your movements, (5) they can cause you to slip and fall to the ground, (6) they disrupt your offensive flow, and (7) they require precise timing with your assailant's movement.

## 83. DON'T THROW OVERHEAD PUNCHES.

The overhead punch is a popular blow thrown by many street brawlers. This punch can be delivered using either hand, and it travels up and over your guarding hand. However, you should never throw this punch in a real fight because: (1) the body mechanics necessary to deliver this punch are telegraphic; (2) it lacks the necessary power to neutralize the assailant; (3) the angle of the blow forces your wrist out of skeletal alignment, and there's a very strong possibility that you can strain or break your wrist; (4) the angle of attack can cause you to strike the top of the assailant's head, and because the top of the human skull is so hard, you could easily break your hand upon impact.

STREET FIGHTING FUNDAMENTALS

# CLOSE-QUARTER TECHNIQUES

**84. MASTER ELBOW STRIKES.**

*Elbows strikes* are devastating weapons that can be used in the grappling range. They are explosive, deceptive, and very difficult to stop. Elbows can generally be delivered horizontally, vertically, and diagonally. Targets include the assailant's temple, throat, chin, cervical vertebrae, ribs, and solar plexus. When delivering elbow strikes, be certain to pivot your hips and shoulder forcefully in the direction of your blow.

(1) Vertical Elbow - The vertical elbow strike travels vertically to the assailant's face, throat, or body. It can be executed from either the right or left side of the body. To perform the strike, raise your elbow vertically (with the elbow flexed) until your hand is next to the side of your head. The striking surface is the point of the elbow. The power for this strike is acquired through the quick extension of the legs at the moment of impact.

(2) Horizontal Elbow - The horizontal elbow strike travels horizontally to the assailant's face, throat, or body. It can also be executed from either the right or left side of the body. To perform the strike, begin from the on-guard hand position, then rotate your hips and shoulders horizontally into your target. Your palms should be facing downward with your hand  next to the side of your head. The striking surface is the elbow point.

(3) Diagonal Elbow (traveling downward) - The diagonal elbow strike travels diagonally downward to the assailant's face, throat, or body. It can be delivered from either the right or

left side of the body. To execute the strike, rotate your elbow back, up, and over while quickly whipping it downward to your desired target. Bend your knees as your body descends with the strike. Your palm should be facing away from when making contact. The striking surface is the elbow point.

## 85. BITE.

When engaged in grappling range, you can use your teeth for biting the assailant's body (e.g., nose, ears, throat, fingers). Although a deep, penetrating bite is extremely painful, it also transmits a powerful psychological message to your assailant. It lets him know that you are willing to do anything to survive. *CAUTION: Biting should only be used as a last resort; you run the risk of contracting communicable diseases.*

## 86. MASTER KNEE STRIKES.

The *knee strike* is another devastating close-quarter grappling-range tool that can bring a formidable assailant to the ground instantly. The knee strike can be delivered vertically and diagonally to a variety of targets, including the common peroneal nerve, the quadriceps, the groin, the ribs, and, in some cases, the face. When delivering the knee strike, be certain to make contact with your patella and not your lower thigh. To guarantee sufficient power, deliver all your knee strikes with your rear leg.

# STREET FIGHTING FUNDAMENTALS

## 87. TOES POINT DOWN.

When delivering the vertical knee strike, keep your rear leg bent with your toes pointed to the ground. This toe position provides the following: (1) it helps maintain proper skeletal alignment, (2) it helps promote muscular relaxation, (3) it helps protect your toes from unnecessary injury, and (4) it facilitates rapid delivery.

## 88. MASTER THE MOUNTED POSITION.

The fighter who establishes the *top-mounted position* has a tremendous advantage in the ground fight. From this position, you can deliver a variety of blows and yet be in a strategic position to avoid most counterstrikes. The mounted position also restricts your assailant's mobility and permits you to generate tremendous power. If you want to be competent in a ground fight, it is critical that you master the four critical aspects of the mounted position, as follows: (1) attack - you must know how to attack your assailant from the mounted position, (2) defend - you must know how to defend an attack from the mounted position, (3) maintain - you must know how to maintain the mounted position, and (4) escape - you must know how to escape from the mounted position.

## 89. USE YOUR HEAD.

When engaged in close quarters combat (CQC), use your head for butting your assailant. *Head butts* are ideal when clinching with your adversary or when a strong attacker has placed you in a hold in which your arms are pinned against your sides. The head butt  can be delivered in the following four directions: (1) forward, (2) backward, (3) right side, and (4) left side.

## 90. STOMP.

The *foot stomp* is a deceptive close-quarter grappling technique that can cause excruciating pain for your assailant. To perform the foot stomp, raise your lead foot approximately 10 inches from the ground and forcibly stomp on the assailant's toes with the heel of your foot. If you doubt the effectiveness of a foot stomp, consider this sobering fact: a woman wearing high-heeled shoes can generate up to 1,600 pounds of pressure per square inch when delivering the foot stomp.

## 91. MASTER THE DOUBLE-THUMB GOUGE.

The *double-thumb gouge* is a nuclear grappling tactic that can produce devastating results. This tactic can be delivered when either standing or fighting on the ground. To perform the gouge, place one hand on each side of the assailant's face. Stabilize your hands by wrapping your fingers around both sides of your assailant's jaw. Immediately drive both your thumbs into the assailant's eye sockets. Maintain and increase forceful pressure. The double-thumb gouge can cause temporary or permanent blindness, shock, and unconsciousness.

*WARNING: The double-thumb gouge should only be used in life-and-death situations! Be certain that it is legally warranted and justified.*

## 92. CRUSH IT.

Crushing techniques are another nuclear ground-fighting tactic that can be used either when standing or ground fighting

STREET FIGHTING FUNDAMENTALS

with your adversary. The two primary crushing targets are your assailant's throat and testicles. When attacking the throat, make certain to drive your fingers deep into the assailant's trachea. Let them envelope the windpipe. Deliberately squeeze the pipe and try to crush it. When crushing the testicles, grab deep into the assailant's groin region, attempting to isolate the testicles. Squeeze and crush them together as forcefully as you can. *WARNING: Crushing techniques should only be used in life and death situations! Make certain that your actions are legally and morally justified.*

## 93. POSSESS GROUND-FIGHTING SKILLS.

Too many martial artists make the erroneous assumption that they can avoid or negate a grappling encounter. This faulty logic will get you killed in a real fight. The bottom line is if a fighter is determined to get you on the ground, he will, despite how good your techniques may be. As a matter of fact, statistics show that nine out of ten fights will end up on the ground. So be forewarned! See Chapter Five for more info.

## 94. WHENEVER POSSIBLE, AVOID SUBMISSION HOLDS.

Don't employ submission holds unless it's absolutely necessary. Although submission holds are significant components of your legal use-of-force response when you're required to control and restrain your adversary, always remember that the safest and most efficient method of neutralizing an assailant (in unarmed combat) is through impact techniques.

## 95. MASTER ANCHORING.

After hitting the opponent with the webbing strike, you must anchor him. Essentially, *anchoring* means controlling and preventing the opponent from disengaging the range of engagement, allowing you to employ the *razing* methodology. Moreover, there are two primary anchor points on the opponent: his neck and/or upper arm.

## 96. MASTER QUARTER-BEAT STRIKES

*Quarter beat strikes* comprise the majority of your *razing* arsenal. Essentially, they are a series of rapid hits that never break contact with the opponent's head targets, and they're primary responsible for creating the psychological panic and trauma for the opponent during a razing assault.

## 97. MASTER ESCAPE TECHNIQUES.

If you want to be prepared for anything, you'd better know escape and counter techniques to every conceivable grab, choke, lock, or hold. The following are 10 standing attacks that you should be prepared for: (1) one-and two-hand wrist grabs, (2) one-and two-hand throat chokes from the front and rear, (3) front and rear bear hugs with and without pinned arms, (4) standing side headlocks (both right and left sides), (5) finger pokes, (6) one-and two-hand shoulder grabs, (7) one-and two-hand chest pushes, (8) rear arm locks (both right and left arms), (9) one-and two-hand lapel grabs, and (10) body tackles. *REMEMBER: Escaping from various chokes and holds requires intuitive reaction. It must be second nature the instant you feel contact.*

STREET FIGHTING FUNDAMENTALS

# DEFENSIVE TECHNIQUES

### 98. DEFENSE IS A LAST RESORT.

Ideally, your best defense is a strong and powerful offense, but there will be situations that demand a defensive response. However, don't misunderstand the necessity of a strong defense by becoming a defensive fighter. A defensive fighter is one who lets his assailant seize and maintain offensive control. This is not what you want. Defense is a temporary setback that will eventually allow you to counter with offensive viciousness. There is a strategic line between offense and defense, victory and defeat, and life and death.

### 99. THE SEVEN COMPONENTS OF DEFENSE.

The seven components necessary for a sound defensive structure are as follows: (1) distance - the spatial relationship between you and your adversary, (2) stance - the strategic posture you assume prior to or during combat, (3) mobility - the ability to move your body quickly and freely while balanced, (4) blocking - various defensive tools designed to intercept your assailant's oncoming blows, (5) parrying -various defensive tools that redirect your assailant's blows, (6) evading - defensive maneuvers strategically designed to neutralize your assailant's attack without making contact, and (7) attacking - offensive action can be a defensive approach designed to control, injure, cripple, or kill your assailant.

### 100. BLOCK.

Blocks are defensive techniques designed to intercept your assailant's circular attacks. Blocks are executed by placing a non vital body part between the assailant's strike and your anatomical body target. Although blocks require significant deviation from your centerline, they are an essential component of defense. Blocks are divided into the following two general categories: (1) arm blocks - serve as protective barriers that intercept punches and kicks directed to your head and torso and (2) leg block - specifically designed to stop kicks directed to targets below your waist. There are seven blocks, as follows: high blocks, mid blocks, low blocks, elbow blocks, leg blocks, cross blocks, and reinforced low blocks (the last two are used only in rare circumstances).

## 101. NEVER BLOCK STRAIGHT BLOWS.

The quickest and most efficient strikes are those that travel in a straight line. Never attempt to block an assailant's linear punch. A block simply does not have the mechanical speed or efficient mechanics to intercept a linear blow. Always use parries to defend against linear punches.

## 102. MAINTAIN YOUR BALANCE WHEN BLOCKING.

When blocking, it's essential to maintain a strong center of balance. Balance is the ability to maintain equilibrium while attacking or defending and while stationary or moving. Since most circular punches carry significant force, you must make an extra effort to maintain your position and avoid being knocked off balance.

To avoid being knocked off balance when blocking an assailant's blow, apply the following: (1) increase your torso rotation to enhance the power of your blocking structure, (2) make certain to set your feet on the ground, and (3) time your blocking movement properly.

## 103. WITHDRAW IT.

Whenever executing an arm block, make certain to withdraw it back to the original on-guard position. This is

# STREET FIGHTING FUNDAMENTALS

important for the following reasons: (1) it places you in a better position to effectively counter your assailant, (2) it minimizes centerline exposure (3) it will help prevent your assailant from grabbing or controlling your arm.

## 104. BLOCKS ARE FOR UNARMED ENCOUNTERS.

Blocking techniques are intended for unarmed encounters. Don't make the tragic mistake of attempting to use blocking techniques to stop an attack from a stick, bludgeon, or any edged weapon. Such action can cause you severe injury and even death.

## 105. INTERCEPT IT AS SOON AS POSSIBLE.

Whenever attempting a block, try to intercept the assailant's attack as soon as possible. In most cases, try to intercept the assailant's blow when it reaches approximately two-thirds (75 percent of maximum impact) of the way to its target, or sooner. This is important for the following reasons: (1) it minimizes balance disruption, (2) it minimizes the contusions on your arm, (3) it quickly arrests the assailant's attack, and (4) it minimizes the assailant's impact power. *WARNING: When blocking, don't let your assailant's blow make contact when it is 100 percent completed.*

## 106. MASTER THE HIGH BLOCK.

The *high block* is used to defend against overhead punches. To execute the lead high block, simply raise your lead arm up and extend your forearm out and above your head. Be careful not to position your arm where your head is exposed. Make certain that your hand is open and not clenched. This will increase the surface area of your block and provide a quick counterattack. The mechanics for the rear high block are the same for the lead high block. Raise your rear arm up and extend your forearm out and above your head.

## 107. MASTER THE MID-BLOCK.

One of the most important blocks in a street fight is the *mid-block,* which is used to defend against circular blows to your head or upper torso. To perform the block, raise either your right or left arm up at approximately a 90-degree angle while simultaneously pronating it in the direction of the strike. Make contact with the belly of your forearm at the assailant's wrist or forearm. This movement will provide maximum structural integrity. Make certain your hand is held open to increase the surface area of your block. Also, be certain to time the rotation of your arm with the attack. Don't forget that the mid-block has both height (up and down) and a width (in and out) fluctuations that are relative to the characteristics of the assailant's blow. Once you deliver the block, immediately counter.

## 108. BEWARE OF THESE MID-BLOCK ERRORS.

There are two common errors that are associated with the mid-block. They are: (1) Making contact with the back of your forearm - this mistake can injure your arm and significantly weaken your blocking structure. To remedy this error, be certain to rotate your forearm into a palm-out position prior to intercepting the assailant's punch. (2) Inadequate shoulder and trunk rotation - you will fail to generate sufficient force to

# STREET FIGHTING FUNDAMENTALS

effectively intercept the oncoming blow. This mistake can cause your assailant's blow to come crashing through your block. To remedy this problem, increase your shoulder and trunk rotation and sweep your arm aggressively in the direction of the attack.

### 109. MASTER THE ELBOW BLOCK.

The *elbow block* is used to stop circular blows to your midsection, such as uppercuts, shovel hooks, and hook kicks. To execute the elbow block, drop your elbow down and simultaneously twist your body toward your centerline. Be certain to keep your elbow perpendicular to the floor and your hands relaxed and close to your chest. The elbow block can be used on both the right and left sides.

### 110. MASTER THE LOW BLOCK.

Though seldom called into action, the *low block* is used to defend against linear attacks to your midsection. To execute the lead low block, drop your lead arm so your forearm is parallel to the ground and ensure that your fingers are pointing up to protect against jamming or breaks. With the low block, contact is made with the belly of the forearm and not the palm. The mechanics are the same for the rear low block. Simply drop your rear arm down to meet the assailant's strike.

### 111. BLOCK WITH YOUR LEGS.

If your assailant attacks with low-line kicks or attempts a sweeping technique, you only have one or two possible options: (1) Evasion - you can evade the kick by stepping out of its range or by moving to the right or left. This is accomplished through quick and explosive footwork, (2) Leg block - you can execute a leg block to intercept/ choke/deflect the oncoming kick. The leg block can be delivered from either your lead or rear leg, and it can be positioned at a variety of angles, heights, and vantages. Generally, the leg block should be used only when you can't evade the attack. Realistically speaking, you don't want to absorb the force of any kick if you have the option of evading it.

### 112. MASTER THE LEG BLOCK.

The *leg block* is used when your assailant executes either a foot sweep or a low-line kick. To perform the leg block, raise your lead leg up to intercept and deflect your assailant's kick. Make contact with the sides of your calves, not your shinbone. Also, make certain that your toe is pointed to the ground to increase the surface area of  your defensive tool. The leg block can be executed in the following three general directions: (1) forward, (2) at a right angle, and (3) at a left angle.

### 113. DON'T BOB OR WEAVE.

The bob and weave are popular defensive techniques. The bob drops your body down from the waist, and the weave pulls you to the other side. Bobbing and weaving works great for boxers in the ring, but it should not be used in a street fight. The bob and weave are dangerous for the following reasons: (1) they leave you open to knee or elbow strikes, (2) they lack overall economy of motion, (3) they inhibit your vision.

## STREET FIGHTING FUNDAMENTALS

### 114. DON'T DUCK.

Ducking is the process of dropping your body down and forward to avoid the assailant's blows. This defensive maneuver is dangerous for the following reasons: (1) it's a relatively slow defensive move, (2) you can unintentionally move yourself into knee or elbow strikes, and (3) it prohibits evasive and explosive footwork.

### 115. DON'T FEINT OR FAKE.

Feints and fakes are setup techniques that can draw either offensive or defensive reactions from the adversary, thereby opening him up for a real blow. These and other deceptions are commonly used in tournament competitions and sparring matches to test the opponent, wear him down, and score valuable points. In real combat, however, you cannot afford the risk and uncertainty of such techniques. Any initiating tool delivered with less than maximum speed, power, and commitment will be countered with viciousness. In combat, you cannot afford to gamble that your assailant will react in the manner intended. *WARNING: Experimentation in the face of danger is an invitation for disaster!*

### 116. DON'T USE STOP-HITS.

A stop-hit is a method of hitting the assailant before his tool reaches full extension. Unfortunately, however, stop-hits are unsafe for combat. Take, for example, the shoulder stop. This defensive technique is especially dangerous because it moves you closer to the assailant's striking limb. This can be particularly problematic if the assailant has longer appendages than you. Worse yet, the shoulder stop can promote a grappling situation. Most importantly, the shoulder stop will only work if you're confronted with an inferior fighter who dramatically telegraphs his blows.

## 117. DON'T USE DESTRUCTIONS.

A "destruction" is a technique that attacks the assailant's attacking limb on the first beat. Destructions are risky and shouldn't be used in unarmed combat. Here are a couple reasons why: (1) in unarmed combat, it makes no sense to attack the assailant's striking limb when you have a wide variety of weaker targets available; (2) in almost all cases, you won't have the necessary psychomotor speed to strike the assailant's limbs (biceps or hand) effectively. The bottom line is that destruction techniques are geared for sparring scenarios, not vicious street fights.

## 118. DON'T FEINT OR FAKE.

Feints and fakes are setup techniques that can draw either offensive or defensive reactions from the adversary, thereby opening him up for a real blow. These and other deceptions are commonly used in tournament competitions and sparring matches to test the opponent, wear him down, and score valuable points. In real combat, however, you cannot afford the risk and uncertainty of such techniques. Any initiating tool delivered with less than maximum speed, power, and commitment will be countered with viciousness. In combat, you cannot afford to gamble that your assailant will react in the manner intended. *WARNING: Experimentation in the face of danger is an invitation for disaster!*

## 119. DON'T SHOULDER ROLL.

The shoulder roll is a defensive technique that rocks your body away from a punch in order to nullify its force. This maneuver is risky because it's predicated on the assumption that the assailant is just going to throw a single blow and wait for you to counter. Furthermore, rolling with any punch takes you out of strategic position, exposes your targets, and eliminates mobility and offensive deployability.

## 120. MASTER THE STIFF-ARM JAM.

The *stiff-arm jam* is defensive technique specifically used to negate the destructive force of both the *upper and mid body tackles*. To perform the technique, simultaneously lower your base (height change to level of entry) and extend both of your arms forward. Both of your palms should make contact with the assailant's upper chest and shoulder. Be certain to pull your fingers back to avoid accidental sprains or breaks. Your objective is to instantaneously negate or "jam" the overwhelming force of the takedown.

## 121. ADAPT TO HIS LEVEL OF ENTRY.

In order for your adversary to perform an effective takedown, he must lower his base and get his hips under you. This means he will need to bend his knees and torso to lower his *level of entry*. Therefore, when your adversary gets within his "shooting range" for the takedown and lowers his level of entry, it's critical that you immediately adjust and match his height change. This action will dramatically reduce the effectiveness of his takedown.

## 122. CLINCH DEFENSIVELY.

*Clinching* is used for both offensive and defensive purposes. For defense, clinching should be employed immediately after you have performed a specific defensive technique such as a block, parry, stiff-arm jam, webbing technique, etc. When defensively clinching, you negate the grappler's offensive flow by bypassing his assault and re-establishing offensive control.

## 123. MASTER THE PARRY.

The *parry* is a quick, forceful slap that picks off and redirects your assailant's linear strike (jab, lead straight, or rear cross). There are two general types of parries: horizontal and vertical. Both can be executed from the right and left hands. (1) Horizontal Parry - to properly execute a horizontal parry, from a stance, move your lead hand horizontally across your body (centerline) to deflect and redirect the assailant's punch. Immediately return to your guard position. Be certain to make contact with the palm of your hand. With sufficient training, you can effectively incorporate the horizontal parry with your slipping maneuvers. (2) Vertical Parry - to execute a vertical parry, move your hand vertically down your body to deflect and redirect the assailant's blow. *Never parry with your fingers! The fingers provide no structural integrity, and can be jammed or broken easily.*

## 124. BE EVASIVE.

Evasive techniques are designed to nullify your assailant's attack without making contact. Evasive techniques include the following: (1) sidestepping - stepping laterally (right or left) to avoid contact with the adversary, (2) retreating - stepping back to avoid contact with the assailant, (3) slipping - swaying your head and torso (right, left, and back) to avoid the assailant's blow, and (4) escaping - running or escaping from the scene to avoid contact with the adversary.

## 125. SLIP IT.

*Slipping* is a quick defensive maneuver that permits you to avoid an assailant's linear blow (jab, lead straight, rear cross, or palm heel) without stepping out of range. Safe and effective slipping requires precise timing and is accomplished by quickly snapping the head and upper torso sideways (right or left) or backwards to avoid the oncoming blow. One of the best advantages to slipping is that it frees your hands so that you can simultaneously counter.

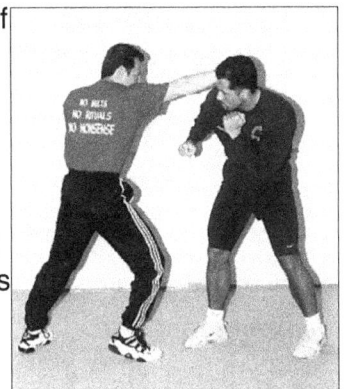

There are three ways to slip. They include the following: (1) Slipping right - start from a stance and quickly sway your head and upper torso to the right to avoid the assailant's blow. Quickly counter or return to the starting position. (2) Slipping left - start from a stance and quickly sway your head and upper torso to the left to avoid the assailant's linear blow. Quickly counter or return to the starting position. (3) Slipping back (also called the snap back) - start from a stance and quickly snap your head back far enough to avoid being hit. Quickly counter or return to the starting position.

## 126. KNOW HOW TO STOP A POSTAL ATTACK.

*Going postal* describes an adversary who's gone off the deep end and unexpectedly attacks you with an explosive and frenzied flurry of blows. Adrenaline, rage, and fear are the three primary ingredients that fuels a postal attack, and the most effective way to deal with this type of assault is the shielding wedge.

## 127. MASTER THE SHIELDING WEDGE

When your adversary "goes postal", your objective is to get from point A to B as quickly and safely as possible, because danger and vulnerability can be found in time and distance.

Your tactical objective is to reduce both of them as quickly as possible, and the shielding wedge is your best option.

$$A \xrightarrow{\dfrac{\text{TIME+DISTANCE}}{\text{VULNERABILITY}}} B$$

The *shielding wedge* technique is found in my F*eral Fighting Program* and it's predicated on the ancient Greek military formation known as the Phalanx. When used correctly, this technique will effectively protect your face, neck, and throat from the opponent's postal attack.

While the shielding wedge technique is a gross motor skill movement, it still requires specific arm, shoulder and head articulation. Proper body mechanics and correct timing are also crucial. However, once mastered, the shielding wedge maneuver will become an instinctual defensive tool that can be deployed under the stress of a ballistic postal attack.

Don't confuse the shielding wedge with its cousin the webbing strike that's featured in my *Widow Maker Program*. While both look similar, they possess antithetical objectives and require significantly different hand and arm configurations.

*Here, Franco demonstrates the Shielding Wedge technique.*

# FOOTWORK & MOBILITY

### 128. MOBILITY IS ESSENTIAL.

Here's seven strategic reasons why mobility is essential for combat, as follows: (1) a moving target is harder to hit, (2) your assailant can misjudge your proximity, (3) it throws the assailant's timing off, (4) it helps prevent multiple assailants from surrounding you, (5) it helps you locate escape routes, (6) it enhances the overall power of your blows (remember that movement is a natural power generator), and (7) it sometimes aids in acquiring superior positioning.

### 129. MASTER THE FOUR DIRECTIONS OF FOOTWORK.

Basic footwork is structured around four general directions: (1) forward (advancing) - from your stance, first move your front foot forward (approximately 12 inches) and then advance your rear foot an equal distance; (2) backward (retreating) - from your stance, first move your rear foot backward (approximately 12 inches) and then move your front foot an equal distance; (3) moving right (sidestepping right) - from your stance, first move your right foot to the right (approximately 12 inches) and then move your left foot an equal distance; and (4) moving left (sidestepping left) - from your stance, first move your left foot to the left (approximately 12 inches) and then move your right foot an equal distance.

### 130. ACQUIRE EXPLOSIVE FOOTWORK.

Explosive footwork is important for both offensive and defensive purposes. In offense, explosive footwork allows you to maintain compound attacking range. In defense, explosive footwork allows you to disengage quickly from a range of overwhelming assault.

The explosiveness of your footwork is predicated on the

following factors: (1) footwork - you must master the basics of footwork before incorporating explosiveness, (2) proper body posture - maintaining correct body posture through footwork movements will prevent loss of balance, (3) powerful legs - strong legs allow you to launch your body effortlessly, (4) equal weight distribution - noncommittal weight distribution allows you to move instantly in any direction, (5) raised heel - creates a springlike effect in your movements.

### 131. PRACTICE SAFE FOOTWORK.

The safest footwork for combat involves quick, economical steps performed on the balls of your feet while you remain relaxed and balanced. When moving on the balls of your feet, always try to keep your legs shoulder-width apart and your weight evenly distributed. Moving on the balls of your feet does not mean haphazardly dancing around your assailant. This type of showboating will get you into serious trouble. Always move with a strategic purpose in mind.

### 132. LUNGE.

During a postal attack situation, you will most likely be using *lunging footwork* to quickly close the distance gap between you and your frenzied attacker. To perform the lunge, move your front foot forward (approximately 24-26 inches) and then move your rear foot an equal distance. Explosive forward movement is generated by pushing off the ball of the back foot.

### 133. STEP AND DRAG.

Use the *step and drag* footwork when standing on slippery and unstable terrain. Some examples of unstable terrain include ice, snow, wet grass, wet concrete, wet leaves, wet metal, wet wood, sand, gravel, mulch, mud, and rock.

## 134. MASTER SIDESTEPPING.

Since many street fighters attack by charging or lunging forward, it's important to master sidestepping. Sidestepping is the process of quickly moving your body laterally (right or left) to evade your charging assailant. When sidestepping, avoid dropping your hand guard. Your hands must be up to protect and counter the assailant. Also, don't bend at your waist. Keep your torso erect and avoid unnecessary shoulder shifting.

## 135. AVOID THESE SIDESTEPPING ERRORS.

(1) Your assailant runs over you - this is because you are moving too slowly. To remedy this problem, keep your weight evenly distributed and explode off the balls of your feet. (2) Your assailant tracks you - this is because you are moving too soon. To remedy this problem, avoid premature movements and wait until the very last second before you explode laterally.

## 136. MASTER STRATEGIC CIRCLING.

*Strategic circling* is an advanced form of footwork where the fighter uses his lead leg as a pivot point. Strategic circling can be used defensively to evade an overwhelming assault or offensively to strike the adversary from a strategic angle. It can be performed from either the southpaw or orthodox stance: (1) circling right (from a southpaw stance) - from a right lead stance, step 6 to 8 inches to the right with your right foot, then use your right leg as a pivot point and wheel your entire rear leg to the right until the correct stance and positioning is acquired. Remember to keep both of your hands up in case your adversary counters; (2) circling left (from an orthodox stance) - from a left lead stance, step 6 to 8 inches to the left with your left foot, then use your left leg as a pivot point and wheel your entire rear leg to the left until the correct stance and positioning is acquired.

### 137. BE DYNAMIC.

No form of combat (armed or unarmed) is ever going to be a static encounter. There is always going to be some type of movement. Be prepared for it!

### 138. NEVER CROSS-STEP.

Cross-stepping is the process of crossing one foot in front or behind the other when moving. Such sloppy footwork makes you vulnerable to a variety of dangers and risks, including: (1) severely compromising your balance, (2) restricting tool and technique implementation, (3) prohibiting explosive and evasive footwork, (5) promoting structural breakdown, and (6) contorting your stance.

The best way to avoid cross-stepping is to follow this basic footwork rule of thumb: *always move the foot closest to the direction you want to go first and let the other foot follow an equal distance.* In other words, no matter what direction you elect to travel, the foot nearest to your intended direction will always lead the way.

### 139. DON'T BE AIRBORNE.

Exploding off the balls of your feet is a critical aspect of an effective offensive attack. However, when moving forward, always keep at least one foot in contact with the ground. You never want to be "airborne" in a fight.

# CHAPTER TWO
## Training and Conditioning

*"If you are unfit or out of shape, you won't stand a chance against a vicious assailant. It's that simple."*

TRAINING & CONDITIONING

# GOALS AND OBJECTIVES

**140. DEFINE YOUR GOALS.**

Before you invest a lot of time and money in self-defense training, it's important to first define your goals. What do you hope to accomplish by studying and training for the next 12 months? For example, do you want to get in better shape? Build up your confidence? Handle a vicious street thug? Or do you want to be capable of fighting multiple assailants? Now is the time to sit and write down all of the goals that you hope to achieve in the course of your self-defense training.

**141. MAKE THE TIME.**

Although the academic aspects of combat are important, physical practice is critical. If you want to be prepared for a life-threatening encounter, you've got to set aside some time from your busy schedule to practice and refine your skills. This will obviously require a bit of discipline and planning on your part. To really progress in self-defense, you'll need to train at least three times per week. However, more frequent training sessions will not only accelerate your progress, but also ensure that your current skills and tactics are razor-sharp.

Real-world self-defense training is not just limited to unarmed combat. If you own a firearm, you have a responsibility to visit the firing range on a consistent basis. This also applies if you rely on a knife, pepper spray, or defensive baton. You have to practice using it on a regular basis, or you will lose your strategic edge.

**142. COMMIT 100 PERCENT.**

Always train with total commitment. The bottom line is that there are no shortcuts to achieving combat mastery.

# TRAINING PRELIMINARIES

### 143. SEE A DOCTOR.

Before you begin an exercise program, make certain that you have been cleared by your doctor. Since there is always some risk involved in self-defense training, and because each person is unique, it's important that before beginning any type of training program you have a complete physical exam.

### 144. TAKE YOUR PULSE.

The only real way to know if you're exercising in your training zone is to take your pulse. There are two primary locations for taking your pulse: (1) Wrist - specifically the radial artery. Place both your index and middle fingers below the base of your thumb, just above the tendons. Press lightly against the inside of the wrist until you feel a steady beat. (2) Neck - specifically the carotid artery. Place both your index and middle fingers on either the right or left side of your Adam's apple in front of the muscles running down the side of the neck. Press firmly against the neck until you feel a steady pulse.

Once you find the pulse on either your neck or wrist, count the number of beats for 10 seconds, then multiply that number by six. This will give you your heart rate for one minute. *REMEMBER: If your heart rate is below 70 percent of your maximum heart rate, increase the intensity of your workout. (See secret number 155 in this chapter for the formula to calculate your training zone.)*

### 145. DETERMINE YOUR TRAINING ZONE.

To benefit from any aerobic workout (e.g., running, skipping rope, stationary bicycling), you must elevate your heart rate to its proper *training zone*. The training zone (or target heart rate) is a safe and effective level of physical activity that produces cardiorespiratory fitness. Your training zone can be anywhere between 70 and 85 percent of your maximum heart rate.

To find your training zone, use the following formula: (1) calculate your base training level by subtracting your age from 220, then multiply that number by 70 percent, or .70; (2) to calculate your upper training level, repeat the first step but multiply by .85 (85 percent) instead of .70.

For example, a man who is 30 years of age would calculate his training zone as follows: (1) 220 - 30 = 190 and 190 x .70 = 133 beats per minute (bpm); (2) 190 bpm x .85 = 162 bpm. Therefore, our 30-year-old man's training zone ranges from 133 beats per minute to 162 beats per minute. Keep in mind that exercising below 70 percent of your maximum heart rate does little for improving your cardiovascular fitness level. *WARNING: Stop exercising immediately if you experience: (1) chest pain, (2) shortness of breath when not exercising hard, (3) nausea, (4) dizziness, and (5) irregular heartbeat.*

### 146. WARM UP.

Every workout should begin with a series of mild exercises, stretches, and movements designed to prepare the fighter for more intense exercise. Properly warming up before a tough workout is important for the following reasons: (1) it gradually increases your body temperature, (2) it safely increases your heart rate, (3) it helps prevent muscle and tendon strains, and (4) it provides psychological preparation for your workout.

# EQUIPMENT

### 147. USE A CLOCK APP.

A clock app can significantly enhance your skills and

abilities. You can use it for the following: (1) to accurately measure your current level of fitness and conditioning, (2) to monitor your progress in your training, (3) to test the speed of your techniques (i.e., drawing and shooting speed, punching and striking speed, escaping speed, and threat-assessment speed), and (4) to add a bit of healthy competition to your training routine. *REMEMBER: When selecting a clock for your training, make certain that the numbers are clear and visible and that the clock has a second hand.*

### 148. SPARE NO EXPENSE.

When purchasing training gear, spare no expense. Combat training is a serious matter, and your training gear should reflect it. Good equipment will provide years of reliable use and enhance your skills. Here's a brief list of the training gear that you'll need: 28-inch gym bag, leather headgear, mouthpiece and carrying case, groin cup, leather boxing gloves (12 ozs. minimum), leather bag gloves, leather skip rope, two 26-inch rattan sticks, rubber training knife, and mock training pistol.

### 149. VIDEO YOUR WORKOUTS.

If you really want to see your skills and abilities, video your workouts. The video will provide you with a more accurate picture of what you are doing in your training. You'll be able to observe mistakes and recognize your combat strengths and weaknesses. The video will also motivate you to train harder. Date each video clip; later on you will be able to compare and see marked improvements in your fighting performance.

### 150. VARY THE EQUIPMENT.

Equipment is a vital part of training. It will systematically develop your tools, skills, and attributes of both armed and unarmed combat. However, to maximize your training, you should use a wide variety of equipment. For example, mannequin heads are ideal for finger jabs, eye rakes, and thumb gouges. Kicks and knee strikes can be developed on striking shields. Focus mitts will sharpen all of your striking tools as well as the fundamental attributes of combat. A full-length mirror will help you critique and refine your stances, maneuvers, and de-escalation skills. Boxing gloves, durable headgear, and other protective equipment will permit effective and safe sparring. The heavy bag is excellent for developing power in all of your natural body weapons. Foam and plastic baseball bats are a must for bludgeon defenses. Chalkable rubber knives are essential for practicing edged-weapon defenses and knife-fighting skills. Trigger-sensitive (mock) pistols should also be used to practice disarming techniques, quick-draw skills, firearm stances, and firearm fundamentals. Dummy cartridges are also excellent for speed-loading drills.

### 151. FOLLOW THESE IMPORTANT GUIDELINES.

To maximize your training and minimize the possibility of injury, follow these important guidelines when using impact equipment (i.e., striking shields, heavy bags, focus mitts) for the first time: (1) begin with light impact and progressively build up to approximately 75 percent power and speed, (2) be cognizant of your form when delivering your blows, (3) be aware of proper skeletal alignment, (4) be especially careful when executing open-hand techniques on impact equipment.

### 152. MOVE, MOVE, MOVE.

When working out on various pieces of training equipment (e.g., heavy bag, focus mitts, striking shield, double-end bag), try to avoid remaining stationary. Get into the habit of constantly moving around with quick, economical steps. Remember, combat is fluid and dynamic, not static!

### 153. HIT THE BAG.

For unarmed combat training, the heavy bag is the single most important piece of training equipment. Its primary purpose is to develop power in all of your offensive techniques. This cylindrical-shaped bag is approximately 40 inches in height and is constructed of either top-grain leather, heavy canvas, or vinyl. The interior of the bag is generally filled with some type of cotton fiber. Heavy bags can weigh anywhere from 35 to 200 pounds; however, the average bag weighs approximately 85 pounds.

Here are some important tips when working out on the bag: (1) gradually build up the force of your blows - a beginner's wrists are generally too weak to accommodate full-force punches; (2) maintain your balance - never sacrifice balance for power; (3) snap your blow - avoid "pushing" the bag; (4) keep your wrists straight when your fists hit the bag; (5) maintain proper form when striking the bag; (6) move around - avoid remaining stationary when striking the bag; (7) harmoniously integrate your kicks, punches, and strikes to develop devastating compound attacks; (8) pace yourself - avoid premature exhaustion; (9) wear protective bag gloves; and (10) stay relaxed - avoid unnecessary muscular tension.

### 154. AVOID SKINNING YOUR KNUCKLES.

If you're skinning your knuckles on the heavy bag, you are most likely dropping your fist slightly during the retraction phase of your technique. Learn to retract your fist through the same trajectory that you used in initiating the punch.

## TRAINING & CONDITIONING

**155. USE HAND WRAPS.**

When engaged in all-out heavy bag sessions, it is wise to protect your hands and wrists with hand wraps. Hand wraps are sold at sporting goods stores. They are long strips of cloth measuring 2 inches wide and 9 feet long. They are washable and should be cleaned after every couple workouts.

## 156. LEARN FROM BIO FEEDBACK.

When working out on the heavy bag (or any piece of equipment for that matter), learn from the negative or painful feedback, such as strains or sprains on your joints or wrists. They are telling you something about your technique.

## 157. HIT BOB.

The body opponent bag or BOB is a great piece of equipment for reality-based training. Compared to the heavy bag, the BOB is a specialized punching bag that develops a broader scope of techniques, including a wide variety of kicks, punches, and strikes. However, the primary purpose of the BOB is to develop target accuracy.

This bag is also ideal for weapons training. For example, you can practice stick strikes, knife attacks, kubotan techniques, and even pepper spray training on the bag. Just be certain to use the right equipment when training or you can permanently damage the bag. Finally, the body opponent bag is perfect for developing your *razing* skills and techniques, by providing realistic facial targets.

## 158. DRAW Xs.

To develop more precise targeting, draw small Xs on your heavy bags, focus mitts, and striking shields. This practice will help develop accuracy in your striking techniques.

## 159. USE THE STRIKING SHIELD.

The striking shield is a versatile piece of training equipment that develops power in most of your kicks, punches, and strikes. This rectangular-shaped shield is constructed of foam and vinyl and is designed to withstand tremendous punishment. As with focus mitt training, your partner plays a vital role in a good striking shield workout. He must hold the shield at the proper height and angle while simultaneously moving in and out of the ranges of combat. The intensity of your workout will depend on his ability to push you to your limit. More importantly, your partner must learn how to absorb a powerful kick without losing his balance or injuring himself.

**160. USE THE DOUBLE-END BAG.**

The double-end bag is a small leather ball suspended by a bungee cord. It is a valuable piece of training equipment that develops timing, accuracy, rhythm, coordination, footwork, and speed. The bag requires considerable practice and a lot of patience. In fact, it is probably one of the most difficult pieces of training equipment to master. Most beginners become very frustrated when working with the double-end bag. To properly control the movement of the bag, you must hit it directly in the center. If you don't strike it dead center, it will bounce uncontrollably to the right and left.

**161. WEAR BAG GLOVES.**

Bag gloves offer excellent protection to the hands when working out on the heavy bag or focus mitts. Most are constructed of either top-grain cowhide or durable vinyl, and some have a metal weight sewn into the palm grip area to aid in punching power. Sizes available are usually small, medium, large, and extra large.

**162. TAKE THEM OFF.**

Although bag gloves are important for protecting your hands when training, every once in a while you should work out without them. This will give you a much more realistic feeling for punching.

**163. USE MANNEQUIN HEADS.**

To sharpen eye strikes while moving about, use mannequin heads. These creepy-looking cosmetology mannequins can be manipulated at different heights and vantages, allowing you to sharpen your eye strikes. Best of all, they're inexpensive and can be purchased online.

**164. TRAIN WITH FOCUS MITTS.**

The focus mitt is an exceptional piece of training equipment that can be used by anyone. It develops accuracy, speed, target recognition, target selection, target impact, and timing in all offensive techniques. By placing the mitts at various angles and levels, you can perform every conceivable kick, punch, or strike. Properly utilized, focus mitts will refine your defensive reaction time and condition your entire body.

Focus mitts are constructed of durable leather designed to withstand tremendous punishment. Compared to other pieces of training equipment, the focus mitt is relatively inexpensive. However, an effective workout requires two mitts (one for each hand). Your training partner (called the feeder) plays a vital role in focus-mitt workouts by controlling the tools you execute and the cadence of delivery. The intensity of your workouts will depend largely upon his or her ability to manipulate the mitts and push you to your limit. *REMEMBER: There's an old saying in CFA regarding focus-mitt feeders. A good focus-mitt feeder is one step ahead of his training partner, whereas a great focus-mitt feeder is two steps ahead of his partner.*

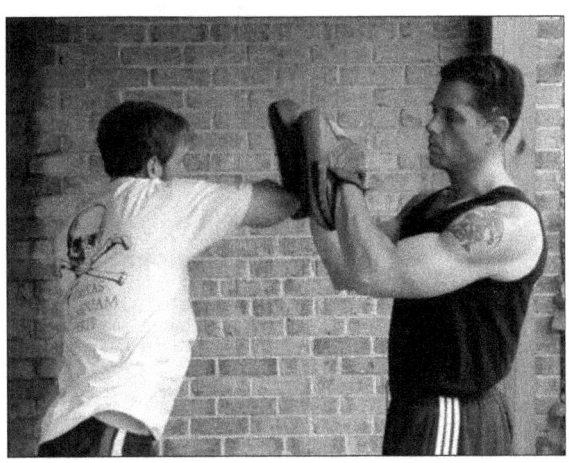

To truly benefit from any focus mitt workout, you must learn to concentrate intensely throughout the entire session. Block out all distractions. Try to visualize the mitt as a living, breathing assailant, not an inanimate target. This type of visualization will make a big difference.

## 165. COMMUNICATE WITH YOUR TRAINING PARTNER.

When training with a focus mitt feeder, give feedback and let your training partner know how he's doing. Remember, communication is vital during your training sessions.

## 166. WEAR DIFFERENT SHOES.

Practice footwork skills and kicking techniques with the following types of footwear: combat boots, hiking boots, running shoes, cross-trainers, sandals, cowboy boots, and loafers. Also practice when barefoot.

## 167. USE THE MEDICINE BALL.

The medicine ball is a large, heavy leather ball that is stuffed with cotton waste. It is used to strengthen and condition the abdominal wall and obliques. When used properly, the medicine ball also develops proper breathing, endurance, and the ability to withstand powerful body blows. Avoid overtraining on the ball. Practice no more than two times per week. Two of the best ways to train with the medicine ball is to have a training partner throw it into your stomach while you are standing, or to lie down on your back and have him drop it repeatedly onto your abdomen.

## 168. AVOID THE SPEED BAG.

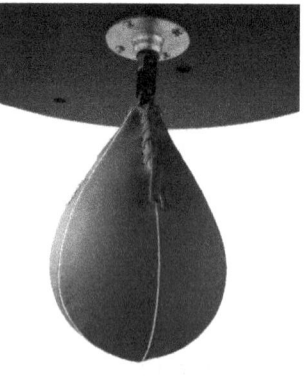

The speed bag is a popular piece of equipment used to develop coordination, endurance, timing, and rhythm. But it's a poor training tool that can endanger a fighter by developing the following poor habits: (1) centerline exposure - to strike the speed bag effectively, you must expose your centerline completely; (2) unrealistic rhythm - the impact rhythm generated on a speed bag isn't remotely close to that generated in a real fight, because there is no real rhythm in a street fight; (3) improper fist positioning - speed striking requires you to "roll" your fists and strike the bag at an unrealistic angle; (4) poor body mechanics - to maintain a rhythm on the bag, the practitioner must abandon proper body mechanics; (5) mobility inhibition - the speed bag platform restricts general mobility; and (6) lack of power - to develop a proper rhythm on the bag, the practitioner must strike the bag with light to moderate force, a habit you don't want when you're involved in a real fight.

### 169. WEAR DIFFERENT CLOTHES.

Make it a habit to train and work out in different types of clothes. This type of "attire training" will teach you a lot about the limitations of clothing when fighting. For example, do you notice a difference in your kicking technique when wearing shorts as compared to a suit? What is it like to fight in a robe, full-length coat, or bathing suit? What is it like to ground fight while wearing a heavy jacket? Do winter gloves affect your accuracy with a firearm? Can you fight effectively when wearing a motorcycle helmet? Do sunglasses impair your vision during a compound attack? Are your kicking techniques restricted when wearing boots or loafers?

### 170. DRESS APPROPRIATELY.

It's important to dress appropriately for your workouts. If your body is too cold or hot, you won't perform to the best of your ability. For example, dehydration and heat stroke can occur if your body's internal temperature gets too hot, whereas an extremely cold internal temperature can lead to a variety of muscle injuries. Always wear loose-fitting clothing that allows freedom of movement and maintains a normal body temperature.

## SPARRING

### 171. GET QUALITY BOXING GLOVES.

You won't benefit completely from your full-contact sparring sessions if you're not using top-quality gloves. The ideal boxing glove is one that provides comfort, protection, and durability. Depending on your training objective, the glove weight can range from 10 to 16 ounces.

Following are some other important features to be aware of when purchasing a pair of boxing gloves: (1) the glove should be composed of multilayered foam padding, (2) the glove should have a curved or attached thumb that will prevent thumb and eye injuries, (3) the glove should have a sufficient palm grip that provides comfort and fist stabilization, (4) the glove should be double-stitched to ensure durability, (5) the entire glove should be constructed of top-quality leather to increase its durability, (6) the glove's design should permit quick opening for defensive purposes, (7) the glove should be fairly easy to slip on and off, and (8) gloves should be bought from a reputable manufacturer. *WARNING: Never use karate-style gloves. These rubberized foam gloves are not designed for real combat training.*

### 172. WEAR HEADGEAR.

Headgear is designed to protect your head against kicks, punches, and strikes during sparring sessions. Generally, headgear is constructed of shock- absorbing foam covered by durable leather. Headgear comes in different sizes and styles. When purchasing headgear, remember that it is important that it fit just right. If it  is too tight, it can interfere with blood circulation. If it is too loose, it can twist over your face and seriously obstruct your vision. For reasons of hygiene, a fighter should not share headgear. Make certain that you purchase your own.

When purchasing headgear, look for the following important features: (1) offers adequate protection without losing visibility, (2) has a padded chin to protect your jawbone, (3) is of solid construction but lightweight, (4) has top-quality leather construction, (5) has an adjustable buckle or strap to facilitate proper fit, (6) has a rugged design that will provide years of use, (7) has a rear safety pad in case of accidental knockdown, and (8) has built-in cheek and nose protectors.

### 173. USE A MOUTHPIECE.

The mouthpiece is a durable rubber protector used to cover one's teeth when sparring. There are two types that can be used: single and double. The mouthpiece is a vital piece of safety equipment that can help prevent the following injuries: (1) broken jaw - the mouthpiece helps prevent a broken jaw by bracing it together when you are hit on the chin, (2) getting your teeth knocked out, and (3) biting your tongue or lips. Always wear a mouthpiece when engaging in any type of sparring drill or full-contact exercise.

### 174. CARRY IT WITH YOU.

If your occupation requires you to regularly engage in physical altercations with the public (i.e., bouncer, city beat cop, security officer, etc.), get into the habit of carrying your mouthpiece in your pocket. This serves two purposes: (1) the mouthpiece offers excellent protection to your teeth in case your adversary lands a lucky blow and (2) the act of nonchalantly putting a mouthpiece in your mouth prior to a fight can be psychologically intimidating to your adversary.

### 175. AVOID PREMATURE SPARRING.

While full-contact sparring is an important component of self-defense training, it's important to integrate this training methodology at the proper time. Never introduce students to full-contact sparring drills until they have acquired the following skills: (1) a variety of offensive and defensive tools and techniques that can be applied effectively, (2) the ability to control the force of their offensive tools and techniques, (3) the fundamental attributes of unarmed combat (speed, timing, coordination, accuracy, balance, and the ability not to telegraph), and (4) a safe attitude toward training. *CAUTION: Prematurely engaging in full-contact sparring exercises is dangerous and counterproductive.*

### 176. SPAR REGULARLY.

Sparring is probably the best training exercise. It develops many combat attributes and completely conditions your body for fighting. More importantly, sparring teaches you the importance of timing and judgment of distance in relation to your offensive and defensive techniques.  Sparring also conditions your body to withstand the impact of blows and kicks. However, don't be misled. Never forget that sparring does not represent the violent dynamics and real danger of a vicious street fight. Sparring is nothing more than a training methodology used to develop combat attributes. In sparring, a fighter develops rhythm. He can pace himself and create rest periods. In the streets, however, anything goes; nothing is sacred. Rhythm is destroyed. It is simply a question of survival.

Keep in mind that point-contact sparring is completely out of the question. Such training is impractical and simply stupid. Nevertheless, here are three effective sparring methods that you can incorporate into your training immediately: (1) stick and move, (2) blitz and disengage, and (3) counter fighting. Make it your mission to master the blitz and disengage methodology. It's the only one that remotely resembles a street fight.

# TRAINING & CONDITIONING

## 177. TRY HANDICAPPED SPARRING.

*Handicapped sparring* is an excellent training methodology that teaches the importance of adaptability while also sharpening individual appendages. This type of sparring is conducted by having two practitioners fight one another with only one appendage (the right arm for example). Keep in mind that all techniques (offensive and defensive) must be executed from one appendage throughout the course of a round.

For more advanced training, you can have one practitioner fight with only one arm while his partner can use both of his. This is especially difficult and should only be used by advanced students who want to take their training to an entirely new level.

## 178. HIP FUSE.

If you're fearful of getting hit, consider adding *Hip Fusing* to your workout program. Essentially, this full-contact sparring drill forces you to "stand your ground" and overcome the fear of exchanging blows with a stronger opponent. In essence, this exercise is performed by connecting two fighters with a 3-foot chain, forcing them to fight in the punching and grappling range.

*Here, two students engage in hip fusing training.*

## 179. TRY CIRCLE FIGHTING.

*Circle fighting* is an advanced form of training that requires a minimum of five participants. It is conducted by having all the participants form a circle (approximately 12 feet in diameter) with one person standing in the center. The instructor then randomly selects participants from the circle to attack (with sparring gear) the practitioner in the middle. The duration of the fight can last anywhere from 30 seconds to 5 minutes. It's up to the instructor. Once the attacker is finished, he returns to the circle, and the instructor immediately selects another participant to attack the person in the middle. Once the practitioners become familiar with this drill, the instructor can speed up the selection of attackers, call out multiple attackers, incorporate bludgeon and knife attacks, and even have the attackers take the fight to the ground.

## 180. DON'T PANIC IF YOU GET HIT.

If and when you get hit in a sparring session, stay in control of the situation and don't panic. Keep both hands up, stay mobile, and remain defensively alert. Maintain proper breathing and don't allow any negative thoughts to contaminate your mind. Stay focused on the task at hand and continue to look for openings in your opponent's defenses.

## 181. AVOID THESE SPARRING MISTAKES.

Here are 10 common mistakes that are made when sparring: (1) defending but failing to counterattack, (2) only fighting from one side (i.e., a right stance), (3) remaining stationary, (4) random hitting or failing to select the appropriate target, (5) lack of commitment when attacking, (6) hesitating to strike, (7) turning the head or closing the eyes when a blow is delivered, (8) turning the body completely sideways from the sparring partner, (9) running away from an attack, (10) swatting at the opponent's glove.

**182. KEEP A FIRST-AID KIT NEARBY.**

If you are going to engage in any type of full-contact training, it's a good idea to have a first-aid kit readily available. A first-aid kit is intended for both minor and major injuries. The kit should be kept in a well-sealed box away from children. Don't forget to write down the emergency number for your local hospital on the box. Most first-aid kits can be purchased at your local drugstore.

# ROUTINES AND WORKOUTS

**183. USE THE HARD DAY/EASY DAY ROUTINE.**

You can't train hard all the time. You must also incorporate easy days into your training schedule. This is important for the following reasons: (1) it helps significantly reduce the chances of getting injured, (2) it helps prevent overtraining, (3) it adds a bit of variety to your training, and (4) it allows your body to properly recuperate and adapt to the demands of the hard-core training. The following is just one sample of a hard day/easy day training routine:

Monday - hard day (ground fighting, sparring, and stick fighting)

Tuesday - easy day (shadow fighting, footwork, and escapes)

Wednesday - off day (rest)

Thursday - hard day (focus mitts, simulated street fighting, proficiency training)

Friday - hard day (knife fighting, heavy bag training, impact tolerance)

Saturday - easy day (firearms training, weapon disarms) or off day (depending on how you feel)

Sunday - off day (rest)

## 184. DEVELOP COMPOUND ATTACK SEQUENCES.

The truth in offense rests in the compound attack. The following are 10 compound attack sequences you can add to your training (these should be practiced when shadow fighting or working out on the heavy bag, double-end bag, or focus mitts): (1) finger jab/rear cross/lead hook punch/rear hook punch; (2) lead straight/rear cross/lead straight/rear cross; (3) hook kick/rear hook punch/lead hook punch/rear uppercut; (4) push kick/rear uppercut/lead uppercut/rear vertical knee strike; (5) vertical kick/rear vertical hammer fist/rear vertical knee strike; (6) rear horizontal elbow/lead horizontal elbow/rear vertical knee strike; (7) side kick/rear hook punch/lead uppercut/rear diagonal elbow/lead diagonal elbow; (8) finger jab/rear palm heel/lead palm heel/rear hook punch; (9) double thumb gouge/foot stomp/rear vertical knee; and (10) lead straight/rear cross/lead straight/rear cross/lead straight/rear cross.

## 185. BIG OR SMALL, FIGHT THEM ALL.

The only way to be truly prepared for the street is to train with a variety of partners, each with different somatotypes. For example, see what it is like to spar someone who is a foot taller than you, or experience what it is like to ground fight someone who is 100 pounds heavier than you. These different body types will help you understand your strengths and limitations in combat.

## 186. BE ON THE LOOKOUT.

In the course of training, you are likely to encounter a wide variety of personality types in class. When training, try to avoid the following types of students: (1) the conversationalist - this one talks too much and often disturbs others in class; (2) the challenger - this student is naturally argumentative and tries to test the instructor's knowledge and patience; (3) the ego tripper - this one will do anything in class to prove just how tough he is, and usually enjoys full-contact drills and likes to injure others; (4) the shy one - this type of student is hesitant to participate in training; (5) the know-it-all - this type of student thinks he knows anything and everything about self-defense training; and (6) the dilettante - this type of student is training for the fun of it and fails to understand the importance of self-defense training.

## 187. TRAIN TO MUSIC.

Your physical performance and mental attitude can be enhanced dramatically by training to music. It is my experience that training to fast, rhythmic music works wonders for conditioning training, whereas hard-driving aggressive rock music works best for proficiency and street training methods. Also try listening to classical music when stretching out and warming up.

## 188. KEEP ACCURATE TRAINING RECORDS.

Record keeping is one of the most important and often neglected aspects of effective training. Make it a habit to keep accurate records of your workouts in a personal journal. This type of record keeping is important for the following reasons: (1) it will help you monitor your progress, (2) it will keep you organized, (3) it will keep you motivated in your training, (4) it will help prevent potential injuries, and (5) it will help you guard against overtraining.

## 189. TRAIN IN ADVERSE WEATHER.

Training outdoors in adverse weather conditions will give

you a substantial edge over your assailant. Here are a few suggestions: (1) practice de-escalation scenarios in the rain, (2) work out on the focus mitts in freezing winter temperatures, (3) execute compound attacks in hot, humid summer weather, (4) ground fight in the snow, (5) spar when it's foggy outside, (6) practice kicks on the striking shield in gusty wind, (7) try firing your gun in poor lighting conditions, and (8) try speed-loading your gun when your hands are wet from rain.

## 190. VISUALIZE REGULARLY.

Visualization is the purposeful formation of mental images to improve your combative performance. This natural and relatively simple exercise serves many purposes, including the following: (1) it improves your general reaction time, (2) it develops sharper psychomotor skills, (3) it improves your confidence, (4) it helps cultivate the killer instinct, (5) it helps you maintain motivation during tough workouts, and (6) it improves shadow fighting workouts. *NOTE: When visualizing, it's important that your mental images are clear, strong, and consistent. There are generally three different mental speeds in which you can visualize: (1) slow, (2) moderate, and (3) fast, as well as in reverse.*

## 191. TRAIN WHEN YOU'RE SICK.

Now is the time to see if you can defend yourself when you're handicapped or ill. This is known as disability training. Here are a few suggestions that will help get you started: (1) practice compound attacks when you're plagued with a migraine headache, (2) practice close-quarter techniques when sitting in a wheelchair, (3) spar with one arm in a sling, (4) practice combat skills while standing on crutches, (5) practice kicks when you have the flu, (6) attempt to yell when you have a sore throat, (7) work out on the heavy bag when you have a bad cough, (8) try ground fighting when you're

TRAINING & CONDITIONING

fatigued and exhausted, (9) fight multiple assailants with a hangover, and (10) practice escaping from grabs, chokes, locks, and holds while you are blindfolded.

### 192. PREPARE FOR MULTIPLE ASSAILANTS.

Here are a few suggestions to get you started with multiple-assailant training: (1) try sparring three assailants at the same time, (2) experience what it is like to ground fight two opponents at the same time, (3) conduct a simulated street fight with three attackers, (4) try to knife fight two assailants simultaneously, and (5) defend against two bludgeon-wielding assailants at the same time. Whatever scenario you choose, you'll acquire a greater understanding and appreciation for the dynamics of multiple-assailant assaults.

### 193. PRACTICE THE SOLO BLOCKING DRILL.

The solo blocking drill is used to sharpen and refine basic blocking movements without the pressure of timing. To begin the drill, apply the following: (1) assume a proper fighting stance in front of a full-length mirror, execute a high block at moderate speed, note any flaws in the execution of the movement, alternate right and left arms, and return to the starting position; (2) next, execute a mid-block at moderate speed, note any mistakes in the execution of the movement, alternate right and left arms, and return to the starting position; (3) now, execute a low block at moderate speed, note any flaws in the execution of the movement, alternate right and left arms, and return to the starting position; (4) finally, execute an elbow block at moderate speed, note any flaws in the execution of the movement, alternate right and left arms, and return to the starting position. *NOTE: The solo blocking drill can also be conducted with the eyes closed to develop a kinesthetic feel for the technique.*

### 194. PRACTICE THE 360-DEGREE BLOCKING DRILL.

The 360-degree blocking drill is excellent for developing defensive reaction time. To begin, apply the following: (1) have your training partner stand approximately three feet from you, (2) position yourself in a 45-degree stance with both of your arms hanging at your sides, (3) without him telegraphing his intentions, have your training partner deliver a random swing at your head or torso, (4) immediately respond with the appropriate block, (5) return your arm to the starting position, (6) have your partner immediately attack with another swing at a different angle. As you become more proficient with this drill, your training partner should deliver a sequence of random swings with greater speed and force. In addition, you can have your partner incorporate linear blows into the drill. *CAUTION: Remember to start out slowly and progressively build up the speed and force of your strikes.*

### 195. SHARPEN YOUR SENSES.

Your five senses (sight, smell, touch, sound, and taste) can be sharpened through a variety of exercises designed to develop both raw detection and learned identification abilities. For example, sit on a park bench for a given period of time and catalog the various objects and actions your five senses detect, then list the possible sources of the sensory data. With sufficient practice, you will make significant progress from being unable to detect a particular sound or smell to not only detecting it quickly and accurately, but also identifying its source. Remember that sensory development increases as these exercises are performed in different environmental settings.

### 196. DEVELOP EMOTIONAL RECOGNITION.

The objective of this drill is to sharpen your ability to recognize and identify various emotional states in people, especially those that are associated with violence. To apply the drill, spend approximately 20 minutes in a busy public place (sporting events, courtroom, shopping mall, emergency room, protest, etc.) sitting back and observing people's emotional states. Pay close attention to their posture, voice, demeanor, hand movements, and facial expressions.

## 197. SHADOW FIGHT.

*Shadow fighting* is the creative deployment of offensive and defensive tools and maneuvers against imaginary assailants. It requires intense mental focus, honest self-analysis, and a deep commitment to improve. For the fighter on a tight budget, the good news is that shadow fighting is inexpensive. All you need is a full-length mirror and a place to work out. The mirror is vital. It functions as a critic, your personal instructor. If you're honest, the mirror will be too. It will point out every mistake - telegraphing, sloppy footwork, poor body mechanics, and even lack of physical conditioning.

Proper shadow fighting develops speed, power, balance, footwork, compound attack skills, sound form, and finesse. It even promotes a better understanding of the ranges of combat. As you progress, you can incorporate light dumbbells into shadow fighting workouts to enhance power and speed. Start off with one to three pounds and gradually work your way up. Weighted vests can also be worn to develop footwork, kicks, and knee strikes. Traditional martial artists will notice that shadow fighting is much more difficult than katas because of its arbitrary nature.

## 198. REST.

Resting the body is just as important as training. Training intensely day after day will lead to either burnout (overtraining) or injury. The body needs time to recoup and replenish itself from grueling workouts. Remember, there is growth in rest.

## 199. AVOID BURNOUT.

Burnout is defined as a negative emotional state acquired by physical overtraining. Some symptoms of burnout include physical illness, boredom, anxiety, disinterest in training, and general sluggish behavior.

Whether you are a teacher or student, novice or expert, you're susceptible to burnout. Here are a few suggestions to help avoid burnout in your training: (1) make your workouts intense but enjoyable; (2) vary your training routine (i.e., hard day/easy day routine); (3) train to different types of music (i.e., hard rock, classical, techno, classic rock, and new age); (4) pace yourself during your workouts—don't try to do it all in one day; (5) listen to your body—if you don't feel up to working out, skip a day; (6) work out in different types of environments; (7) use different types of training equipment; (8) work out with different training partners; (9) keep accurate records of your training routine; and (10) vary the intensity of your training throughout your workout.

## 200. PRIORITIZE OFFENSE.

When working out, make it a habit to begin your training with offensive tools and techniques. This is important because it helps reinforce the offensive mentality and guarantees that training time will be applied to the most important aspect of street survival - offense.

## TRAINING & CONDITIONING

**201. CLOSE YOUR EYES.**

If you want to make your movements instinctual, practice them in a slow and controlled fashion with your eyes closed. Closing your eyes when training will help you develop a complete kinesthetic feel for the movement.

**202. DUMBBELL POWER TRAINING.**

*Dumbbell Power Training* is a great way to develop knockout power by strengthening the specific muscles that are recruited when punching. This type of training allows you to focus on either a specific punch or a punching combination. It's entirely up to you.

A dumbbell power workout can be structured around a prescribed number of repetitions or a period of time. They key is to perform the drill in a *slow and deliberate manner.* Unlike shadowboxing, your goal is to be slow and steady. Remember, throwing your punches too quickly with a lot of weight can damage your joints. Finally, if you are going for time, strive for at least 5 rounds lasting three minutes in duration.

**203. PRACTICE YELLING.**

A strong and powerful yell can be a very effective tool in a fight, and a good place to practice yelling is in your car. The interior of the car insulates and amplifies your voice, giving you a good sense of its effectiveness. Practice prolonged yells and intermittent, explosive ones. The yell should also be used judiciously in sparring and simulated combat scenarios to test its effectiveness.

**204. TRY PROFICIENCY TRAINING.**

If you are looking for a surefire method of perfecting your technique, try *proficiency training.* This method of training is designed to sharpen one particular tool, technique, tactic, or maneuver at a time by executing it over and over again for a prescribed number of repetitions. Each time, the tool or technique is executed with form and at various speeds. Techniques can even be practiced with the eyes closed to develop a kinesthetic "feel" for the movement. Remember to take your time with each repetition. Proficiency training can be performed on all training equipment.

## 205. TRY CONDITIONING TRAINING.

*Conditioning training* sharpens a fighter's tools and conditions his entire body by developing cardiorespiratory endurance and muscular strength. It also develops rhythm, balance, speed, agility, and footwork. This method of training should be practiced in controlled environments, such as a martial arts studio, basement, or garage, to allow sufficient room for you and your training partner to really move around.

In conditioning training you execute kicks, punches, and strikes in different combinations for three or four-minute rounds. Once the round is over, rest for 30 seconds and then go again. A good workout consists of five rounds. Remember to pace yourself through each round, because "pouring it on" in the beginning will lead to premature fatigue. It is also essential to maintain a proper breathing pattern; under no circumstances should you hold your breath. Conditioning training can be performed when sparring or when working out on focus mitts, striking shields, heavy bags, double-end bags, or against imaginary assailants in shadow fighting.

## 206. TRY STREET TRAINING.

*Street training* is the final preparation for the real thing. Since most physical confrontations last approximately 20 to 30 seconds, you must prepare for this type of scenario. Street training requires you to deliver explosive and powerful compound attacks with vicious intent for 20 to 30 seconds, rest for one minute, then repeat the process. In the street training methodology, it is essential to attack with 100- percent conviction and give it all you've got.

Street training prepares you for the stress and fatigue of a real fight. It also develops speed, power, explosiveness, target selection, timing, footwork, and even balance.

## 207. DO THE CYCLONE.

The *cyclone drill* develops bone-crushing hook punches. The objective of the exercise is to assault the heavy bag with a continuous flurry of hook punches delivered in a back and forth fashion, at both high and low heavy bag targets. To perform this drill, follow these steps: (1) face the heavy bag and assume a fighting stance, (2) deliver the lead and rear hook punches in a fluid, back and forth fashion. Concentrate on striking the bag as fast and hard as possible, (3) perform the drill for a minimum of three rounds. Each round can last anywhere from 10 to 90 seconds.

## 208. USE THE SIDESTEPPING DRILL.

Once a week practice sidestepping with a training partner. This drill is important for refining evasion skills and for enhancing your sense of range and timing. To practice the sidestepping drill, employ the following: (1) begin with your training partner standing approximately 10 feet from you; (2) assume a stance (i.e., fighting, de-escalation, natural, knife defense); (3) without telegraphing his intentions, your training partner should charge at you full-speed; (4) if you're standing in a right (southpaw) stance, quickly step with your right foot to the right and have your left leg follow an equal distance. Your partner should miss you and you should be balanced and ready to effectively counterattack. Practice the sidestepping drill with different stances, at various distances, in different lighting conditions, and while standing on different surfaces.

## 209. PUMMEL IT.

The *Pummel drill* is designed to develop and refine the pummel technique, which is used when ground fighting (see Chapter 5: Grappling and Ground Fighting for specific details). To execute the pummel drill, apply the following: (1) place the heavy bag or body opponent bag on the floor, (2) have your training partner tie a rope (approximately five feet long) to the top of the bag, (3) mount the heavy bag (the same way you would mount an assailant in a ground fight), (4) for 30 seconds employ full-speed, full-force strikes (linear blasts, hammer fists, and hook punches) on the upper portion of the heavy bag, (5) have your partner pull vigorously (side to side, and up and down) on the rope while you deliver the blows, (6) maintain your balance when your partner tugs the bag.

## 210. ELEVATE IT.

The *Elevation drill* is one of the most demanding exercises you can perform on the heavy bag. Besides requiring muscular endurance, this drill also requires a significant amount of mental resilience and attention control. The objective of this exercise is to keep the heavy bag elevated at a 45-degree angle by continuously punching it. This drill is brutal on the arms. In fact, the average person can barely last 30 seconds.

To perform the drill follow these steps: (1) face the heavy bag and assume a fighting stance. (2) deliver lead straight and rear cross combination continuously. Concentrate on delivering full-speed, full-force punches. (3) maintain a rapid-fire cadence to keep the bag elevated at a 45-degree angle from the floor. (4) avoid pushing the bag and remember to snap each blow. If the heavy bag spins when performing this exercise, it means your punches are not landing at the center of the bag. Remember to focus your blows at a single target point. (5) perform the drill for a minimum of three rounds. Each round can last anywhere from 10 to 90 seconds. If you are exceptionally conditioned, go for 90 seconds.

# TRAINING & CONDITIONING

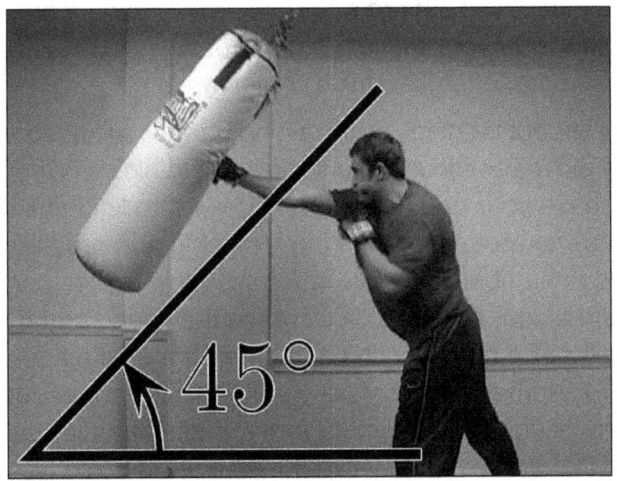

*Here, a student performs the elevation drill.*

## 211. FEEL THE IMPACT.

*Impact training* is a series of exercises that condition your mind and body to withstand the trauma of kicks and blows. In unarmed combat, there are two types of striking impact: snapping and breaking. Snapping impact shocks the head or body but does not fully penetrate it. It's quick but lacks substantial follow-through. A snapping blow usually makes a brisk, sharp cracking sound when it connects with its target. In contrast, breaking impact shocks and moves the head or body. It can break or fracture bones easily because it follows through its target (approximately three inches). You must be physically and psychologically prepared to tolerate both types of impact.

Impact training requires both forms of impact to be administered to specific body parts, including the shoulders, back, chest, biceps, triceps, abdominals, thighs, and calves. Striking these targets will not cause serious or permanent injury. *WARNING: Never strike the face, neck, throat, solar plexus, spine, groin, or joints during impact training. These anatomical targets are very sensitive and cannot be conditioned to withstand deliberate impact. Striking these targets can cause severe and permanent injury. It is imperative that your training partner deliver accurate blows and avoid these targets during training.*

For impact training, your training partner will need a pair of boxing gloves or focus mitts to deliver the blows. When you begin, have your partner start off slowly with light strikes to your muscle groups, alternating snapping and breaking blows. Always remember to exhale when the blow makes contact. Over time, your partner can increase the speed and force of the strikes. Be patient with each other. It will take time and some experimentation before you and your partner can properly gauge the amount of force. Impact training sessions should last approximately five minutes and should be conducted at least twice a month.

### 212. TRAIN IN DIFFERENT ENVIRONMENTS.

A prepared fighter is an adaptable fighter. Make it a habit to work out in different types of environments. For example, experience what it is like to train in a dark and unfamiliar alley, in a bathroom stall, between two parked cars, in a swimming pool, on a flight of stairs (be careful), or while sitting behind the wheel of your car. Find out what it's like to execute a compound attack while standing in your shower stall. This dynamic form of environmental training will provide you with the experience necessary to handle the unpredictable nature of street fighting.

### 213. PARTICIPATE IN PSYCHO EMOTIONAL TRAINING.

Train when you are experiencing different types of emotional states. For example, work out when you feel angry and frustrated. Is there a noticeable difference in your performance? Are your skills and techniques enhanced when you're happy and energetic? What is your energy level when you're sad or depressed? Does your emotional state change

TRAINING & CONDITIONING

after a taxing training session? If so, how? Experiment and see how well you ground fight when slightly intoxicated, tired, or drowsy. *WARNING: Always have a sober and trustworthy training partner with you when experimenting with alcohol. And never experiment with alcohol and firearms. They are a deadly combination.*

### 214. EXPERIENCE DIFFERENT TERRAINS.

Now is the time to see what will work on different types of terrain and surface areas. Try sparring in tall grass. What happens to your balance when performing kicks on ice or wet grass? Does the snow or sleet affect your visibility when you execute a compound attack? What happens when you ground fight in the mud or sand? Experiment and find out. The more varied the terrain you train on, the better prepared you will be.

### 215. CONFRONT YOUR FEARS.

Write down ten of your biggest fears. They can be anything from financial worries to a knife fight with a vicious psychopath. Once you have made your list, put them in an envelope, seal the envelope, and put it in a safe place where no one will find it. After one year has passed, open the envelope and see if you have conquered any of those fears. If so, congratulations are in oder. If not, get back to work.

### 216. SAFETY IS PARAMOUNT.

When it comes to martial arts training, safety is of paramount importance. Some martial artists will avoid using safety equipment because of big egos, laziness, ignorance, and a variety of other reasons. However, it behooves you to take the proper safety precautions. Here are a few suggestions to help minimize the possibilities of injury: (1) buy the best training equipment that you can afford, (2) know the proper way to use training equipment, (3) regularly inspect your equipment for wear and defects, (4) avoid ego-driven training partners, (5) be especially aware when training with someone of superior size, skill, or experience, (6) always warm up before training, (7) drink plenty of water during training sessions to avoid dehydration, and (8) be cautious when performing training drills for the first time.

### 217. BE RUTHLESSLY REALISTIC WHEN TRAINING.

Whether you are training for armed or unarmed combat, your training sessions must be completely realistic. You must methodically integrate the frightening and spontaneous elements of fighting safely into your routines. Such reality-based training is a surefire method of preparing you for the real thing.

For example, conduct simulated street fights with fully padded assailants. Work out in dark, cramped, and unfamiliar environments. Train with focus mitts, mannequin heads, chalkable rubber knives, trigger-sensitive mock pistols, and foam and plastic baseball bats. Strategic histrionics should be developed through countless de-escalation scenarios.

Since no two attacks are ever the same, you need to incorporate a wide variety of combative scenarios into your training program. This realistic and dynamic form of training will provide you with the experience necessary to handle the unpredictable nature of combat. *WARNING: Inadequate or unrealistic training is a complete waste of time and extremely dangerous. Always train for the reality of combat.*

### 218. TRY SPORTS MASSAGE.

A complete workout program also includes caring for the wear and tear on your body. The physiological benefits of sports massage make it a significant component of any conditioning program. Sports massage benefits a fighter for the following reasons: (1) it helps your body recover more quickly from your workouts, (2) it improves blood circulation, (3) it promotes muscular relaxation, (4) it promotes faster healing from injuries, and (5) it aids in the removal of cell waste products and promotes better cell nutrition.

# SUPPLEMENTAL EXERCISES

### 219. KNOW THE 11 REASONS TO EXERCISE.

Here's 11 reasons why you should exercise on a regular basis: (1) to be prepared for combat, (2) to lose excess weight, which shortens life, (3) to improve your circulation, (4) to tone and firm muscles to acquire the physical proportions nature intended, (5) to relax from tensions causing undue fatigue and loss of sleep, (6) to stay physically fit and mentally alert, (7) to improve your metabolism, (8) to help build body resistance, (9) to acquire a more positive outlook through the feeling of good health and well- being, (10) to help maintain a youthful appearance, and (11) to get more enjoyment out of life.

### 220. BE AEROBICALLY FIT.

Since a rapid and effective response to a vicious fight imposes tremendous strain on your heart and lungs, you're going to have to do aerobic exercise, including running, biking, swimming, skipping rope, sparring, or a little of each to develop sound cardiorespiratory conditioning. Cardiorespiratory conditioning is a component of combative fitness that deals with conditioning the heart, lungs, and circulatory system for both armed and unarmed fighting.

## 221. RUN.

Running is one of the best ways to get into top physical condition. Running on a consistent basis improves wind capacity, endurance, circulation, and muscle tone. It strengthens the legs, burns a significant amount of calories, and stimulates the metabolism.

Running sessions should always start with a brisk jog, working up to a faster pace. Start off slowly and progressively build up speed. Try to run a minimum of five times per week for a duration of approximately 50 minutes. Later on you can consider adding hills or step running to your training routine.

## 222. TEST YOUR SHOES.

The most important piece of equipment when running are your shoes. Before you hit the pavement in a new pair of running shoes, be certain you get the best fit. The following guidelines should help: (1) test your new shoes for a minimum of one hour to make sure you have a comfortable fit, (2) your shoes should fit properly if there is a thumbnail width of space between the end of your toe and the tip of the shoe, (3) your heel and instep should feel snug, but not tight, (4) your arch should match the shoe's arch pad.

## 223. RUN CORRECTLY.

Running style is another important consideration. Avoid stomping on the ground. Try running lightly and rhythmically with your arms and shoulders relaxed. Let your feet glide across the floor. Running should be practically silent. In fact, if you hear your feet hit the ground you'll know that you're running incorrectly. Every running session should include the following stages: warm up, main workout, cool down, and stretches. And always buy the best running shoes you can afford. Your feet will thank you later.

## 224. RUN IN THE MORNING.

If possible, run in the morning. This is important for the following reasons: (1) the air is usually cleaner, (2) during the hot summer months, it's cooler, (3) there's more privacy, (4) it's quieter, (5) it accelerates your metabolism for the rest of the day, (6) your aerobic workout is taken care of so you can go about your day with peace of mind, and (7) you are mentally cleansed and energized for the rest of the day.

## 225. DRESS PROPERLY.

Dressing correctly for your run is also very important. Here are some important points to consider: (1) wear clothes that don't restrict movement; (2) wear a good pair of running shoes; (3) in the summer months, dress to keep cool and comfortable; (4) in the winter months, dress warmly and in layers - sweatpants, sweatshirt, windbreaker, gloves, and hat are all important articles of clothing; and (5) wear light or bright colors for maximum visibility.

## 226. 10 REASONS WHY YOU SHOULD RUN.

Here are 10 good reasons why you should incorporate running into your training program: (1) it's one of the most efficient methods of cardiovascular conditioning, (2) it's the most easily accessible aerobic activity, (3) it's inexpensive, (4) running dramatically reduces daily stress and anxiety, (5) running is a vital component of weight management, (6) it's exhilarating, (7) running prepares you for the "escape" tactical option, (8) running is for individuals of all ages, (9) running prepares you for the tremendous physical strain of combat, and (10) running slows down the aging process.

## 227. JUMP ROPE.

If you want to be quick and light on your feet, you'll need to jump rope on a regular basis. Jumping rope is also one of the most effective ways of conditioning your heart and improving coordination, endurance, balance, agility, and body composition. One of the most important factors to consider when selecting a rope is the length. A simple method to measure the rope properly is to stand on the center of the rope with one foot. The handles of the rope should reach your armpits.

Here are some other guidelines that will help you: (1) relax your arms and shoulders when jumping, (2) push off your toes and land gently on the balls of your feet, (3) use your wrists and forearms to turn the rope, (4) maintain good posture and bend naturally at the knees and hips, (5) jump low - approximately one inch off the ground, (6) keep your head up - avoid the tendency to look down at your feet, (7) keep both elbows close to your sides, (8) never jump rope barefoot, (9) don't get frustrated by a tangled rope, and (10) jump to different types of music.

## 228. CYCLE.

Stationary bicycling is an excellent low-impact exercise that requires very little room. Along with conditioning the cardiorespiratory system, the exercise bike stimulates your metabolism and gives your legs a vigorous workout.

One important consideration when using an exercise bike is adjusting the seat so it fits your body properly. If the seat is too low, you'll limit your legs' range of motion and ultimately develop knee problems. If the seat is too high, your hips will rock side to side and you won't be able to pedal smoothly. The seat should be adjusted so that when you fully extend your leg, your knee is slightly bent. Also be careful when adjusting the tension of the flywheel. Too much tension will damage your knees and inhibit your workout. My best advice is to keep the tension at a level that will allow you to maintain approximately 80 revolutions per minute (RPM) for 30 to 40 minutes. Remember, if you are to benefit from the bike, you must keep your heart rate elevated for a minimum of 30 minutes.

## 229. LIFT WEIGHTS CONSISTENTLY.

A smart weight training program, combined with consistent stretching exercises, will significantly improve power, endurance, speed, coordination, body composition, and even pain tolerance. When training, be certain to execute all the exercises in a slow and controlled fashion. Hoisting and swinging movements will lead to serious injury and should be avoided. If you are unfamiliar with a particular exercise, ask a certified fitness instructor for assistance.

## 230. STRETCH EVERY DAY.

Muscular flexibility is another important component of combative fitness. You need a stretching program designed to loosen up every major muscle group. Remember that you can't kick, punch, ground fight, or otherwise execute necessary body mechanics if you are "tight" or inflexible. Stretching on a regular basis will increase the muscles' range of motion, improve circulation, reduce the possibilities of injury, and relieve tension.

Stretching should be performed in a slow and controlled manner. Always hold your stretch for a minimum of 60 seconds, and avoid all bouncing movements. Always remember to stretch before and after your training sessions. The following six stretches will help get you started.

(1) Neck stretch - from a comfortable standing position, slowly tilt your head to the right, holding it for a count of 20 seconds. Then tilt your head to the left for approximately 20 seconds. Stretch each side of the neck at least three times.

(2) Triceps stretch - from a standing position, keeping your knees slightly bent, extend your right arm overhead, bent at the elbow, then hold the elbow of your right arm with your left hand and slowly pull your right elbow to the left. Keep your hips straight as you stretch your triceps gently for 30 seconds. Repeat this stretch for the other arm.

(3) Hamstring stretch - from a seated position on the floor, extend your right leg in front of you with your toes pointing toward the ceiling. Place the sole of your left foot in the inside of your extended leg. Gently lean forward at the hips and stretch out the hamstrings of your right leg. Hold this position for a minimum of 60 seconds. Switch legs and repeat the stretch.

(4) Spinal twist - from a seated position on the floor, extend your right leg in front of you. Raise your left leg and place your left foot on the floor on the outside of your right leg. Place your right elbow on the outside of your left thigh. Stabilize your stretch with your elbow and twist your upper body and head to your left side. Breathe naturally and hold this stretch for a minimum of 30 seconds. Switch legs and repeat this stretch for the other side.

(5) Quad stretch - assume a sitting position on the floor with your legs folded underneath you. Your toes should be pointed behind you, and your insteps should be flush with the ground. Sit comfortably into the stretch and hold for a minimum of 30 seconds.

(6) Prone stretch - lie on the ground with your back to the floor. Exhale as you straighten your arms above your head.

Your fingers and toes should be stretching in opposite directions. Hold this stretch for 15 seconds.

### 231. DEVELOP YOUR NECK.

The neck is one of the most neglected components of combat conditioning. Besides acting as a shock absorber against head blows, strong neck muscles control the whipping motion of the head, thereby controlling the velocity of the brain moving inside the skull. You can develop and strengthen your neck muscles by regularly using a neck harness.

### 232. DO PUSH-UPS.

Push-ups are excellent for strengthening your upper body (chest, shoulders, and triceps). To properly perform the push-up, lie on your stomach with your feet slightly apart. Place your hands shoulder-width apart, keep your back straight, and place your elbows close to your sides. Exhale as you push your body up from the ground. From the upward position, inhale and slowly lower your body down approximately three inches from the floor. Repeat this movement until your chest muscles become fatigued. Push-ups should always be performed in a slow and controlled manner.

### 233. STRENGTHEN YOUR ABDOMINALS.

Strong abdominal muscles are essential to a fighter. They protect internal organs, maintain proper posture, and support the lower back. One of the best exercises to develop the abdominal muscles is the crunch. To perform this exercise, start by lying with your back on the floor, arms folded across your chest, with your feet on a bench. Now pull your chin to your chest and contract your abdominals to move your torso (upper body) upward. Avoid lunging forward and lifting your lower back off the ground. Be certain to exhale as you approach the upward position. Remember to pause momentarily at the top. Return to the starting position in a controlled manner by inhaling and slowly lowering your shoulders to the floor. Repeat this exercise until your abdominal muscles fatigue. Strive to perform this exercise at least four times per week.

**234. STRENGTHEN YOUR HANDS.**

Since the majority of your fighting techniques are delivered with your hands, it's important for you to strengthen your fingers, wrists and forearms. Powerful hands and forearms will improve tearing, crushing, and gouging techniques as well as overall grappling skills. In addition, they make knife-disarming techniques safer and weapon-retention techniques more effective. Strong fingers and hands also tend to improve the structural integrity of your fists.

**235. TRAIN YOUR FOREARMS.**

Condition your wrists and forearms by performing various forearm exercises with free weights. Exercises like: hammer curls, reverse curls, wrist curls, and reverse wrist curls are great for developing powerful forearms. When training your forearms, be certain to work both your extensor and flexor muscles.

**236. USE HAND GRIPPERS.**

A very effective way to strengthen your hands, wrists and forearms is to work out with heavy duty hand grippers. While there are a wide selection of them on the market, I personally prefer using the *Captains of Crush* brand. These high quality grippers are virtually indestructible and they are sold in a variety of different resistance levels ranging from 60 to 365 pounds.

### 237. USE A WEIGHT VEST.

Weight vest training is an effective way to develop explosive fighting skills and mental resilience. By practicing your skills with additional weight attached to your torso, you'll be strengthening the muscles in your body while simultaneously improving your conditioning. Weight vest training can be incorporated into just about any drill, here are just a few ways you can add it to your program: (1) Shadow fight with your weight vest, (2) Perform footwork drills, (3) Spar with the vest on, (4) Consider taking long walks or hikes while wearing the vest. In order to get the best results from your workout, you'll need to invest in a high-quality vest that provides both comfort and durability. The vest must also be able to support a good deal of weight, ranging anywhere from 25-75 pounds.

### 238. TREAT STRAINED MUSCLES.

Despite effective warm-ups and safe training, injuries can still occur. One of the most common types of training injuries is a muscle pull or strain, which is simply a partial tear in the width of the muscle fiber. It is a painful injury that can set you back significantly in your training. The best way to treat it is by applying ice to the injured area as soon as possible. Icing the injury helps control internal bleeding and swelling. Apply ice treatment until the bleeding and swelling stop. Approximately 48 hours later, apply heat to the injured muscle. This will help increase circulation and accelerate the natural healing process.

### 239. COOL DOWN.

Cooling down from a strenuous workout is just as important as warming up. A cool-down is a series of light exercises and movements that immediately follow a workout. The purpose of the cool-down is to hasten the removal of metabolic wastes and gradually return the heart to its resting rate. A proper cool-down will also reduce the likelihood of stiffness. Simply halting your workout can cause sluggish circulation, blood pooling, and slow waste-product removal. Some experts say that it contributes to muscle soreness and cramping. Here are a few suggestions: (1) make your cool-down last a minimum of five minutes, (2) light stretching exercises are the best way to cool down, (3) brisk walking is another effective cool-down method.

### 240. AVOID CRAMPING.

Muscle cramping is the result of a particular muscle contracting for too long. It is often recognizable as a sudden and painful tightening of the muscle. The three primary causes of muscle cramping are (1) salt depletion because of excessive sweating, (2) muscle fatigue, and (3) injury. The best way to avoid cramping is to hydrate properly. Drink plenty of water before and during your workout. If you do get a muscle cramp, the best method of relieving it is to relax the muscle by either stretching it or massaging it with the fingers. Keep in mind that the muscle can be worked again after the cramping subsides.

# NUTRITION

### 241. CONSUME CREATINE.

Creatine is a fantastic natural supplement that can benefit anyone who wants to boost their strength, endurance and build lean muscle mass. It may also increase brain function, fight certain neurological diseases, and accelerate muscle growth. Best of all, this white powder is tasteless, odorless, and relatively inexpensive.

## 242. EAT RIGHT.

A fighter's diet is one of the most neglected aspects of combat fitness. A true diet refers to a life- style of eating right.

Sixty percent of your daily caloric intake should consist of complex carbohydrates. Carbohydrates, the body's primary source of energy, are found in vegetables, fruits, potatoes, pasta, and all grain products.

Next we have proteins, which are essential for muscle and tissue growth. Poultry, fish, and legumes are excellent sources of low-fat proteins. Unless you are on a serious weight-gain program, you should devote no more than 30 percent of your daily caloric intake to proteins.

Finally, unsaturated fats are vital to proper metabolic function and vitamin absorption and should make up 10 percent of your calories. Don't confuse unsaturated fats with their nasty relatives, saturated fats. Saturated fats, found in ice cream, chocolate, cakes, and so on, are a big NO. Forget them. They will only make you fat and sluggish. Look for natural unsaturated fats in such foods as nuts, seeds, and various grains.

Keep in mind that nutritional supplements should also be taken to ensure that you get all the necessary vitamins and minerals.

## 243. TAKE YOUR VITAMINS.

A vitamin is any of various fat-soluble (stored in the body fat) or water-soluble (dissolve in water) organic substances essential for the growth and maintenance of the body. Vitamins are a necessary part of the fighter's diet. As a matter of fact, the word "vitamin" comes from the Latin word *vita*, meaning "life." A well-balanced diet will ensure that you are taking in the necessary amounts of vitamins. However, vitamin deficiencies can occur, and they can have a negative effect on your performance. *WARNING: Avoid excessive amounts of fat-soluble vitamins, they can cause severe toxicity.*

**244. LIGHTEN UP.**

Excessive body fat will only be a hindrance when fighting. It interferes with agility, speed, and endurance, and it continually taxes the heart. If you are overweight, here are 10 suggestions to help you lighten the load: (1) set a realistic caloric deficit level, (2) lose weight slowly (no more than one pound per week), (3) avoid foods that are high in fat, (4) eat four small meals per day, (5) drink plenty of water throughout the day, (6) avoid diet fads, (7) weigh yourself only once per week, (8) partake in at least four aerobic workouts (running, biking, rope skipping, etc.) per week and make certain each one is a least 45 minutes in duration, (9) if you slip up with your diet or workout program, don't beat yourself up; realize that you are only human and try again, and (10) limit red meat consumption to only once per week.

# READING AND RESEARCH

**245. READ, READ, READ.**

The intellectual or academic aspects of combat training cannot be overlooked. You must possess an insatiable desire to learn. Effective academic research involves voracious reading. The body of printed materials on combat has grown astronomically. Read anything you can get your hands on. Don't make the common mistake of passively reading material. Get into the habit of dissecting and noting literature. Strategically sound theories and concepts should be noted and remembered. Books should be read over and over again until practical concepts are intellectually solidified. Always read material with an open mind balanced with healthy skepticism.

### 246. BUILD YOUR CFA LIBRARY - ONE BOOK AT A TIME.

I've dedicated my life to authoring a massive self-defense library. With over 55 CFA book titles in circulation, you have everything you need to acquire the intellectual and academic aspects of combat training and preparedness. Happy reading!

### 247. READ *THE ART OF WAR BY SUN TZU*.

Read this book frequently, and don't forget to make notes in the margins.

### 248. DON'T LEND THEM OUT.

The books you own are precious. Don't lend them out. Speaking from experience, people won't treat them with the same care and respect that you would. And many times you'll never see them again.

### 249. FOLLOW THE NEWS.

Your local news feed can provide you with a wealth of information about violence and crime. Depending on how much you can stomach, get into the habit of reading or watching it regularly. Pay close attention to what you are reading and find out the motivations, mentalities, and methods of street criminals.

### 250. STUDY INSTRUCTIONAL VIDEOS.

One aspect of self-defense training that is often overlooked is instructional training videos. Too few people are aware of the advantages of regularly watching and studying instructional reality-based videos. Be certain to add them to your training regimen.

### 251. BE SKEPTICAL YET OPEN-MINDED.

When reading self-defense books or watching training videos, always observe with a skeptical eye and look for the combative utility of every technique. Whenever you learn a new self-defense technique, ask yourself, "Will this really work in the unpredictable conditions of a real fight?"

## THE INSTRUCTOR

### 252. LISTEN TO YOUR INSTRUCTOR.

Your instructor is there to evaluate your performance during your workouts. Listen carefully to what he has to say. A good combat instructor will be brutally honest and tell you what you are doing correctly and what you are doing wrong.

### 253. BE SELECTIVE.

Choose a self-defense instructor the very same way that you would choose a surgeon to perform a difficult operation. In both cases, your life is in his hands. Here are the questions to get answers to when selecting a competent instructor: (1) How long has he been studying martial sciences? (2) How long has he been teaching self-defense? (3) Exactly what aspects of combat is he qualified to teach? (4) What agency, institution, or person certified him? (5) Is he well known for his expertise? (6) Is he articulate with combative nomenclature? (7) Does he practice what he preaches? (8) Is the instructor published? (9) Does the instructor answer all of your questions? (10) Does he injure his students? (11) Does he project a professional image? (12) Does his attitude show patience and respect toward his students? (13) What is his temperament - is he friendly and serious or cynical and negative? (14) Does he seem oriented toward safety?

## 254. TRAINING DOs AND DON'Ts.

Here are 10 training DOs and DON'Ts for self-defense instructors: (1) DO encourage friendly and healthy competition between your students, (2) DO try to find out what causes your students to make mistakes and take action to prevent recurrences, (3) DO admit your mistakes, (4) DO maintain a professional attitude at all times, (5) DO let every one of your students know what is expected of him, (6) DO encourage your students to overcome their weak points, (7) DON'T expect beginner students to be perfect, (8) DON'T expect your students to progress as quickly as you do, (9) DON'T allow misinformation to be disseminated in the ranks, (10) DON'T let incorrect habits go uncorrected in class.

## 255. TEACH OTHERS TO TEACH THEMSELVES.

If you're a combat instructor, teach your students to teach themselves. Avoid spoon-feeding information. Consider the *Socratic method of teaching*. Make your students answer their own questions through mental and physical inquiry.

## 256. BE RESPECTFUL.

Always treat your instructor or mentor with the highest level of respect. Display a willingness to show consideration and appreciation for his teachings. Make it a habit to be polite and courteous whenever you are in his presence. Polite expressions of consideration or deferential regard are also in order. Courteously yield to his opinions, wishes, and judgments. Never violate his rules or interfere with his teaching. Remember, your life is in his hands.

### 257. GOOD INSTRUCTORS ARE HARD TO FIND.

A good self-defense instructor knows how to push his students. He also knows how to motivate the weak and browbeat the arrogant.

### 258. TALK TO COPS.

If you ever have the opportunity, talk to law enforcement officers about their encounters with street criminals. Law enforcement people are generally very candid, and they can teach you a lot about the realities of street violence.

# SCHOOL SELECTION

### 259. FIND AN ECLECTIC SCHOOL.

When looking for a realistic self-defense school, choose one that is strictly devoted to the science of combat. The school you select should also be eclectic, drawing from such fields as martial science, criminal justice, military and police science, psychology, sociology, conflict management, histrionics, kinesics, anatomy, firearms, and emergency medicine. Also be sure that the tools, techniques, and tactics are all predicated on efficiency, effectiveness, and safety.

### 260. FIND THE ANSWERS TO THESE QUESTIONS.

Here are some important questions to ask when selecting a self-defense school: (1) Is the training practical and realistic?

(2) Are questions permitted in class? (3) Does the school stress the importance of range proficiency? (4) Is safety stressed during training? (5) Does the instructor discuss the legal ramifications of self-defense? (6) Are training materials available for the students? (7) Are full-contact exercises conducted? (8) Are ground fighting techniques taught? (9) What types of weapons are taught? (10) Is the information presented in a methodical and organized fashion? (11) How proficient are the advanced students of the particular system? (12) What is the general atmosphere of the school? (13) Does the instructor seem to be in control of the studio? (14) Can you afford the membership fees?

### 261. CHOOSE CAREFULLY.

You must be cautious when choosing a martial art or self-defense school. They don't all have the same objective. Here are some important points to keep in mind.

(1) If you are looking for practical self-defense training, stay clear of traditional martial arts. A karate or kung-fu instructor is no more qualified to teach you street combat than a ballet teacher or fitness trainer. When all is said and done, the traditional martial arts have absolutely nothing to do with real world fighting. (2) Don't select a school simply because of geographical proximity. Don't let your laziness force you to sacrifice quality training. (3) Look for a reputable school that instructs students in both armed and unarmed self-defense.

### 262. BELIEVE NOTHING YOU HEAR, AND ONLY ONE HALF THAT YOU SEE.

Martial artists are notorious for exaggerations and blatant lies. Don't believe what you hear in the martial arts community - especially stories about so-called *ancient masters*. They're grifters who exploit the dreams and aspirations of weak-minded people.

### 263. BOYCOTT MARTIAL ART TOURNAMENTS.

Martial art tournaments are for egotistical martial artists who are too afraid to fight. They parade around in bizarre clothing and win the admiration of ignorant spectators who have absolutely no idea of what real combat is about. It's a million-dollar business that perpetuates the myth of martial arts. And don't be impressed by martial arts demonstrations. They prove nothing. If you must watch a spectator sport, try attending MMA, boxing, wrestling, or kickboxing matches.

# LEARNING AND TESTING

### 264. KNOW THE SEQUENCE OF LEARNING.

There is a proper sequence for learning any combat technique. First, you must acquire knowledge of the specific technique. Second, you must develop the proper timing to execute the technique smoothly. The third and final component to the sequence is to apply the attributes (i.e., speed, power, accuracy, etc.) that make the technique effective.

### 265. THE SEVEN Ps OF TRAINING.

Here's one principle of training that you should never forget: Proper Planning and Preparation Prevent Piss-Poor Performance.

### 266. PRACTICE.

Practice makes perfect, and perfect makes survivors. The only way to be truly prepared for combat is to practice on a regular basis. You must perform the task, technique, maneuver, or tactic repeatedly to acquire or polish a particular skill. Don't make the common mistake of thinking that expensive equipment will compensate for practice. It won't!

## TRAINING & CONDITIONING

### 267. DON'T GET COMPLACENT.

The longer you study the combat arts, the greater your chance of falling victim to complacency. Complacency signals a downfall in your training. Always strive to improve your skills and abilities. Stay hungry for knowledge and training and don't lose your drive for personal improvement. Remember, if you think you have arrived, you haven't.

### 268. TAKE A TEST.

Cognitive and physical testing is a vital component of elite combat training. A complete self-defense exam should challenge the student in two domains: (1) cognitive - the student is tested orally and then required to take a written examination and (2) psychomotor - the student must physically demonstrate the skills and techniques, with emphasis placed on his instinctive ability to apply the correct technique.

### 269. EXPERIENCE IS ALWAYS THE BEST TEACHER.

There's no real substitute for actual fighting experience.

### 270. TRAIN THE WAY YOU WILL FIGHT, FIGHT THE WAY YOU HAVE TRAINED.

Never forget that under stress, in a real fight, you will instinctively revert to the way you have been trained.

### 271. REMEMBER WHAT YOU'VE LEARNED.

Unless you have ingrained your combat skills into your psyche by imprinting your memory through repetition, you'll often forget what you have learned.

## 272. CONTEMPLATE HYPOTHETICALS.

Analytical exercises should be a regular part of your training. During idle times, practice problem-solving skills. For example, move hypothetical criminals into different ranges of combat and select and visualize appropriate targets, and combinations. Mentally gauge openings and ranges of attack, or scrutinize the five tactical responses (comply, escape, de-escalate, assert, and fight back) as they relate to a variety of possible scenarios, such as the following: (1) being held at knife point, (2) being kidnapped, (3) being held at gunpoint.

## 273. ACQUIRE THE THREE TRAINING DOMAINS.

There are three general training domains that must be acquired in order to master the skills and tools of combat, as follows: (1) cognitive domain - encompasses the specific knowledge related to the tool or technique; (2) psychomotor domain - includes the physical skills necessary to execute the tool or technique; and (3) affective domain - includes the attitudes, philosophies, ethics, values, discretionary use of force, and the spirit (killer instinct) required to use the tool or technique appropriately.

# CHAPTER THREE
## Attributes of Combat

*"A kick, punch, block, or any other technique is useless unless accompanied by specific combative attributes."*

ATTRIBUTES OF COMBAT

# COGNITIVE ATTRIBUTES

**274. TOUGH IT OUT.**

*Mental toughness* is a combat performance mechanism utilizing a collection of mental attributes that allow a person to cope, perform and prevail through the stress of *extreme adversity*. Generally, extreme adversity will include most of the following six elements: (1) a degree of danger, (2) the element of risk, (3) the presence of fear, (4) the possibility of loss, (5) a challenge to your self-confidence, (6) the experience of pain (emotional or physical).

Regardless of your occupation, profession or personal goals, mental toughness has three primary objectives. They include: (1) to cope with adversity, (2) to perform during adversity, (3) to prevail from adversity.

**275. COPE WITH ADVERSITY.**

Mental toughness requires you to accept adverse circumstances. This is counter intuitive for most people because we are born with a natural instinct to avoid conflict and discomfort. In fact, we often make our situations worse by avoiding them. Therefore, the first step to coping with adversity is to identify and embrace it. Recognize it for what it is - a legitimate obstacle to your goal. Effectively coping with adversity also means you must immediately manage and control the stress that comes with it. This is critical because it determines whether or not you'll be able to perform at the right moment.

### 276. BE DECISIVE.

Combat demands that you be decisive about your decisions and actions. *Decisiveness* is your ability to be unwavering and focused when following a tactical course of action. Remember that indecisiveness in combat can lead to dangerous vulnerabilities.

### 277. BE PERCEPTIVE.

*Perception* is the interpretation of information acquired from one's senses when faced with a dangerous situation. You gather information through your five senses. Your eyes, ears, nose, and senses of touch and taste will provide a wealth of vital information about a threatening assailant and the environment. With adequate training, your senses can be sharpened and your powers of observation enhanced.

The ability to process information varies from person to person. In fact, two people who witness the same event are likely to report it differently. This is referred to as "individual perception." In part, previous experiences can determine the manner in which a person will interpret stimuli. When it comes to effective self-defense, you must attempt to remove preconceived notions, assumptions, and biases that may lead to dangerously incorrect conclusions or oversights. These false reactions form barriers to your ability to grasp reality.

### 278. CONTROL AROUSAL

For most people, the *fight-or-flight response* is debilitating. They panic or freeze up, and fear then becomes a powerful weapon of the opponent. Therefore, it's important that you learn to control the physiological and psychological response to make it work for you and not against you in an emergency crisis situation. This is referred to as *arousal control*.

The first step to controlling arousal is to accept the fact that the fight-or-flight response is a natural human response. Second, harness the fight-or-flight response by preparing yourself thoroughly for the danger that may one day confront you. Third, actively employ coping techniques, such as positive self-talk, and controlled breathing skills to manage the immediate effects of stress, anxiety, and fear. Fourth, develop a keen sense of self-awareness.

### THE FIGHT-OR-FLIGHT RESPONSE

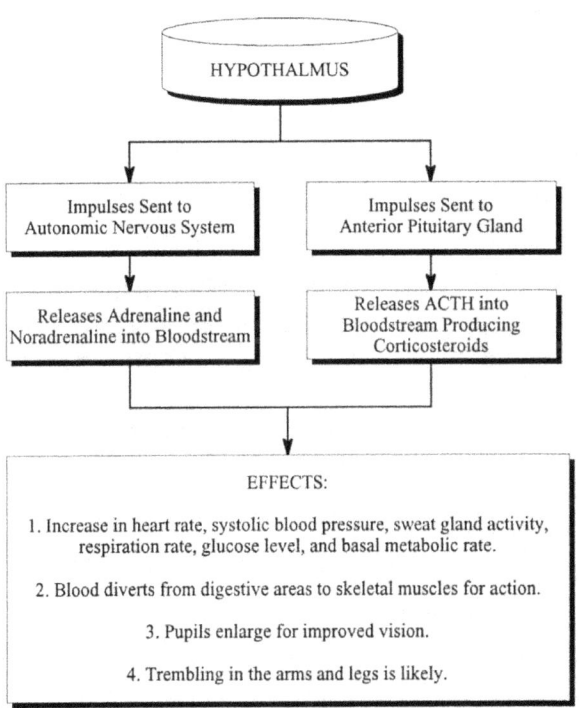

### 279. BE RESILIENT.

*Resilience* is the ability to recover quickly from various forms of adversity. Essentially, it provides the mental strength to "bounce back" or "get back on your feet" and continue pursuing your goal or objective. For example, an athlete might sustain a physical injury or embarrassing performance mistake. A soldier might experience psychological trauma from war, or a police officer might experience post-traumatic stress from a deadly shootout with the criminal. As diverse as these examples might be, all of them require a substantial amount of mental resilience to recover and get back on track.

## 280. EMBRACE INSTRUMENTAL AGGRESSION.

Human aggression is a necessary behavior trait that has ensured the survival of our species, and it's also a vital component of combat preparedness. Essentially, *Instrumental aggression* is the purposeful and controlled aggressive action designed to help achieve a particular objective or goal. A police officer arresting a criminal suspect, or a bouncer physically ejecting a belligerent patron from a bar, are good examples.

Instrumental aggression is particularly important for occupations and activities that require you to administer physical force, such as military service, police work, private security, and self-defense. Full-contact sports like boxing, MMA, kickboxing, wrestling, football, rugby, lacrosse, and ice hockey will also benefit from this form of controlled aggression.

## 281. BE SELF-DISCIPLINED.

*Self-discipline* is considered the single most important trait required to achieve personal excellence. As a matter of fact, it's self-discipline that separates the novice from the expert and the highly accomplished person from the underachiever. Self-discipline is the ability to work methodically and consistently toward a personal goal until it is achieved. In some instances, it might require you to work tirelessly day after day, week after week, and month after month until your objective is actualized.

Self-discipline requires you to control and manage your impulses, emotions and desires so you can effectively pursue and ultimately reach your goals. It means having the self-control to ignore the deleterious temptations of instant gratification, in favor of acquiring a more meaningful and sometimes arduous goal.

## 282. BE RESPONSIBLE.

*Responsibility* is another core component of mental toughness. Essentially, it means being morally accountable for your own behavior. For example, a self-defense practitioner is responsible for his training and performance as well as his relentless drive to improve himself. He or she must consistently evaluate their performance and determine what must be done to eliminate mistakes in order to achieve peak performance. Consequently, they must take full responsibility for each and every decision and action they make during a crisis situation. They must take credit and responsibility for both victories and losses alike.

However, warriors are only responsible for what they control. Unnecessarily blaming yourself for things that are clearly out of your control is fruitless, and self-destructive. The truth is you can still lose a battle, despite your best efforts.

## 283. BE VICIOUS.

If you want to prevail in a fight, you must be more vicious and ruthless than your assailant. At the same time, you must calculate your tools and tactics strategically to maximize efficiency and effectiveness. *Viciousness* is the propensity to be extremely violent and destructive. It is characterized by intense savagery.

Viciousness is also a vital component of the killer instinct that can be instilled mentally by pseudospeciating your adversary. *Pseudospeciating* means assigning inferior qualities to your adversary. Viciousness should not be misinterpreted as wrong, evil, immoral, or depraved. Some of you may wonder how I can reconcile viciousness with virtue. The concept of viciousness conjures up images of helpless victims being preyed upon by cruel aggressors. But it is this erroneous perception that must be reversed. The bottom line is that there are times when viciousness must be met with greater viciousness. Viciousness is a necessary means to achieve and sustain safety, justice, and peace. This may sound paradoxical and extreme, and you may challenge the compatibility of virtue and the capacity for brutal destructiveness. But there is, in fact, no inherent incompatibility. The advanced fighter must be virtuous and yet altogether capable of unleashing a controlled explosion of viciousness and brutality.

## 284. BE INTUITIVE

Learn to rely on your innate ability to *sense* something without the use of rational thought. In many circumstances, immediate cognition will provide you with the necessary time to respond to a threatening situation. In some situations, going with your "gut" reaction can be just what is called for. Remember, when something doesn't seem right or the objective data doesn't add up, then chances are something is wrong.

## 285. BE ASSERTIVE.

In order to perform at your best, you must possess a healthy degree of assertiveness. *Assertiveness* is a form of behavior characterized as a confident and positive expression of your thoughts, feeling, and needs. On the other hand, it doesn't mean being pushy, intrusive, or confrontational.

Assertiveness is also a vital trait in the world of self-defense. The immutable fact is humans, by nature, take full advantage of weak and timid personalities. And it's no surprise that meek people get manipulated and exploited by shrewd and psychologically dominant individuals. Through effective communication skills, you can thwart a person's efforts to intimidate, dominate, and control you.

### 286. BE TELEGRAPHICALLY COGNIZANT.

A seasoned fighter is aware of everything, including his assailant's intentions to attack. *Telegraphic cognizance* is the ability to recognize both verbal and nonverbal signs of impending aggression or assault. (1) Verbal signs (assault is imminent): abnormal stuttering, rapid speech, incoherent speech, extreme sarcasm, threats, challenging statements, screaming and yelling, and swearing. (2) Nonverbal signs (assault is possible): increased breathing and pulse rate, excessive sweating, pulled shoulders, clenched teeth, direct and uninterrupted eye contact, acting as if he is ignoring you, drunken behavior, immediately changing from uncooperative to cooperative. (3) Nonverbal signs (assault is imminent): clenched fists, quivering hands, cessation of all movements, reddened face (from blood surge), protruding veins (from face, neck, or forearms), extreme body tension, shoulder telegraph, target stare (looking at groin, jaw, etc.), finger pointing, pacing, quick turning, fist threats with arm bent, hands on hips, 1,000-yard stare (looking through you), hand concealment, rocking back and forth, and a change in stance.

### 287. ADAPT.

During combat, factors change like the wind. A poor fighter will expect his environment to adapt to him, whereas a smart fighter adapts to his environment. *Adaptability* allows you to adjust to new or different conditions or circumstances both physically and psychologically. In the heat of combat, a fighter should not question change, or scrutinize a particular situation excessively. A fighter must simply conform to the necessary demands of his immediate predicament.

### 288. BE SELF-AWARE.

*Self-awareness* is a critical attribute of combat. This means knowing and understanding aspects of yourself that may provoke criminal violence, and which, if any, would promote a proper response in a self-defense situation. The following questions are designed to get you started on the important process of developing self-awareness. Use them to form a profile of yourself.

(1) Physical attributes. What are your physical strengths and weaknesses? Do you possess the physical skills and attributes necessary for effective self-defense? Are you a natural athlete or a klutz? Are you overweight or underweight? Are your body language and the manner in which you carry yourself more likely to provoke or deter a violent attack? Are you in good shape? Do you smoke or drink excessively?

(2) Mental attributes. What are your mental strengths and weaknesses? Do you possess the specific concepts, principles, and knowledge related to self-defense and combat? Are you quick and intelligent? Can you think on your feet in a dangerous situation? How do you handle stress and anxiety? Do you panic or frighten easily? Can you make proper "use-of-force" decisions?

(3) Affective attributes. What are your emotional strengths and weaknesses? Are your attitudes, philosophies, ethics, and values congruent to the realities and rigors of combat? Do you know how to tap the proper fighting spirit for combat (killer instinct)?

(4) Communication attributes. What are your strengths and weaknesses in communicating with others? Do you possess the ability to effectively defuse a hostile situation? Can you communicate effectively under stressful and dangerous

situations, or do you become nonplused?

(5) Occupation. Does the nature of your occupation make you or your family vulnerable to different forms of criminal violence? Are you involved with the military or law enforcement? Are you a celebrity? Do you have diplomatic or political connections? Do you control large sums of money or valuable drugs? Does your political affiliation make you a likely target for kidnapping or terrorism?

(6) Personality traits. What type of person are you? Are you passive or aggressive? Are you opinionated and argumentative or open-minded and deliberative? Are you fiery, loud, and boisterous or quiet, subdued, and calm? Are you quick to anger? Do you harbor grudges? Are there sensitive issues, remarks, or statements that may cause you to lose control?

(7) Gender and age. What are the different types of violent crimes that may be directed toward you because of your sex? For example, women are much more likely than men to be raped or abused by their spouses. On the other hand, males are more likely than females to be victims of homicide. Is your age an open invitation for an attack on the street? For example, children and teens are more likely to be molested and kidnapped than adults, and senior citizens are slower, weaker, and more vulnerable to attack than young adults.

(8) Income level. What types of crime may be directed toward you because of your income level? Are you wealthy, comfortable, or dirt-poor? Does your income level make you or your family vulnerable to kidnapping for ransom? Or does your financial situation force you to live in poor neighborhoods that breed violent crime? Are you wealthy and flashy, displaying outward evidence of your wealth?

## 289. BE SITUATIONALLY AWARE.

*Situational awareness* is total alertness, presence, and

focus on virtually everything in your immediate surroundings. It requires you to detect and assess the people, places, objects, and actions that can pose a danger to you.

Don't think of situational awareness simply in terms of the customary five senses of sight, sound, smell, taste, and touch. In addition to these, the very real powers of instinct and intuition must also be developed and sharpened. Situational awareness, in terms of threats posed by human attackers, begins with an understanding of criminal psychology. It's a common misconception that all street criminals are stupid. On the contrary, they can be shrewd, methodical, bold, and dominant. The especially dangerous ones are often expert observers of human behavior, capable of accurately assessing your body language, walk, talk, state of mind, and a variety of other indicators. Street criminals know what to look for and how to exploit it. They are selective predators who employ carefully designed measures to evaluate fear, apprehension, and awareness. Seasoned street criminals are always looking for easy targets. Chronic barroom brawlers, street punks, bullies, and muggers operate in the same basic manner. They look for weak, timid, and unaware people.

As you develop situational awareness, you transmit a different kind of signal to the enemy's radar. Weakness and uncertainty are replaced by confidence and strength. Your carriage and movements change dramatically. You will be seen as assertive and purposeful. You will be less likely to be perceived as an easy mark, and your chances of being attacked will diminish significantly.

Situational awareness also reduces the potency of the street criminal's favorite weapon - the element of surprise. Your ability to foresee and detect danger will diminish the assailant's ability to stalk you or lie in wait in ambush zones. In addition to enhancing your ability to detect, avoid, and strategically neutralize ambush zones, situational awareness allows you to detect and avoid threats or dangers not necessarily predicated on the element of surprise. Some situations will actually afford you the luxury of seeing trouble coming. Nevertheless, it's remarkable how many people fail to heed obvious signs of danger because of poor awareness skills.

Very few people take the time to utilize their situational awareness skills for a variety of reasons. Some are in denial about the prevalence of street violence, whereas others are too distracted by life's everyday problems and pressures to pay attention to the hidden dangers that lurk around them. Whatever the reasons, poor situational awareness skills can get you into serious trouble and could cost you your life.

### 290. UTILIZE ATTENTION CONTROL

While situational awareness provides the raw data of your immediate surroundings, *attention control* is the ability to select what stimuli to pay attention to and what to ignore. Attention control is actually a combination of two mental skills: selective attention and concentration.

*Selective attention* is the ability to filter out and ignore the unnecessary sights, sounds, sensations, thoughts, and emotions and focus exclusively on stimuli that is pertinent to your goal or objective. Simply put, it means selecting and discriminating the valuable data that is critically important to your task, from a considerable amount of junk. *Concentration*, on the other hand, is the ability to sustain attention over a specific period of time.

### 291. BE CRIMINALLY AWARE.

Open your eyes and ears to the many lessons of criminal awareness. *Criminal awareness* is a passive combative attribute that involves a general understanding and knowledge of the nature and dynamics of a criminal's motivations, mentalities, methods, and capabilities to perpetrate violence.

By keeping yourself informed of local and global incidents through the media, official crime reports, and other credible sources, you will gain a necessary grasp of the types and trends of violent acts and the reasons behind them.

When analyzing a violent act you have read about, ask yourself the following six questions: (1) Who? Who was attacked, and who was the attacker? (2) What? What happened? What were the circumstances? (3) Where? Where did the attacker develop the means to carry out the act, and where did the act actually take place? (4) When? When was the act committed? (5) Why? Why did the act take place? Why that perpetrator, why that victim, why that particular act? (6) How? How was the act committed?

The answers to these questions will obviously differ with every violent incident, but through this type of analysis, your ignorance and naiveté will be replaced by an enhanced awareness of potentially violent acts and how they occur. You will become familiar with the personality types of various street aggressors, including information about their age, sex, education, values, cultural eccentricities, and combat mannerisms.

## 292. BE CONFIDENT.

*Self-confidence* means having an unshakable trust in both your judgment skills and abilities. However, it should not be confused with arrogance or false bravado. In fact, you must be self-aware. You must have an accurate and realistic perspective of yourself including both your inherent strengths and weaknesses. When all is said and done, dangerous poisons like egotism, conceit and narcissism will undermine your goals by instilling a false reality.

## 293. BE PHILOSOPHICALLY RESOLUTE.

To be prepared to fight, you must philosophically resolve

issues of combat before you encounter an assailant. Philosophical resolution is essential to a fighter's mental confidence and clarity. In learning the art of war, you must find the ultimate answers to questions concerning the use of violence in defense of yourself or others. To advance to the highest levels of combative awareness, you must find clear answers to such provocative questions as (1) Could you take the life of another in defense of yourself or a loved one? (2) What are your fears? (3) Who are you? (4) Why are you reading this book? (5) What justifies the use of violence? (6) What is good and what is evil? If you haven't begun the quest to formulate the answers to these important questions, then take a break. It's time to figure out just why you want to know the laws and rules of destruction.

## 294. BE PREPARED.

A superior combatant is always ready. He's taken the time to prepare himself for the brutal realities of combat. There are three components of combative preparedness: (1) cognitive preparedness - you are mentally and psychologically prepared for the horrors of combat and equipped with the necessary concepts, principles, and knowledge critical for combat; (2) psychomotor preparedness - you are physically prepared for the rigors of combat and possess all of the physical skills and attributes necessary to fight effectively; and (3) affective preparedness - you are emotionally and spiritually prepared for the demands and strains of combat, you have philosophically resolved issues related to combat, and your attitudes, ethics, and values are congruent with the task of fighting.

## 295. BE TARGET-ORIENTED.

Knowing where to attack your assailant is just as important as knowing how and when to attack him. *Target orientation* means having a workable knowledge of the various anatomical targets presented in both armed and unarmed encounters.

Target orientation is divided into the following six categories: (1) impact targets - anatomical targets that can be struck with your natural body weapons; (2) nonimpact targets - anatomical targets that can be strangled, twisted, torn, crushed, clawed, gouged, or strategically manipulated; (3) edged-weapon targets - anatomical targets that can be punctured or slashed with a knife or edged weapon; (4) bludgeon targets - anatomical targets that can be struck with a stick or bludgeon; (5) ballistic targets - anatomical targets that can be shot with a firearm; and (6) chemical irritant targets - anatomical targets that are vulnerable to chemical irritants.

## 296. BE EMOTIONLESS.

Emotions are extremely powerful feelings that have tremendous influence over our actions. A fighter must not experience emotions while engaged in combat with an adversary. A fighter must learn to eliminate fear, anger, remorse, and ego from his consciousness temporarily. Emotion serves no purpose in combat. In fact, emotions are dangerous because they create indecisiveness, apprehension, and dangerous vulnerabilities.

## 297. BE FAST IN YOUR DEFENSIVE REACTION TIME.

Defensive reaction time is the elapsed time between your assailant's attack and your defensive response to that attack. Excluding a postal attack, your goal is to try to increase the elapsed time by increasing the distance between you and your assailant. Generally, in unarmed combat situations, the neutral zone will provide adequate defensive reaction time. Defensive reaction time can also be enhanced by recognizing telegraphic movement before the assailant launches his strike effectively.

## 298. BE STREET-SMART.

*Street smarts* can be defined as the knowledge, skills, and attitude necessary to avoid, defuse, confront, and neutralize both armed and unarmed assailants. When a self-defense technician strategically integrates the attributes of awareness, assessment, and combat preparedness, he will have acquired street smarts.

## 299. BE PATIENT.

Patience is the ability to endure and calmly await the outcome of a situation. This combat attribute is particularly important when you are "locked up" with your assailant in a ground fight, or when you are held down by suppression fire in a gunfight.

## 300. BE COURAGEOUS.

*Courage* is at the essential core of any fighter. Courage both inspires and validates the warrior. In all times and in all places, courage has been admired and revered, and has become the reason and the rationale for a society's success. But precisely what is courage? In many ways, it is easier to say what courage is not. Courage is not recklessness or foolish risk-taking, nor is it haphazard rage and fury. Instead, courage breeds confidence, resolution, and bravery. As many a fighter will tell you, fear can be intimately entwined with courage. Fear is the stimulus that, biologically speaking, triggers the fight-or-flight response; yet courage is choosing to stay and fight rather than to run away.

Courage is not the absence of fear, rather it's the ability to perform difficult actions or tasks when you are frightened. It requires you to confront a host of negative emotions and sensations including fear, anxiety, pain, intimidation, and trepidation.

## 301. BE INHERENTLY SUSPICIOUS.

In the streets you need to have a suspicious nature. A suspicious nature consists of (1) being distrustful of strangers, (2) always mentally questioning the presence of strangers, and (3) never taking your eyes off strangers, especially those in close proximity.

## 302. KNOW THE LAW.

Developing a deadly capability to protect yourself carries tremendous moral and social responsibility, as well as the risk of civil liability and criminal jeopardy. There is an interesting irony facing most martial artists and self-defense experts: the more highly trained, knowledgeable, and skilled you are in firearms, knives, unarmed combat tactics, martial arts, and other self-defense skills, the higher the standards you must follow when protecting yourself and others. Remember, if you act too quickly or use what others might consider "excessive force" in neutralizing an assailant, you may end up being a defendant in a legal process. If you are involved in a vicious street fight, where do you stand in the eyes of the law? If it becomes necessary to fight, you must know the answers to the following two important questions: (1) Exactly when can I use force? (2) How much physical force is legally justified?

## 303. BE UNIFIED MENTALLY.

A *unified mind* is one that is free and clear of distractions and fully focused on the combat at hand. Distractions can be internal, when the fighter's mind either wanders off or panics prior to or during combat, or external, when an outside source distracts the fighter (e.g., the assailant "psyches you out" or such environmental conditions as poor weather, lighting, terrain, or noise exist). *NOTE: Always remember that in combat, a clouded mind sees nothing.*

## ATTRIBUTES OF COMBAT

### 304. STAY COMPOSED.

If you lose your mental composure in a self-defense situation, you probably won't survive. *Composure* is defined as a quiet and focused mind-set that enables you to acquire your combat agenda. Mental composure can only be acquired by controlling your fear and anxiety.

### 305. CONTROL FEAR.

Fear is a strong, unpleasant emotional reaction to a real or perceived threat. If uncontrolled, fear quickly leads to panic, and then it's too late to protect yourself effectively. Here are a few suggestions to help you control the deleterious effects of fear: (1) learn effective combat skills, (2) be confident with your fighting skills, (3) regularly practice crisis rehearsal (visualization) scenarios, (4) understand and accept the physiological responses of the fight-or-flight syndrome, (5) learn to tap into your killer instinct, (6) trust your instincts, (7) be combat conditioned, (8) maintain a positive attitude in combat, (9) maintain a high degree of awareness, and (10) evaluate past reactions to dangerous or threatening situations.

# PHYSICAL ATTRIBUTES

### 306. LOOK HARD.

The way you appear to others can play a big role on the streets. A formidable fighter is one who possesses a *hard look* that tells everyone, including potential attackers, that you're not to be bothered with. A hard look has two components: (1) facial - when your facial expression appears situationally aware, dead serious, and confident; and (2) physique - when your body appears muscular, and powerful. Remember, if you're fat, underweight, or visibly out of shape, no one will ever take you seriously. This is the law of nature.

## 307. BE REALISTIC ABOUT RHYTHM.

Rhythm is defined as combat movements characterized by the natural ebb and flow of related elements. Although rhythm is considered by many martial art instructors to be a combat attribute, it is really seldom used. Real combat usually does not allow you the opportunity to dance around your assailant and execute a rhythmic combination of strikes. Combat is similar to a car wreck. It's spontaneous, explosive, unmerciful, and bloody. When your assailant explodes through the ranges of unarmed combat in an attempt to rip you apart, it's difficult to maintain a rhythmic flow of strikes.

Furthermore, the concept of "breaking" your assailant's rhythm is absolutely ridiculous. In a vicious street fight, you won't have the time or opportunity to study and analyze your assailant's movements. You don't have time to learn your assailant's pattern of blows prior to breaking them. Such sparring concepts have no place in the world of actual fighting.

## 308. BE AGILE.

Agility is an important attribute that will be called upon in both armed and unarmed encounters. Agility is defined as the ability to move one's body quickly and gracefully. In unarmed combat, you need to move your body through the ranges quickly and easily. Agility is important because it minimizes your target exposure, economizes your offensive and defensive movements, and accelerates the velocity and power of your strikes.

ATTRIBUTES OF COMBAT

### 309. BE FLEXIBLE.

Flexibility is important to a fighter because it ensures muscle suppleness and the ability to move through the maximum range of motion. This is particularly important when ground fighting with an assailant. Muscular flexibility will also allow you to deploy your striking techniques with greater speed and ease.

### 310. TOLERATE PAIN AND SUFFER IN SILENCE.

*Pain tolerance* is the ability to physically and psychologically withstand pain. This is important for both intense training and actual combat. A self-defense practitioner who cannot tolerate pain is in grave danger. In unarmed combat, when a fighter is struck with a powerful blow and his mind goes into shock, his concentration breaks, his spirit weakens, and he begins to panic, he will almost always be defeated. Learn to tolerate the pain, and suffer in silence.

### 311. BE FAST.

Speed is a vital attribute of both armed and unarmed combat. There are two types of speed that you need to be concerned with: (1) mental speed - the rate at which you can employ your cognitive skills (i.e., assessment, awareness, tactical option response, and discretionary use of force) in a self-defense situation and (2) psychomotor speed - the rate at which you can move your body (e.g., to punch, block, evade, draw, and shoot a firearm) in a self-defense situation.

### 312. STAY BALANCED.

Balance is simply defined as a fighter's ability to maintain equilibrium while stationary or moving. In many emergency situations, if you lose your balance, you will lose your life.

Balance is critical for the following reasons: (1) you can

change your direction of movement quickly and efficiently, (2) it enhances your general reaction time, (3) it enhances your mobility, (4) it permits quick recovery from a committed movement, (5) it prevents the assailant from exploiting you in a ground fight, and (6) it prevents unnecessary target exposure to your assailant.

Balance is often lost because of (1) poor body mechanics, (2) poor kinesthetic perception, (3) improper weight shift, (4) excessive follow-through, and (5) improper skeletal alignment.

## 313. BE AMBIDEXTROUS.

You must be able to fight your adversary with equal ability on both the right and left sides of your body. Here's why ambidexterity is essential: (1) your strong hand or might be injured or wounded in combat, (2) you might be assaulted on the weak side of your body, and (3) your strong hand or leg might be occupied the time of the assault.

Ambidexterity must also be mastered in the following components of combat: (1) stances - both armed and unarmed combat stances; (2) submission holds - in both vertical and horizontal grappling planes; (3) natural offensive body weapons - kicks, punches, and various other striking techniques; (4) natural defensive body weapons - blocks, parries, and various other body evasion skills; (5) knives and edged weapon skills; (6) makeshift weapon skills; (7) stick and bludgeon skills; (8) pepper spray; and (9) firearm skills.

## 314. BE COORDINATED.

Coordination is simply the harmonious functioning of muscles in the execution of any fighting technique or maneuver. Coordination is vital because it ensures that your technique is: (1) delivered with maximum accuracy, (2) performed with complete efficiency, (3) performed with balance and control, and (4) delivered with proper timing.

## 315. MASTER THE HIERARCHY OF WEAPONS.

A superior combatant possesses the knowledge, skills, and attitude necessary to master the complete hierarchy of weapons. The hierarchy of weapons includes (1) natural body weapons (offense and defense), (2) chemical irritants (OC), (3) sticks and bludgeons, (4) makeshift weapons, (5) knives and edged weapons, and (6) firearms.

## 316. SPEED IT UP.

If you want to increase the speed of your natural body weapon, try some of the following: (1) focus on retraction speed - concentrate on speeding up the retracting motion of strikes when training, (2) minimize target follow-through - don't allow your strike to completely "settle" in the selected target, (3) step with the strike - step in the direction of the blow to accelerate its velocity, (4) practice psychomotor repetition - repeat the desired movement thousands of times to sharpen and crystallize the physical movement, (5) visualize regularly - envision the strike being delivered at great speed, (6) relax - avoid unnecessarily tensing your body and relax your muscles prior to executing your technique, (7) breathe properly - exhale during the execution of your movement, (8) acquire kinesthetic perception - acquire a keen sense of body mechanics through movement, and, finally, (9) think fast.

## 317. BE DISTRACTIVE.

Distraction is a critical component of combat; you must possess distractive tactics. Distractive tactics can be divided into the following two categories: (1) verbal - utilizing your voice to distract your assailant, including selective semantics (choice words) and voice (tone, pitch, tempo, and volume); (2) physical - utilizing physical movements or gestures to distract your assailant, including eye movements, body shifts, head turns, and appendage movements.

### 318. BE RANGE PROFICIENT.

Combat is unpredictable: it can occur anytime and anywhere. If you want to be prepared to handle any type of situation, you'd better be range proficient. This means that you can fight your adversary in all possible situations. Unarmed range proficiency is the ability to fight and defend from all three distances of unarmed combat.

(1) Kicking range. At this distance, you are usually too far away to strike with your hands, so you would use your legs to strike your adversary. For real-life combat, you should only employ low- line kicks, which are directed to targets below the assailant's waist, such as the groin, thigh, knee joint, and shinbone. Effective low-line kicks include side kicks, push kicks, hook kicks, and vertical kicks.

(2) Punching range. This is the midrange of unarmed combat. At this distance, you are close enough your assailant to strike him with your hands. Hand strikes do not require as much room as kicking strikes, and the surface that you are standing on is not as much of a concern. Punching range tools include finger jabs, palm-heel strikes, lead straights, rear crosses, knife-hand strikes, horizontal hooks, shovel hooks, uppercuts, and hammer-fist strikes.

(3) Grappling range. The third and closest range of unarmed combat is the grappling range. At this distance, you are too close to your adversary to kick or execute most hand strikes, so you would use close-quarter tools and techniques to neutralize your assailant. As we learned in Chapter 1, the grappling range is divided into two planes: (1) vertical - you and your assailant are standing and (2) horizontal - you are ground fighting with your assailant. Grappling range tools and techniques include head butts; biting, tearing, clawing, crushing, and gouging tactics; foot stomps; horizontal, vertical, and diagonal elbow strikes; vertical and diagonal knee strikes; chokes; strangles; joint locks; holds; reversals; and escapes.

ATTRIBUTES OF COMBAT

## 319. BE EVASIVE.

Evasiveness is the ability to avoid threat or danger. There are generally two types of evasion - contact evasion and confrontation evasion. Contact evasion is when you physically move or manipulate your body targets to avoid being struck (i.e., slipping your head to the side or sidestepping away from a charging assailant). The key to a successful contact evasion is proper timing: you should always wait until the very last moment. Move too soon and your assailant will track you. Move too late and he will maul you. Confrontation evasion is when you strategically manipulate the distance or environment to avoid a possible confrontation with an assailant (i.e., crossing the street long before a shoulder-to-shoulder encounter with a pack of street punks moving up the sidewalk). Effective confrontation evasion requires keen situational awareness skills.

## 320. BE INSTINCTIVE ABOUT STANCE SELECTION.

*Stance selection* is the ability to select a stance appropriate for a particular combat situation instinctively. Effective stance selection requires you to understand and master the following stances and postures: (1) natural stance - a strategic stance one assumes when approached by a suspicious person who appears nonthreatening, (2) fighting stance - a strategic posture one assumes when face-to-face with an unarmed assailant, (3) knife defense stance - a strategic stance one assumes when confronted by an edged weapon attacker, (4) knife fighting stance - a strategic stance one assumes when armed with a knife or edged weapon, (5) de-escalation stance (kicking, punching, and grappling ranges) - a strategic and nonaggressive stance one assumes when de- escalating a hostile individual, (6) standing firearms stance - a strategic stance one assumes when standing with a handgun, (7) kneeling firearms stance - a strategic stance one assumes when kneeling down with a handgun, and (8) prone firearms stance - a strategic stance one assumes when lying down with a handgun.

### 321. BE QUICK IN YOUR OFFENSIVE REACTION TIME.

Offensive reaction time is the elapsed time between your target selection and target impaction. In both armed and unarmed combat, your objective is to reduce the elapsed time.

### 322. BE ACCURATE IN YOUR TIMING.

Timing is your ability to execute a technique or movement at the optimum moment to achieve the most desirable effect. Accurate timing is enhanced through (1) accurate and rapid assessment skills, (2) accurate and proper distancing from your selected target, (3) accurate and rapid mental speed, and (4) psychomotor speed and overall proficiency.

### 323. RECOGNIZE TARGETS.

*Target recognition* is the ability to recognize specific anatomical targets immediately during a self-defense situation. This will vary depending on the type of weapon or tool you would use in a self-defense situation. The following are just a few examples.

(1) Natural body weapon targets. When you plan on striking your assailant with your natural body weapons, targets include the eyes, temple, nose, chin, back of neck, front of neck, solar plexus, ribs, groin, thighs, knees, shins, and, in some cases, the fingers.

(2) Submission hold targets. When

you are employing submission holds on your assailant, some targets include the neck and throat, elbow joint, shoulder joint, waistline, wrists, legs, ankles, and fingers.

(3) Edged-weapon targets. When you are utilizing a knife or edged weapon in a self-defense situation, some targets will include the ear cavities, eye sockets, temples, base of skull, cervical vertebrae, jugular vein, underside of the chin, carotid artery, subclavian artery, heart, lungs, wrists, back of knees, Achilles tendons, brachial arteries, radial arteries, third and fourth rib regions, solar plexus, groin, and femoral arteries.

(4) Bludgeon targets. When utilizing a bludgeon in a self-defense situation, some of your targets will include the head, throat, back of neck, clavicle, lower back, elbows, hands and forearms, ribs, thighs, and knees.

(5) Ballistic targets. When you are utilizing a firearm in a self-defense situation, some of your targets will include the head, torso (center of mass), pelvic region, and, in some cases, the thighs.

(6) Makeshift weapon targets. When utilizing a makeshift weapon in a self-defense situation, some targets will include a) striking weapons - head, throat, back of neck, clavicle, lower back, elbows, hands and forearms, ribs, thighs, and knees; b) distracting weapons - face and eyes, groin, and legs; c) cutting weapons - ear cavities, eye sockets, temples, base of skull, cervical vertebrae, jugular vein, underside of the chin, carotid artery, subclavian artery, heart, lungs, wrists, back of knees, Achilles tendons, brachial arteries, radial arteries, third and fourth rib regions, solar plexus, groin, and femoral arteries.

(7) Chemical irritant targets. When utilizing chemical irritants (OC) in a self-defense situation, targets will include the mucus membranes (i.e., eyes, nose, and mouth).

## 324. STAY RELAXED WHEN FIGHTING.

You must be able to relax your body during a threatening

situation. Your body must be free of muscular tension from the psychological pressure of combat. There are four effective ways to reduce nervous tension and enhance physical relaxation during a fight.

(1) Preparation. Be prepared to handle numerous combat situations by possessing the three components of combative preparation: a) cognitive preparedness—you're mentally and psychologically prepared for the horrors of combat, b) psychomotor preparedness—you're physically prepared for the rigors of combat, and c) affective preparedness—you're emotionally and spiritually prepared for the demands and strains of combat.

(2) Proper breathing. Control and pace your breathing during the threatening encounter.

(3) Fight-or-flight response. Control your fight-or-flight response by unleashing your killer instinct at the proper time.

(4) Proper attitude. Always maintain a positive attitude during a threatening situation.

(5) Kinesthetic perception. Kinesthetic perception is important because it allows you to effectively regulate or monitor the muscular tension in your body.

### 325. BE UNIFORM.

One of the most important and often neglected attributes of combat is *uniformity,* meaning that you properly perform a specific task or action the same way every time. Uniformity is important in some of the following aspects of combat: (1) weapon uniformity - you grip or draw your hand-held weapon the same way every time (the grip or draw will depend largely on the weapon of choice), (2) natural body weapon uniformity - you deliver your natural body weapons the same way every time, (3) stance uniformity - the different stances are employed the same way every time, (4) technique uniformity - your technique or maneuvers are performed the same way every time, and (5) attribute uniformity - your attributes (i.e., speed, power, accuracy, balance, etc.) are consistent.

## 326. UNDERSTAND PROBABLE REACTION DYNAMICS.

In my book *Maximum Damage,* I define *probable reaction dynamics (PRD)* as "the opponent's anticipated or predicted movements or actions during both armed and unarmed combat." Knowledge of your assailant's probable reaction dynamics is vital in both armed and unarmed combat. In fact, you must be cognizant of the probable reaction dynamics to every kick, punch, strike, technique, and weapon in your self-defense arsenal. This is what I refer to as *reaction dynamic awareness.*

Probable reaction dynamics will always be the result or residual of your initial action. This action can be in the form of a verbal statement, physical technique, or simple gesture. Regardless of your style of fighting, understanding and ultimately mastering reaction dynamic awareness will give you a tremendous advantage when fighting.

### PRD ADVANTAGES

- Provides fighting foresight
- Compound attack efficiency
- Maintains the offensive flow
- Fight ends faster
- Conserves energy and reduces combat fatigue
- Reduces fear and apprehension
- Improves defensive awareness
- Anatomical target awareness
- Use-of-force accuracy
- Training time saver

## 327. BE DECEPTIVE.

A clever tactician is a deceptive tactician. *Deceptiveness* is an important attribute for combat. Make your techniques as deceptive as your thoughts. Your objective is to delude your assailant into an error in judgment. Deception can be subtle or simply inflammatory. It depends on the self-defense situation.

## 328. BE SKILLED IN KINESICS.

You must understand the science of body language. This means that you must understand the behavioral pattern of nonverbal communication. Nonverbal communication includes your stance and posture, walk, carriage, eye and mouth movements, and arm, hand, and leg movements.

## 329. BE AWARE OF NOMENCLATURE.

You should be able to understand names that fall into the various classifications of combat systems, including(1) natural body weapon nomenclature - the names of various natural body weapons, (2) submission hold nomenclature - the names of various submission hold techniques, (3) edged-weapon nomenclature - the names of component parts of a knife or edged weapon, (4) bludgeon nomenclature - the names of component parts of a stick or bludgeon, (4) firearm nomenclature - the names of component parts of a firearm (long and short guns), (5) ammunition nomenclature - the names of component parts of a firearm cartridge, (6) makeshift weapon nomenclature - the names of component parts of various makeshift weapons, and (7) chemical irritant nomenclature - the names of component parts of a chemical irritant (pepper spray) canister.

## 330. BE FRACTALLY COGNIZANT.

*Fractal cognizance* is an important combat attribute

reserved only for advanced fighters. Fractal cognizance is the awareness and strategic utilization of *sub combat ranges* (armed and unarmed). This combative attribute is important for the following reasons: (1) it bridges the gap between the ranges of armed and unarmed combat, (2) it maximizes the effectiveness of a compound attack by maintaining the offensive flow, and (3) it introduces a completely new dimension to combat.

## 331. BE SKILLED IN TARGET SELECTION.

*Target selection* is the cognitive process of selecting the appropriate anatomical target to attack. Selecting the appropriate target is predicated on three important factors: (1) proximity - how far the assailant is from your tool, technique, or weapon; (2) positioning - exactly where the assailant is positioned and at what angle and height; and (3) use of force - the amount of force (non deadly or deadly) that is legally warranted for the particular situation.

## 332. BE ADROIT.

This means have finesse, which is usually the by-product of the complete harmonious interplay of combative attributes. It is the ability to execute a movement or a series of movements skillfully and with grace and refinement. This attribute is especially important when applying submission holds in the grappling range of unarmed combat.

## 333. BE KINESTHETICALLY PERCEPTIVE.

*Kinesthetic perception* is the ability to feel one's body accurately during the execution of a particular movement. This movement can be a punch, kick, block, or slash of the knife. Kinesthetic perception is important for both armed and unarmed combat for the following reasons: (1) it allows you to effectively regulate or monitor the tension in your body, (2) it enhances speed and minimizes telegraphic movements in combat, (3) it bridges a strong mind and body link for the practitioner, and (4) it informs you of psychomotor disturbances (i.e., balance disruption, equilibrium breakdown, and skeletal misalignment).

### 334. BE ACCURATE.

*Accuracy* is the ability to execute a movement with precision and exactness in combat. There are different forms of combat accuracy. Here are a few examples: (1) striking accuracy - the ability to strike your assailant with precision and exactness (this includes natural body weapons, bludgeons, and some makeshift weapons), (2) cutting accuracy - the ability to cut your assailant with precision and exactness, (3) shooting accuracy - the ability to shoot your assailant with precision and exactness, and (4) manipulation accuracy - the ability to manipulate your assailant's limbs and joints with precision and exactness.

### 335. BE SKILLED AT TRAVERSING.

Traversing skills are essential attributes in both armed and unarmed combat. Traversing is particularly important when under limited environmental conditions or when confronted with multiple assailants who try to outflank you. Traversing skills can be employed when unarmed and fighting multiple assailants or when bludgeon fighting and knife fighting. Also keep in mind that when you are engaged in a gunfight, you can employ traversing skills while standing or kneeling. *REMEMBER: The two primary components of effective traversing (while standing) are to keep your knees bent and flexible while twisting freely at your waist to either your right or left side.*

## 336. MANIPULATE RANGE.

*Range manipulation* is the ability to strategically manipulate the ranges of combat (both armed and unarmed). The following are the two forms of range manipulation that you must master: (1) offensive range manipulation (ORM) - the skillful and strategic exploitation of the ranges of combat for offensive purposes and (2) defensive range manipulation (DRM) - the strategic manipulation of ranges for defensive purposes. Effective range manipulation requires keen awareness skills accompanied by superb timing.

## 337. BE EXPLOITATIVE OF TARGETS.

Once you have acquired awareness of reaction dynamics, you can implement target exploitation. *Target exploitation* is a combative attribute that allows you to strategically maximize your assailant's reaction dynamics during the fight. Target exploitation skills can be applied in both armed and unarmed encounters.

## 338. TROUBLE SHOOT THE PROBLEM.

Sometimes things don't work out as planned. No matter how much you prepare and train, there is always the possibility that there will be a problem or setback in combat. And a prepared fighter is one who anticipates such problems and is equipped to handle them.

Troubleshooting skills can be defined as your ability to diagnose and solve problems immediately when engaged with your assailant. They can be used in the following situations: (1) ground fighting - when a particular submission hold is not working effectively; (2) combat shooting - when you cannot hit your target effectively or when faced with firearm malfunctions; (3) striking techniques - when a particular strike (natural body weapon or bludgeon) is not neutralizing your assailant.

### 339. BE TERRAIN-ORIENTED.

The terrain you're fighting on is a critical environmental factor. Every good fighter should know the strategic implications of the terrain he is standing on. One of the best ways to prepare yourself is through terrain orientation. This means developing a working knowledge of the various types of environmental terrains and their advantages, dangers, and strategic limitations.

Terrains fall into one of the following two categories: (1) stable terrain - principally characterized as stationary, compact, dense, hard, flat, dry, or solid ground; and (2) unstable terrain - principally characterized as mobile, uneven, flexible, slippery, wet, or rocky ground. You should be particularly familiar with unstable terrains, including ice, snow, wet grass, wet concrete, wet leaves, wet metal, wet wood, sand, gravel, mulch, muddy areas, rocky areas, and escalators.

### 340. BE TACTILELY VISUAL.

*Tactile sight* is the ability to *see* through physical contact with your assailant, and it is used predominantly in close-quarter confrontations (i.e., ground fighting with your assailant).

### 341. MASTER DISTANCING.

*Distancing* is your ability to understand spatial relationships. A fighter must understand the strategic extent of space. During both armed and unarmed combat, a fighter must instinctively know the opportunities and limitations of the range he is engaged in.

# CHAPTER FOUR
## Tactics & Strategy

*"Strategic preparedness can make all the difference between life and death."*

# GENERAL TACTICS

**342. BE AWARE AT ALL TIMES.**

When walking the streets, get into the habit of constantly scanning your environment, thoroughly and quickly noting potential problems.

**343. LOOK PEOPLE IN THE EYE.**

When conversing with friends, always maintain direct eye contact. Eye contact in non combative situations shows confidence, internal strength, and, in some cases, respect for the other person.

**344. CROSS THE STREET.**

If you think you're being followed when walking down a street, cross the street at a 90-degree angle immediately and observe the behavior of everyone around you. Remember, you can be surveyed or trailed from directions other than behind you.

**345. TURN WIDE CORNERS.**

When walking on the streets, always turn wide corners. Do not go around corners within five feet of a wall, building, or shrubbery. This tactic will enhance your defensive reaction time if you are ambushed.

**346. SMILE... YOU'RE ON VIDEO.**

Be mindful of your actions and verbal statements in public places. Nowadays, everyone is armed with a smartphone and will likely record your actions and behavior when engaged in a hostile encounter. Always be certain your actions are warranted and justified in the eyes of the law. This is important from both a moral and legal perspective.

## 347. STRATEGIZE WITH YOUR PARTNER.

Sit down with your partner or spouse and strategize what each of you will do in the event of a threat or street assault. Openly discuss your strengths, weaknesses, and what you expect from each other. This type of strategizing also applies to friends who frequently hang out with you in public places.

## 348. LOOK STRONG AND CONFIDENT.

Street thugs and chronic brawlers are expert observers of human behavior. When walking in public places, always keep your head up and walk with confidence and purpose. Also, avoid looking lost, fatigued, uncertain, or preoccupied.

## 349. BE LEERY OF SPECTATORS.

During a fight, always be cognizant and suspicious of all spectators. Onlooker intervention is a common occurrence in a fight. Ironically enough, Americans are inveterate supporters of the underdog. They hate to see anyone lose a fight.
REMEMBER: Never trust anyone in a fight.

## 350. SHORTCUTS ARE DANGEROUS.

Be especially careful when taking shortcuts, including alleys, parking lots, tunnels, construction sites, or abandoned buildings.

## 351. USE WINDOWS TO YOUR ADVANTAGE.

When walking the streets, use store windows or other reflective sources to identify whether you're being followed by someone.

## 352. KEEP AT LEAST ONE HAND UNOCCUPIED.

When walking the streets, always have at least one hand free and unoccupied at all times

## 353. AVOID CERTAIN ACTIONS.

If you want to increase your safety in the streets, avoid the following: (1) counting money in public; (2) openly displaying jewelry; (3) sleeping on public transportation; (4) arguing with strangers; (5) getting into staring contests with others; (6) losing your temper; (7) picking up hitchhikers; (8) laughing at strangers; (9) daydreaming; (10) asking strangers for directions; (11) leaving valuables in your car; (12) tailgating other motorists; (13) getting into shoving matches; (14) fighting over a woman - it's not worth it; (15) overeating when dining out - eat light and you'll move more quickly if a fight occurs; (16) threatening anyone - if something needs to be done, just do it; and, finally, (17) getting drunk - you'll make a fool out of yourself, and you won't be able to protect yourself effectively.

## 354. BE APPROPRIATELY ARMED IN THE WILDERNESS.

When camping or hiking in the woods, always carry a tactical knife with you. Rather than providing refuge from the violence of the city streets, backcountry areas, by virtue of their being so remote, can leave you particularly vulnerable to assault if you're unprepared for potential trouble.

## 355. AVOID AMBUSH ZONES.

*Ambush zones* are strategic locations (in everyday environments) from which an assailant can launch a surprise attack. Ambush zones can be found and exploited in both unfamiliar and familiar environments, even in your home, and in both unpopulated and populated areas. An ambush zone can be set in a dark or poorly lit area as well as in a well-lit location. Ambush zones can be established in a variety of common places, such as under, behind, or around trees, utility boxes, and shrubs, beds, corners, Dumpsters, doorways, walls, tables, automobiles, trash cans, rooftops, bridges, ramps, and mailboxes. Now is the time to familiarize yourself with these various types of ambush zones and avoid them whenever possible.

**356. AVOID CROWDS OR LARGE EVENTS.**

Avoid crowds, especially during political demonstrations, sporting events, and strikes. If panic breaks out, you could find yourself in a riot situation and possibly be trampled in the crowd.

**357. MOVE CAUTIOUSLY IN DARK ENVIRONMENTS.**

When fighting in dark or poorly lit environments, move cautiously. A twisted ankle or a broken leg will take you out of the fight.

**358. PARK STRATEGICALLY.**

Park your vehicle next to the end curb in a parking lot. It will reduce the chance of it getting scratched, and this fact will reduce the possibility of an argument or a fight.

**359. DON'T RETALIATE.**

If another motorist drives aggressively, cuts you off, tails you too closely, gives you a gesture of contempt, or screams at you, don't retaliate. It's just not worth it.

**360. CHECK YOUR MIRRORS.**

When driving in your car, check your side and rearview

## TACTICS & STRATEGY

mirrors to see if you are being followed. If you are unsure, take a diversionary route to make sure you're not.

### 361. DON'T GET TOO CLOSE

When stopped in traffic, stay far enough behind the car in front of you to safely pull around it and drive away. This extra distance will permit you to escape quickly if it becomes necessary.

### 362. KEEP YOUR CAR IN GEAR.

When approaching intersections or stoplights, always keep your car in gear and be prepared to drive away immediately.

### 363. DUCK AND FLOOR IT.

If an assailant is shooting at you while you're driving your car, duck down low, sound the horn, and floor it.

### 364. ACQUIRE BARROOM TACTICS.

Apply these strategies when visiting a bar or nightclub: (1) be aware - of your environment, especially makeshift weapons (glasses, bottles, and dining implements); (2) stand up - when trouble approaches the bar, get out of your seat immediately, because it is very difficult to defend yourself when seated in a chair or on a barstool; (3) expect no space - you will have to employ close-quarter techniques in a bar fight; (4) expect obstacles - people, barstools, pool tables, etc., will get in your way when fighting; (5) appear strong - calm, and confident when you enter a drinking establishment; (6) position yourself strategically - try to keep your back to the bar; (7) assess your environment - take a minute and look around at various possible escape routes; (8) limit your conversation - avoid letting someone lure you into a conversation about a heated subject; (9) keep your hands free - try to keep your hands unoccupied as much as possible; (10) hit hard - since alcohol has a tendency to increase your assailant's pain threshold, strike him harder.

### 365. BEFRIEND THE BOUNCERS.

If you frequent a particular bar or night spot, always befriend the bouncers and know each of them by name.

### 366. KNOW YOUR WAY OUT.

Whenever you enter a bar, always have an emergency escape route in mind in case you need to exit immediately.

### 367. LEAVE IMMEDIATELY.

If a brawl breaks out in a bar or any other drinking establishment, leave immediately. The entertainment value of a fight isn't worth the potential danger of it escalating into something much worse.

### 368. BE CAUTIOUS IN HIGH-RISK SETTINGS.

Be exceptionally alert and cautious in the following environments: (1) 24-hour convenience stores, (2) liquor stores, (3) dive bars, saloons, and night clubs, (3) motorist rest stops, (4) ATMs, (5) banks, (6) public rest rooms, and (7) parking garages, (8) gas stations.

### 369. DON'T CALL ATTENTION TO YOURSELF.

When visiting recreational facilities (beaches, parks, movie theaters, bars, etc.), avoid calling attention to yourself with loud or boisterous behavior.

### 370. ALWAYS EMPLOY THE FOLLOWING.

Here are a few tips and suggestions that you should follow: (1) always keep a low profile when entering a bar or nightclub; (2) always expect the unexpected in a bar fight; (3) always be leery of an assailant who offers peace too soon during a conflict; (4) when sitting in a movie theater, always position yourself close to an exit or in an aisle seat to allow a quick avenue of escape; and (5) always try to keep your back to the wall when sitting in a bar or restaurant.

# CLOTHING & GROOMING

### 371. WEAR COMFORTABLE CLOTHING.

Avoid wearing restrictive clothing in public places. For example, tight pants restrict kicking techniques and the ability to run from danger, dress ties can be used to strangle, manipulate, or throw you off balance, and bulky winter coats can inhibit striking and grappling techniques. Light running shoes offer poor ankle support during lateral or otherwise evasive footwork. Earrings can be torn from the earlobes during a ground fight. Always try to wear clothes and shoes that facilitate quick and free movement. Leather jackets are good protection to the arms and extremities during a knife fight. Heavy athletic shoes can enhance your footwork and kicking techniques.

### 372. KEEP YOUR HAIR SHORT.

Try to keep your hair short, especially at the back of your head. Long hair or trendy ponytails can be dangerous and risky for the following reasons: (1) vision - they can temporarily impair your vision during the course of a compound attack or during a ground fight, (2) manipulation - in a ground fight your assailant can pull your hair and manipulate your balance as well as easily control you and throw you by the hair, and (3) immobilization - your assailant can immobilize you by grabbing your hair.

# ASSESSMENT

### 373. ASSESSMENT IS CRITICAL.

*Tactical assessment* is the process of rapidly gathering and analyzing information and then accurately evaluating it in terms of threat and danger. In general, you can assess people, places, actions, and objects.

Accurate assessment of a self-defense situation is critical for the following reasons: (1) it enhances your overall safety; (2) it helps in determining the appropriate level of force; (3) it helps in choosing the appropriate tactical option (i.e., comply, escape, de- escalate, assert, or fight back); and (4) it will help you to defend yourself if you have to go to court. Accurate assessment skills help promote a "reasonable force" response.

### 374. CHOOSE THE APPROPRIATE FORCE RESPONSE.

Properly assessing a threatening situation will also allow you to select the appropriate level of force for a self-defense situation. What follows are the different levels of force that you must be able to choose and execute correctly.

(1) Presence response - the 1st level of interaction with your assailant. At this level, your presence is known (i.e., you are standing in front of your adversary).

(2) Verbal response - the 2nd level of interaction with your assailant. At this level, you verbally communicate with your assailant (e.g., de-escalation scenario or assertion scenario).

(3) Restraint response - the 3rd level of interaction. At this level, you physically control your adversary by either utilizing chemical irritants or a variety of submission holds.

# TACTICS & STRATEGY

(4) Impact response - the fourth level of interaction with your assailant. At this level, you physically strike your assailant to incapacitate him temporarily (i.e., with natural body weapons, bludgeons, or makeshift weapons).

(5) Deadly force response - the fifth and final level of interaction with your assailant. At this level, you employ deadly weapons (e.g., firearms, edged weapons, makeshift weapons, and, in some cases, natural body weapons) to stop your assailant's threat of death or great bodily harm.

## 375. CHOOSE THE APPROPRIATE TACTICAL OPTION.

Accurate assessment skills will also permit you to choose the appropriate tactical option. There are *five tactical options* to any self-defense situation. They are listed here in order of increasing level of resistance: (1) comply - to obey the assailant's commands, (2) escape - to safely and rapidly flee from the threat or danger, (3) de-escalate - to defuse the situation strategically, (4) assert - to stand up for your rights verbally, and (5) fight back - to use various physical and psychological tactics and techniques to stun, incapacitate, cripple, or kill your attacker.

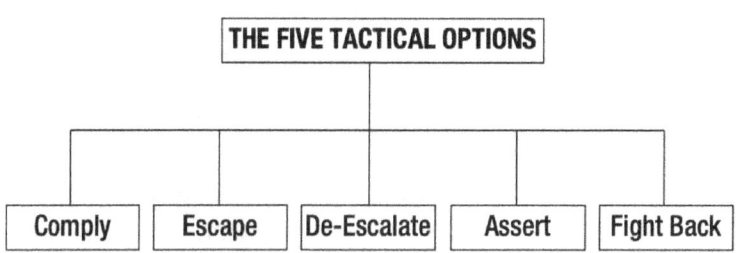

*The five tactical options for any self-defense situation.*

# 1001 STREET FIGHTING SECRETS

**376. ASSESS THE ENVIRONMENT.**

A fight can occur anywhere. In any combative situation you must quickly evaluate the strategic implications of your environment. It can be a bar, street, alley, bedroom, movie theater, airport, grocery store, gas station, elevator, your office, inside your car, or on the beach. There are six essential factors to consider when assessing your environment. They are: escape routes, barriers, makeshift weapons, terrain, positions of cover, and positions of concealment.

(1) Escape routes. These are the various avenues or exits that allow you to flee from the threatening situation safely. Examples of escape routes are windows, fire escapes, doors, gates, escalators, fences, walls, bridges, and staircases. *WARNING: Be careful that your version of a safe escape route doesn't lead you into a worse situation.*

(2) Barriers. A barrier is any object that obstructs the assailant's path of attack. At the very least, barriers give you some distance and some time, and they may give you some safety - at least temporarily. A barrier, however, must have the structural integrity to perform the particular function that you have assigned it. Barriers are everywhere and include such things as large desks, doors, automobiles, Dumpsters, large trees, fences, walls, heavy machinery, and large vending machines. *CAUTION: Barriers should not be confused with positions of cover or concealment.*

(3) Makeshift weapons. These are common, everyday objects that can be converted into offensive and defensive weapons. Like a barrier, a makeshift weapon must be appropriate to the function you have assigned to it. You won't be able to knock your assailant out with a car antenna, but you could whip it across his eyes and temporarily blind him. Although you could knock your assailant unconscious with a good, heavy flashlight, you could not use it to shield yourself from a knife attack. Makeshift weapons can be broken down into the following four types: a) striking, b) distracting, c) shielding, and d) cutting.

(4) Terrain. This is a critical environmental factor. What are the strategic implications of the terrain you are standing on? Will the surface interfere with your ability to fight your adversary?

(5) Positions of cover. A position of cover is any object or location that temporarily protects you from the assailant's gunfire. Some examples include large concrete utility poles, large rocks, thick trees, an engine block, the corner of a building, concrete steps, and so on. Positions of cover are important not only because they protect you from gunfire but because they buy you some time and allow you to assess the situation from a position of safety. When choosing a position of cover, avoid selecting the following objects because bullets can penetrate them: a) internal doors, b) small trees, c) car doors, d) all glass windows, e) drywall, f) tall grass, g) the trunk of a car, h) overturned tables, i) trash cans, j) shrubbery, and k) fences.

(6) Positions of concealment. These are various locations or objects that allow you to hide from your adversary temporarily. Positions of concealment are most commonly used to evade engagement with your assailant, and they permit you to attack with the element of surprise. Positions of concealment include trees, shrubbery, doors, dark areas, walls, stairwells, cars, and other large and tall objects.

*WARNING: Don't forget that positions of concealment do not protect you from gunfire.*

### 377. ASSESS THE INDIVIDUAL.

In a potentially dangerous situation, you must assess the source of danger. Who is posing the possible threat? Is it someone you know, or is he a complete stranger? Is it one guy or two or more? What are his intentions in confronting you? Pay very close attention to all available clues, especially nonverbal indicators. Your answers to these important questions will shape your overall tactical response. Let all of your five senses go to work to extract the necessary information. And don't forget to listen to what your instincts are telling you about the threatening person. The following are five essential factors to consider when assessing a threatening individual: demeanor, intent, range, positioning, and weapon capability.

(1) Demeanor. If time permits, assess the assailant's outward behavior. Be on the lookout for both verbal and nonverbal clues. For example, is he shaking or is he calm and collected? Are his shoulders hunched or relaxed? Are his hands clenched? Is his neck taut? Is he clenching his teeth? Is he breathing hard? Does he seem angry, frustrated, or confused? Does he seem high on drugs? Is he mentally ill or simply intoxicated? What is he saying? How is he saying it? Is he making sense? Is his speech slurred? What is his tone of

voice? Is he talking rapidly or methodically? Is he cursing and angry? All of these verbal and nonverbal cues are essential in accurately assessing the assailant's overall demeanor and adjusting your tactical response accordingly.

(2) Intent. Once you have assessed the assailant's demeanor, you'll be better equipped to assess his intent. In other words, why is this person confronting you? Does he intend to rob or kill you? Is he trying to harass you? Is he seeking vengeance for something you have done? Or is he a troublemaker looking to pick a fight with you? The assailant's intent is perhaps the most important assessment factor, but it also can be the most difficult to determine. Furthermore, in the world of self-defense, things can change very quickly. For example, an intent to rob can quickly turn into an intent to murder. In any event, the appropriate tactical response is highly dependent upon a correct assessment of your assailant's intent.

(3) Range. Range is simply the spatial relationship between you and your assailant in terms of distance. In unarmed combat, for example, there are three possible ranges from which your adversary can launch his attack— kicking, punching, and grappling ranges. When assessing your assailant, you'll need to recognize the strategic implications and advantages of his range immediately. For example, is he close enough to land a punch effectively? Is he at a distance from which he could kick you? Is he in a range that would allow him to grab hold of you and take you down to the ground? Is he within range to slash you with a knife or strike you with a bludgeon? Is the assailant moving closer to you? If so, how quickly? Does the assailant continue to move forward when you step back?

(4) Positioning. Positioning is the spatial relationship between you and the assailant in terms of threat, tactical escape, and target selection. In combat, it's important to understand the strategic implications of the assailant's

positioning prior to and during the fight. For example, is the assailant standing squarely or sideways? Is he mounted on top of you in a ground fight? Or is he inside your leg guard? What anatomical targets does the assailant present you with? Is he blocking a door or any other escape route? Is his back to a light source? Is he close to your only possible makeshift weapon? Are multiple assailants closing in on you? Is your assailant firing his gun from a position of cover or concealment? You must answer these questions before choosing a tactical strategy appropriate to the situation.

(5) Weapon capability. Always try to determine whether your assailant is armed or unarmed. If he is carrying a weapon, what type is it? Does he have an effective delivery method for the particular weapon? Is he armed with more than one weapon? If so, what are they and where are they? There are four general points of concern when assessing the assailant's weapon capability, including hands/fingers, general behavior, clothing, and location.

(a) Hands/fingers. When strategically scanning your assailant for weapons, quickly glance at his hands and all his fingertips. Can you see them? Is one hand behind him or in his pocket? If you cannot see his fingers, he could be palming a knife or some other edged weapon. Be extremely cautious when the assailant's arms are crossed in front of his body or when he keeps his hands in his pockets.

(b) General behavior. How is the assailant behaving? For example, does he pat his chest frequently (as a weapon security check)? Does he act apprehensive, nervous, or uneasy? Or does he seem to be reaching for something? Is your assailant's body language incongruous with his verbal statements.

(c) Clothing. What the assailant is wearing can also clue you in on what he may be concealing. For example, is the assailant wearing a knife sheath on his belt? Could there be a knife concealed in one of his boots? At other times you may have to be a bit more analytical. For example, is your assailant wearing a jacket when it is too hot for one? Could it be to conceal a gun at his waist or shoulder?

(d) Location. Does the assailant seem suspiciously rooted to a particular spot? Or is he running back to his car, possibly to get his gun? Is he close enough to grab that beer bottle on top of the bar? How far is the assailant from a makeshift weapon?

### 378. REMEMBER HE OR SHE LOOKS LIKE.

Accurate assessment skills will allow you to describe your assailant to the authorities. If you do decide to report a criminal assault, notify the police while your recollections are still fresh. Jotting down a few notes immediately after the altercation is also a good idea.

When filing your report with the authorities, try to include the following: (1) number of assailants, (2) sex of assailant(s), (3) somatotype, (4) approximate height and weight, (5) hair color/style, (6) deformations, (7) speech/accent, (8) race/ethnicity, (9) descriptions of eyes/nose/mouth/teeth, (10) facial hair, (11) type of clothing worn, (12) type of weapon used, (13) tattoos, (14) automobile model/color, (15) jewelry, and (16) whether he was right or left handed.

### 379. KNOW WHEN NOT TO ASSESS.

Although assessment skills are a vital component of self-defense, there are times when you must forget about assessment. For example, a street punk lunges from behind a car, grabs you, and throws you to the ground. It's obviously too late for assessment skills. In such a situation, you must act intuitively and immediately to neutralize him, or you're going to be hurt. Time is of the essence, and your instinctive reaction and reflex must take the place of assessment.

# DE-ESCALATION TACTICS

### 380. DE-ESCALATE THE SITUATION IF POSSIBLE.

*De-escalation* is the strategic process of defusing a potentially violent confrontation. Its goal is to eliminate the possibility of an agitated individual resorting to physical violence. Effective de-escalation is a delicate mixture of science and art, psychology and warfare. You must use both verbal and nonverbal techniques to calm the hostile person, while employing tactically deceptive physical safeguards to create the  appearance that you are completely nonaggressive. You must be in total control of yourself, both physically and emotionally, in order to deal effectively with someone on the verge of losing complete control.

You should always try to de-escalate a hostile situation for the following five reasons: (1) violence can often be avoided, (2) you have a moral imperative to prevent violence, (3) de-escalation polices or controls your destructive abilities, (4) it enhances courtroom defensibility, and (5) it helps reduce the possibility of spectator intervention.

### 381. EMPLOY THE SEVEN DE-ESCALATION PRINCIPLES.

There are seven de-escalation principles that you need to master. Let's start with nonverbal principles. They include: (1) emotional control - the ability to remain calm when faced with a hostile person, (2) proximity - the ability to maintain a safe distance from a hostile person, (3) strategic positioning - the ability to tactically position oneself to either escape, move behind a barrier, or utilize a makeshift weapon, (4) nonaggressive physiology - strategic body language used to defuse a potentially violent person, and (5) perception - the ability to accurately interpret vital information acquired from one's senses when confronted with a hostile person. Verbal principles of de-escalation include: (1) voice control - the ability to control and manipulate your voice when faced with a hostile person, and (2) selective semantics - the ability to select and utilize choice words when faced with a hostile person.

### 382. KNOW THE DIFFERENT STATES OF MIND.

De-escalation skills are best applied with the following states of mind: (1) egomaniac - a hostile person who simply has a big ego, (2) drunkard - a hostile person who is intoxicated and fueled with "liquid courage," (3) frustrated - a hostile person who is frustrated or irritated, (4) frightened - a hostile person who is afraid, (5) angry - a hostile person who is generally angry by nature.

### 383. CHOOSE YOUR WORDS CAREFULLY.

Words are powerful. In fact, great nations have gone to war over mere words. Likewise, in individual combat, a poorly chosen word can provoke an immediate attack by a hostile individual. It behooves you to employ *selective semantics*. Selective semantics can be defined as the strategic manipulation of choice words to de-escalate a hostile situation effectively. Your objective is to convince a hostile person that you are willing to compromise. Avoid commands like "relax, " "calm down," "shut up," "stay back," "keep your distance," or "chill out." Such statements will likely provoke hostility and anger. Instead, get into the habit of saying, "Hey, I'm really sorry," "Please, let's talk this out," or "I can understand your anger." Also use phrases like "Pardon me," "OOPS - my fault," or "Excuse me" when someone accidentally bumps into you.

### 384. MASK YOUR EMOTIONS.

When faced with a hostile individual, you must be capable of *masking* your emotions with a neutral looking face. The *poker face* is a neutral and attentive facial expression that is used when de-escalating a hostile situation. It is critical because it prevents the hostile person from reading your true intentions and feelings. Most importantly, masking personifies control and clarity and instills emotional control.

### 385. BE VOCALLY CONTROLLED.

The quality of your voice is naturally linked to your demeanor and psychological state. You can easily hear anger, fatigue, and many other emotions in the emanations of the voice. This is why it is essential that you remain calm and in complete control of a potentially hostile situation, or your voice will give you away. Voice control requires you to have complete control over the four components (tone, pitch, volume, tempo) of your voice during a threatening situation.

(1) Tone is the overall quality and character of your voice. The tone of your voice projects your emotions and feelings. When confronted with a hostile person, you must remove all threatening aspects from your voice. Always maintain a tone of voice that is serious and nonthreatening.

(2) Pitch is the relative highness or lowness of your voice. We all have a natural range or average pitch for our voices. However, when we become anxious, frustrated, or excited, our pitch usually goes up. When talking to a potential adversary, try to maintain a moderate voice pitch.

(3) Volume is the amplitude, or loudness, of your voice. Loud voices are often associated with anger, hostility, and aggression, whereas soft voices could be associated with fear, apprehension, or weakness. When confronted with a

# TACTICS & STRATEGY

threatening individual, always try to maintain a moderate voice volume. Speak loudly enough to be heard clearly under the immediate circumstances, but avoid yelling. If you're in a situation where you'd have to yell to be heard - like on a busy street or in a nightclub - you would be better off to attempt nonverbal communication techniques.

(4) Tempo is the speed or rate at which one speaks. Rapid speech usually indicates excitement, high energy, fear, nervousness, or anger. A slow tempo can be interpreted as being condescending, unsure, depressed, or ambivalent. When de-escalating a hostile person, speak at a moderate tempo to convey calmness, confidence, and control.

## 386. NEVER DROP YOUR HANDS TO YOUR SIDES

When facing a hostile person and attempting to de-escalate the situation, never drop your hands to your sides; put your hands in your pockets or cross your arms. Keeping your hands down at your sides won't provide you with the necessary reaction time to defend against your assailant's attack effectively. You've got to have your hands up to protect your anatomical targets and, if necessary, to strike your assailant with your natural body weapons. Don't point your finger or clench your fists. Keep your hands open loosely, both facing the hostile person.

## 387. BE CONGRUENT.

Effective de-escalation can only be achieved when you harmoniously orchestrate your verbal and nonverbal skills. This is known as *congruency*. Significantly neglecting any one of the de-escalation principles will result in incongruence, which can lead to disaster. For example, if you're pointing your finger in someone's face, your selective semantics really won't matter. If your body language is perfect and your voice exact, but your choice of words is poor, you won't be congruent. Remember, for effective de-escalation, your entire body, mind, voice, choice of words, and emotions must be unified into a congruent whole.

## 388. BE A GOOD ACTOR.

In some self-defense situations, you may need to act or modify your behavior until you reach your desired objective. For example, you might have to play a diplomatic and concerned role when de-escalating an angry and threatening individual. Or you may have to act out compliance to achieve a strategic position over your firearm-wielding assailant before you attempt to disarm him. Mastering histrionics will allow you to act successfully in a threatening encounter. Histrionics and combat deception go together.

Deceptive acting during a potentially dangerous encounter is no simple task. Effective histrionics will require you to control both your verbal and nonverbal behavior. Your emotions, physiology, and voice tone, pitch, volume, and tempo must all be congruent to the role that you have chosen.

## 389. DON'T TOUCH HIM.

When de-escalating, never attempt to console a hostile person by putting a comforting hand on his shoulder or offering a peaceful handshake. This act will reduce your tactical advantage and may, contrary to your intentions, be interpreted as an invasion of the other person's space.

## 390. DE-ESCALATION DOESN'T ALWAYS WORK.

There is no real guarantee that de-escalation skills will

work on every person. There are people who are going to attack you no matter how skillful and sincere you are in your efforts to avoid violence. Always keep in mind that when you're dealing with human behavior, anything can happen. So be alert and be prepared for the worst possible scenario.

# YOUR ADVERSARY

### 391. DON'T DISHONOR HIM.

Never make your adversary feel cowardly in front of people he loves or respects. Do not appear dominating, threatening, abrasive, condescending, or challenging. Remember, people will go to great lengths to protect their egos.

### 392. DON'T UNDERESTIMATE HIM.

Never assume that your adversary is stupid or incompetent. Always treat him as if he is an expert in both armed and unarmed combat.

### 393. GIVE YOUR ADVERSARY AN AVENUE OF ESCAPE.

Give your assailant the opportunity to escape with his ego and pride intact. In some cases, violence is symptomatic of someone who feels powerless or backed into a corner.

### 394. BE AWARE WHEN HE TURNS HIS BACK TO YOU.

He may be setting you up for a "sucker punch."

### 395. LET HIM BE THE FOOL.

The next time your adversary invites you outside to fight, agree with him and let him walk out first. Once he turns his back to you, knock him out. Just be certain your actions are legally justified in the eyes of the law!

### 396. BE AWARE OF THE THREE UNPREDICTABLE Ds.

The three most unpredictable types of assailant that you will come across are as follows: (1) drunk, (2) drugged, and (3) deranged.

### 397. FOLLOW ACTIONS, NOT WORDS.

During the pre-contact stages of self-defense, it's always more important to focus on what your adversary is *doing*, instead of what he is saying.

### 398. PREPARE FOR THE BEST AND THE WORST.

Always prepare for the best and the worst type of assailant. It's a big mistake to prepare yourself only for a refined fighter. There are many poor fighters out there who have a unique and unpredictable style of fighting that can cause you severe bodily injury. For example, a fighter with erratic movements can throw off the most seasoned fighter.

### 399. KNOW THE THREE BODY POSITIONS.

There are three general body positions that your assailant can assume when standing in front of you. They include: (1) zero-degree position - this is when his entire body is facing you, including the majority of his anatomical impact targets. (2) 45-degree position - this is when his body is bladed 45 degrees to you. He can effectively attack and defend from this position. (3) 90-degree position - this is when his body is sideways to you. His rear appendages (arm and leg) are severely limited, but he can strike effectively from his lead side.

TACTICS & STRATEGY

# RANGES OF COMBAT

### 400. KNOW WHAT YOU'RE DOING.

One of the highest levels of combative mastery requires a precise understanding of how specific striking tools relate to ranges of unarmed combat. The chart below will help you with this important association.

| KICKING RANGE | PUNCHING RANGE | GRAPPLING RANGE |
|---|---|---|
| Vertical Kick | Finger Jab | Head Butt |
| Side Kick | Palm Heel | Biting Tactics |
| Push Kick | Knife Hands | Thumb Gouge |
| Hook Kick | Lead Straight | Foot Stomp |
| | Rear Cross | Horizontal Elbow |
| | Hook | Vertical Elbow |
| | Uppercut | Diagonal Elbow |
| | Shovel Hook | Vertical Knee |
| | Hammerfist | Diagonal Knee |
| | | Tearing Tactics |
| | | Clawing |
| | | Crushing Tactics |
| | | Linear Blasts |

### 401. SPECIALIZE IN A RANGE.

Although range proficiency is a critical component of fighting, it's also important to specialize in a particular range of combat. This is known as range specialization. For all intents and purposes, you should specialize in the punching range for the following strategic reasons: (1) the assailant's defensive reaction time is reduced in the punching range; (2) unlike with the kicking range, you can efficiently neutralize your adversary in punching range; (3) punching-range tools are more efficient than those for the other ranges of unarmed combat; (4) punching-range tools are less telegraphic than kicking-range tools; (5) compared to grappling range (vertical and horizontal planes), punching range only requires moderate bodily commitment; (6) there is less of a "space requirement" necessary to deploy most of your punching range tools; (7) terrain is not so critical a factor in the punching range; (8) since there is no bodily entanglement, multiple assailants can be fought in the punching range; (9) punching range tools can be executed while moving, and (10) punching range tools require moderate weight transfer and shifting and are therefore faster than kicking techniques.

### 402. UNDERSTAND RANGE CHARACTERISTICS.

The ability to master the ranges of unarmed combat requires that you acquire a foundational understanding of each range. The following chart will give you strategic insight into the pros and cons of each range of unarmed combat.

For example, the grappling range of unarmed combat: (1) requires a very high degree of commitment to the assailant, (2) offers a reduced amount of defensive reaction time, (3) provides enhanced offensive reaction time, (4) has a very low potential for telegraphing an attack, (5) has a very high potential for neutralizing an assailant, (6) has a very high risk of danger for the practitioner, (7) requires a very high degree of energy expenditure, (8) has a very high likelihood of engagement, (9) has a very high potential for maintaining its range during the course of the fight, (10) the average layperson has a very low level of awareness and ability in this combat range, (11) it has a moderate terrain stability requirement, and (12) it has a very low preference for engagement.

# TACTICS & STRATEGY

| RANGE CHARACTERISTICS | KICKING RANGE | PUNCHING RANGE | GRAPPLING RANGE |
|---|---|---|---|
| 1. Commitment level | very low | moderate | very high |
| 2. Defensive reaction time | enhanced | reduced | reduced |
| 3. Offensive reaction time | reduced | enhanced | enhanced |
| 4. Telegraphic potential | very high | moderate | very low |
| 5. Neutralizing potential | very low | very high | very high |
| 6. Risk of danger | low | moderate | very high |
| 7. Energy expenditure | moderate | moderate | very high |
| 8. Likelihood of engagement | low | high | very high |
| 9. Maintainability | very low | moderate | very high |
| 10. Layman awareness/ability | low | very high | very low |
| 11. Terrain stability requirement | high | low | moderate |
| 12. Preference for engagement | moderate | very high | very low |

## 403. USE OFFENSIVE RANGE MANIPULATION.

This is the skillful and strategic exploitation of the ranges of combat for offensive purposes. Since punching range is the most advantageous range of unarmed combat, your objective is to maintain this distance while delivering an overwhelming compound attack.

Here is an example: if the fight commences from the neutral zone, take the initiative and close the distance between you and your assailant with a quick, non telegraphic low-line kick. When your kick hits its target, explode into the punching range. Proceed with a flurry of full-force, full-speed blows. Be absolutely certain your blows are appropriate to the assailant's targets and reaction dynamics. If your assailant freezes in his tracks, stay in punching range and keep the pressure on. However, stay defensively alert because some fighters may decide to counterpunch or charge forward in an attempt to take you to the ground. If your adversary decides to move into grappling range (vertical), immediately employ a flurry of elbow strikes, knee strikes, and head butts with the same overwhelming speed of your punching tools. Don't allow your adversary to break your offensive flow. If the assailant retreats into the kicking range, immediately respond with a quick low-line kick and explode into the punching range. Continue your blitzkrieg until your adversary is out of commission.

### 404. UTILIZE DEFENSIVE RANGE MANIPULATION.

If you're confronted with a vicious compound attack, defensive range manipulation is your only hope for survival. A well-executed compound attack is simply too fast, unpredictable, and powerful to block, parry, or slip. Attempting to coordinate a defensive response for each one of the assailant's blows is absurd and impossible. If you want to protect yourself effectively, you must disengage the range of assault. Defensive range manipulation will allow you to strategically disengage the assailant's compound attack quickly and safely so that you can counter the assault.

Here's an example of defensive range manipulation: if your assailant's attack begins from the punching range, immediately retreat to the kicking range. Once you are balanced, counter with a quick low-line kick. This will disrupt your assailant's balance and impede his offensive flow. However, be certain your kick is accurate, powerful, and properly timed. Once your kick impacts with its target, seize the opportunity to commence with your own flurry of full-speed, full-force blows. Keep the pressure on until the adversary is neutralized.

## TACTICS & STRATEGY

### 405. STAY AWAY FROM HIM.

Proximity is a vital consideration in both armed and unarmed combat. The farther away you are from an assailant, the greater your defensive reaction time, and the greater the visual picture you will have of your assailant. The closer you are to your assailant, the fewer options you have. For example, in grappling range, any strike delivered by your assailant will most likely land, no matter how fast you can react. You simply cannot defeat the laws of nature.

### 406. USE THE NEUTRAL ZONE TO YOUR ADVANTAGE.

Contrary to what some people might think, the *neutral zone* is not a range of unarmed combat. It is simply the distance at which neither you nor your assailant can strike or kick each other. The strategic implication of the neutral zone is that it creates distance between you and the assailant. This, in turn, will provide you with enhanced reaction time so that you can protect yourself adequately. However, don't become complacent; not all situations or environments will afford you the luxury of maintaining a neutral zone.

The neutral zone should be used primarily (1) to safely assess a potential threat, (2) to de-escalate a hostile situation, and (3) to assert yourself to someone.

# VISUAL CONSIDERATIONS

### 407. USE MONITORING POINTS.

Most fighters don't know where to look when fighting an adversary. *Monitoring points* are specific locations on your assailant's body that you should be focused on, including the throat triangle, shoulder region, hands, torso, and knees. The monitoring point that you choose in a fight will depend on the three important factors: (1) range of combat, (2) type of confrontation, and (3) type of combat (i.e., armed or unarmed).

### 408. AVOID DIRECT EYE CONTACT.

When actively engaged with an assailant, avoid direct eye contact. A quick glance is fine, but avoid becoming transfixed. Looking into the assailant's eyes is dangerous for several reasons: (1) it provides no vital data about his attack, (2) it draws your attention away from the immediate threat, (3) you can be "psyched out," (4) you can fall victim to a variety of visual feints, (5) you cannot assess the assailant's weapon capability effectively, (6) it limits your target recognition, and (7) it inhibits accurate assessment of the combat environment.

# OFFENSIVE TACTICS

### 409. RAZE HIM.

In my WidowMaker Program, R*azing* is defined as a series of vicious close quarter techniques designed to physically and psychologically extirpate a criminal attacker. These close quarter techniques are executed at various beats: (half beat, quarter beat and zero beat) and they include the following:

# TACTICS & STRATEGY

- Eye raking
- Tearing
- Biting
- Elbow strikes
- Head butts
- Bicep pops
- Finishing chokes

- Eye gouging
- Crushing
- Hair pulling
- Shaving forearms
- Hair Pulling
- Neck cranks

*Razing* is the most devastating form of unarmed fighting. Its brutal and invasive characteristics are both physically and psychologically traumatic for the recipient. The overwhelming nature of razing invokes instantaneous panic by delivering a destructiveness exceeding that of a deadly and evil criminal aggressor. When razing is properly performed, it accomplishes the following objectives during a fight:

1. Cognitive Brain Shutdown - The brutal and overwhelming nature of razing overrides the opponent's cognitive brain preventing him from any lucid thought process. Since razing is so fast and ferocious, the opponent's cognitive brain can't process what is actually happening to him.

2. Instant Damage - Razing is simply indefensible! The speed and proximity at which these quarter beat hits are delivered is truly overwhelming. The bottom line is, they're just too fast and too close for the opponent to react defensively. In many ways, razing is likened to an angry swarm of wasps, your only hope is to try and escape from the pain.

Finally, because of its devastating power, razing should only be used in self-defense situations that warrant the application of deadly force.

*From left to right, a basic razing sequence.*

# TACTICS & STRATEGY

## 410. ENERGY IS LOST QUICKLY.

Your body can only sustain delivering a compound attack for so long. Initially, your brain will quickly release adrenaline or epinephrine into your blood stream, which will fuel your fighting and enhance your strength and power. This boost of energy is known as an *adrenaline dump*. However, your ability to exert and maintain this maximum effort in a compound attack will last no more than 30 to 60 seconds if you're in above average shape. If the fight continues after that, your strength and speed may drop by as much as 50 percent. When all is said and done, you don't have much time in a street fight, so the battle needs to be won fast before your energy runs out!

## 411. KEEP YOUR COOL.

If you are going to prevail in a fight, then you must learn to be in control of the situation and keep your cool. In extremely hostile situations, losing control, showing fear, or expressing frustration or anger will only exacerbate matters greatly. In many ways, it's like pouring gasoline on a fire. You must learn not to take it personally if someone says something offensive or makes an insulting gesture toward you. The bottom line is, if you have a high degree of self-esteem and confidence, you'll be far less inclined to lose control.

## 412. KNOW THE DEADLY FORCE FORMULA.

There are many combat situations that justify and warrant the use of deadly force. It's imperative that you know the two factors that determine the lethality of a natural body weapon. They are: (1) target selection - the anatomical target that you select and (2) amount of force - the amount of force that is delivered to the selected target.

## 413. PSEUDOSPECIATE YOUR ADVERSARY.

*Pseudospeciation* is the ability to assign inferior and subhuman qualities to another person immediately in a threatening encounter. This psychological stance is important in combat because it blinds the fighter from the limitations of combat etiquette. It allows you to fight the assailant with vicious intent and determination, and permits you to unleash your killer instinct, while freeing you from the inherent dangers of apprehension. Simply put, pseudospeciation allows you to get the job done.

## 414. GHOST HIM.

Preceding a first strike and during a compound attack, it's important to "ghost" your adversary. *Ghosting* is the process of mentally eliminating all the facial features on your opponent (particularly his eyes) so that he appears completely faceless. Besides eliminating gazing, ghosting also enhances your ability to pseudospeciate your adversary.

## 415. STRIKE BEFORE YOU CONTROL.

Try to strike your assailant before you even attempt a control and restraint technique. This is critical for the following reasons: (1) striking temporarily stuns your assailant, (2) striking buys you some time to apply the control technique effectively, (3) striking disrupts the assailant's balance, (4) striking will temporarily distract the assailant, (5) striking disorients the assailant, (6) striking causes extreme pain for the assailant, (7) striking creates motor dysfunction, (8) striking creates a reflex response that you can exploit, and (9) striking often will loosen the assailant's limbs, permitting easier manipulation.

## TACTICS & STRATEGY

### 416. KNOW THE FOUR ELEMENTS OF ATTACK.

The following four elements must exist if your assailant is to commit an attack: (1) intent - the assailant must have the state of mind to execute the action, (2) opportunity - the assailant must have the time and necessary circumstances to attack effectively, (3) weapon - the assailant must have a weapon to attack (e.g., natural body weapon, knife, bludgeon, gun, or makeshift weapon), and (4) delivery method - the assailant must have an effective vehicle or method of delivering his weapon.

### 417. KICK HIM WHEN HE'S DOWN.

There are situations that legally warrant kicking a man when he's down. However, it's not as easy as it seems. It requires a considerable amount of skill and technique. Here are some important targets to look for: (1) posterior impact targets, including the temple, back of the neck, spine, fingers, elbow joint, ribs, back of the knee, and ankle and (2) anterior impact targets, including the face, throat, solar plexus, front of the ribs, groin, and the front and side of the knee. *WARNING: Be careful! A skillful ground fighter can pull you down to the ground during the course of your assault.*

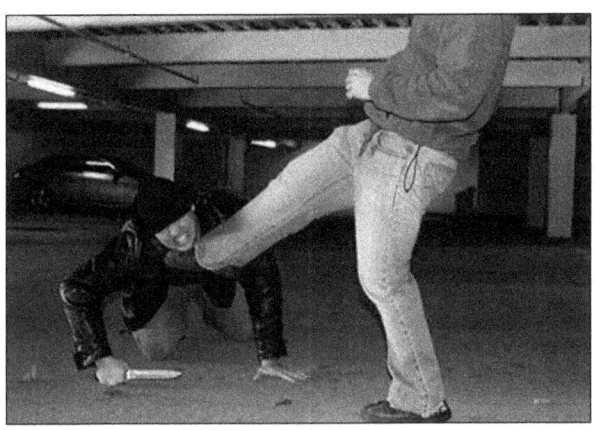

## 418. STRIKE FIRST.

Whenever you are squared off with your assailant and there is no way to escape safely, you must strike first, fast, and with authority and keep the pressure on. This offensive strategy is called the *first strike principle (FSP)*, and it is essential to the process of neutralizing a formidable adversary. Allowing the assailant the opportunity to deliver the first strike is tactical suicide. It's like allowing a gunslinger to draw his weapon first. In unarmed combat, if you allow the assailant to strike you first, he might injure or possibly kill you, and he will most certainly force you into an irreversible defensive flow that will inhibit you from issuing a counterattack. *WARNING: When employing the FSP, you must also be certain that your initial strike is warranted and justified in the eyes of the law.*

## 419. EXPLODE.

When attacking your assailant, explosiveness is the vehicle for a compound attack. The offensive tools that barrage your assailant should possess a sudden and immediate outburst of violent energy. A compound attack should never be progressive; it does not build in speed and power. It begins and ends explosively. Explosiveness is not just limited to the natural body weapons of unarmed combat. The fuel of explosiveness should also be used with footwork, firearms, knives, and bludgeons.

## 420. COMPOUND IT.

To neutralize a vicious assailant effectively, you will almost always have to do more than execute a single punch or strike. Most unarmed combat situations will demand that you initiate a compound attack against your adversary. A *compound attack* is the logical sequence of two or more tools strategically thrown in succession. The objective is to take the fight out of the assailant and the assailant out of the fight by overwhelming his defenses with a flurry of full-speed, full-force strikes.

Based on speed, power, target selection, and target exploitation, the compound attack also requires calculation, control, and clarity. To maximize your offensive attack, you must have a thorough knowledge and understanding of the anatomical targets presented by your adversary. Unless your assailant is in full body armor, there are always targets. It simply is a question of your recognizing them and striking quickly with the appropriate body weapons.

### 421. MAINTAIN THE OFFENSIVE FLOW.

When you proceed with a compound attack, always maintain the offensive flow. The *offensive flow* is defined as continuous offensive movements designed to neutralize or terminate your adversary. When attacking your adversary, keep the pressure on and don't stop until he is completely neutralized. *WARNING: Stagnating your offensive flow will open you up to numerous dangers and risks. Avoid it!*

### 422. DELIVER CLOSEST WEAPON TO CLOSEST TARGET.

In most self-defense situations, the *closest weapon/closest target* (CWCT) principle should be applied. This principle states that when physical danger is imminent, you should launch your closest weapon to the assailant's closest target. This is strategically viable for the following reasons: (1) it creates the most direct and efficient route of travel, (2) it accelerates your offensive reaction time, (3) it reduces telegraphing, (4) it reduces your assailant's defensive reaction time, (5) it improves the overall accuracy of your strike, and (6) it's safer for you.

## 423. END IT AS QUICKLY AS POSSIBLE.

Every physical confrontation should end quickly. Remember, the longer a fight lasts, the greater your chances of serious injury. A fight should be over as quickly as it begins. Your tools, techniques, and tactics must be quick and decisive. There is no time to design a battle plan or test the assailant's ability with probing techniques.

Here is a brief list of things that can occur during the course of your fight: (1) spectators can intervene, (2) you can make a tactical error that can cost you your life, (3) your immediate physical condition may worsen, and (4) the level of force between you and the assailant will escalate progressively.

## 424. NEVER DRAW AN ATTACK.

*Attack by drawing* is a method of fighting where you offer the opponent an intentional opening designed to lure his attack. Two common drawing techniques are a wide hand positioning and a low hand guard, as if to say, "Come on, take your best shot!" Once the opponent takes the bait, you swiftly defend and counter. Beware! This fighting strategy is risky and ineffective for the following reasons.

(1) Who is to say you can stop and counter the assailant's first strike? For example, would you try this technique against a professional boxer who has lightning-fast hands?

(2) By allowing the assailant to act and forcing yourself to react, you automatically put yourself at a disadvantage.

(3) Who is to say that the assailant will go for the bait? He may attack a completely different target zone.

(4) What happens if the assailant attacks with a flurry of vicious blows? You will find yourself in an irreversible defensive flow that could get you killed. Deception is an important combat skill; however, the drawing method is a gamble that might get you killed.

## TACTICS & STRATEGY

**425. DON'T COUNT ON SINGLE-STRIKE VICTORIES.**

The *single attack* is a method of fighting where the fighter delivers a solitary offensive tool to either terminate the fight or "probe" the assailant. Advocates of this method of attack argue that is the safest method of attack because it does not require full commitment to the adversary. Others profess it to be the highest form of combat when one quick, powerful blow ends the fight. *Both theories are dead wrong.* First, you cannot neutralize an assailant by lingering at the perimeter of the encounter. In real fights, you must always commit yourself 100 percent with the most effective flow of offensive tools appropriate to the range, angle, force level, and targets the assailant presents. Second, never assume one kick, punch, or strike will end a fight. Subscribing to this type of faulty logic could get you killed in a vicious fight. The bottom line is that single-strike victories are few and far between.

**426. AVOID HAND TRAPPING.**

Don't attempt immobilization attack (trapping) techniques in a fight. The immobilization attack is a complex system of moves and countermoves that allows you to control and manipulate the assailant's limbs (usually his arms and hands) temporarily in order to create an opening to attack. Hand trapping techniques require lightning-quick reflexes, highly developed touch sensitivity, and they're ineffective for a variety of reasons, including:

(1) The ability to use trapping techniques is based on the assailant presenting a proper structure in response. His hands must accept your feed in just the right way. The trapping feed or *attachment* may be either a linear or circular tool to engage the assailant's counter or guard. Once the initial lockup takes place, the trapper can go to work with parries, blocks, energy reversals, and other techniques aimed at neutralizing the assailant and creating openings. All of this may sound impressive; however, you simply cannot rely on your

assailant's presentation of the predefined structure necessary for various trapping techniques to succeed.

(2) If your attachments are not adequately engaged by the assailant, you can't build a trapping structure.

(3) If your adversary disengages, which is extremely likely in a real fighting situation, your trap disintegrates immediately.

(4) Your assailant can easily counter with a series of head butts, elbows, knees, and other close-quarter tools.

(5) Trapping techniques can lead to a ground fight, which is the last thing you want in a street fight. *NOTE: Don't confuse hand trapping techniques with the functional limb trapping movement that can be applied in a ground fight.*

**427. DON'T USE THE INDIRECT ATTACK.**

The *indirect attack* is a progressive method of attack. It always involves more than one technique. Do not, however, confuse the indirect attack with its superior cousin, the compound attack.

The indirect attack builds through stages. The initial technique is not the coup de grace, i.e., the knockout weapon. In fact, in many indirect attacks, the initiating technique is not even a weapon, but one of any number of feints or other deceptions designed to open the assailant up for the follow-up blow. Even when the initiating tool is an actual kick, punch, or strike, it serves merely as a setup for the finishing blow.

In competition or sparring, the initiating technique sets up or accumulates valuable points, wears down the assailant, and opens him up to more devastating blows. In real combat, however, where points are of no consequence and setups are not safe, the progressive indirect attack should never be employed.

In the explosive and dangerous situation of a fight, you cannot afford the risk of a setup technique. Any initiating tool or technique delivered with less than maximum speed and power will likely be ignored and will certainly be countered with viciousness.

As stated earlier, assumptions and experimentation in the face of danger are invitations to disaster. The indirect attack involves far too much risk and uncertainty. It lacks the all-out explosiveness, power, and commitment required to face an assailant hell-bent on your destruction. Remember, in real combat, no rules apply. You are subject to an attack from anywhere and anything. You cannot allow your assailant even the slightest opportunity to gain the upper hand. You've got to go full force all the way to ensure victory. By definition, the indirect attack is inconsistent with this approach and should not, therefore, be used in a real fight.

### 428. HEAD-HUNT.

*Head-hunting* means strategically pursuing and selecting the assailant's head as your primary impact target. Remember, if you have the option of attacking your assailant's head or torso, go for his head. The incapacitation potential in much greater. Just be certain your actions are warranted and justified in the eyes of the law!

### 429. CALL THE SHOTS.

Contrary to what many theoreticians may say, you must call the shots in a fight. Your decision to launch a particular tool or technique (in stand-up combat) should not be influenced by your assailant's technique, method of fighting, or form of defense. Rather, it is the angle of attack, range of combat, and use-of-force justification that sets the standard for weapon selection in a fight.

## 430. YOU WON'T KNOW TILL IT'S OVER.

The concept of avoiding your assailant's strengths and exploiting his weaknesses is a competition-oriented strategy (often used in sparring) that can't be effectively employed in real fighting. Since a street fight is so dynamic and explosive, you will not have the time to assess your adversary's fighting method. There simply isn't enough time. By the time you recognize his strengths and weaknesses, the fight will be over.

## 431. NO MINOR BLOWS.

A minor blow is defined as a strike or kick (i.e., boxer's jab, hand slap, back fist punch, roundhouse snap kick, etc.) that is not used as a knockout or finishing blow. Minor blows are generally used for the following reasons: (1) to irritate your assailant, (2) to throw your assailant off balance, (3) to set your assailant up for a finishing blow, (4) to offset or prevent a possible counterattack, and (5) to test or probe your assailant's fighting abilities. *WARNING: Minor blows are combatively deficient and have no business in a real fight. Completely eliminate them from your arsenal of striking tools.*

## 432. YELL.

The voice is a very powerful tool. When fighting, the yell is a natural manifestation of the voice. Yelling actually serves several strategic purposes in combat. Yelling while fighting can distract, startle, and temporarily paralyze your assailant. It can cause the adversary to freeze in his tracks, allowing you a split-second advantage to deliver the first debilitating strike and thus gain offensive control. Yelling can also be used to *psyche out* the assailant and synchronize your state of mind with the physical process taking place. It is the catalyst that sets off the killer instinct and the primal expression that harbors the killer instinct. In addition, yelling actually may draw attention to your fight.

## TACTICS & STRATEGY

### 433. ATTACK PRESSURE POINTS.

A *pressure point* is a specific area on the human body where a nerve lies close to the surface and is supported by bone or a muscle mass. Direct pressure can be applied to a pressure point area by striking it with a natural body weapon. Some effective pressure point areas include the common peroneal nerve, the femoral nerve, and the infra orbital. A powerful strike to a pressure point area will cause the following physiological responses: (1) extreme pain, (2) a stunning effect, (3) motor dysfunction, (4) balance disruption, and (5) reflex response.

### 434. KNOW WHEN TO ESCALATE.

Know how and when to escalate your level of force quickly and accurately in a fight.

# POSITIONING TACTICS

### 435. UTILIZE STRATEGIC POSITIONING.

During combat, always try to position yourself strategically from your adversary. For example, when faced with a threatening assailant, try to subtly maneuver yourself into a position that will allow you to escape safely. Or, if the ability to escape is not in the cards, then quickly check for any physical barriers and try to position yourself behind one.

There are other important considerations of strategic positioning, such as keeping a keen eye out for possible makeshift weapons and positioning yourself accordingly. Or, when faced with multiple assailants, avoiding backing yourself into a wall and letting them surround you. Lighting is another important component of strategic positioning. Try to position yourself so that the immediate light source (sun, auto headlights, street lamp, etc.) glares into your adversary's eyes and not yours. Terrain is also important. Try to force your assailant to stand on unstable terrain.

### 436. MOVE TO HIS DEAD SIDE.

When squared off with your assailant, try to move strategically to your assailant's dead side. The dead side is the lead side of the assailant's body. It is the safest direction to move toward because it is farthest away from the assailant's rear appendages.

### 437. STEP FORWARD.

When someone aggressively taps you on the shoulder from behind, be certain to step forward and then turn around with both of your hands up and be ready to defend or attack.

### 438. KEEP THE LIGHT BEHIND YOU.

Always have a powerful light source (e.g., sun, moon, street lamp, auto headlights, reflection source, etc.) behind you and facing your adversary. This is important for two reasons: (1) it helps illuminate your target, and (2) it inhibits your adversary's vision.

### 439. STRONGER SIDE FORWARD.

If you have the option of assuming a stance in a fight, always try to face your assailant with your stronger and more coordinated side. This will position your more powerful and coordinated limbs closer to the assailant. If you are right-handed, generally your right side is stronger and more coordinated. *NOTE: This combat axiom excludes firearm stances.*

## TACTICS & STRATEGY

### 440. MANEUVER TO AN ESCAPE ROUTE.

When squared off with an assailant, always try to subtly maneuver yourself into a position to safely escape, or close to avenues of escape (windows, gates, open doors, stairs, etc.).

### 441. BEWARE OF THE INSIDE POSITION.

One of the most dangerous areas is your assailant's inside position. The inside position is the area between both of his arms where he has the greatest amount of control.

### 442. GET BEHIND YOUR ADVERSARY.

If you want the greatest and safest position in a fight, attack your assailant from behind. A rear assault is generally effective for the following two reasons: (1) the assailant cannot see what you are doing, and (2) the assailant has the least amount of control when assaulted from the rear.

### 443. DON'T TURN YOUR BACK.

Avoid turning your back on a potential assailant unless he is so far away he can't grab, punch, kick, slash, or club you. Turning your back to someone is a sign of trust; remember, trust no one in the streets.

## ANATOMICAL TARGETS

### 444. ATTACK HIS EYES.

Eyes are ideal targets for street combat because they are one of the most important organs your assailant needs to fight effectively, not to mention that they are extremely sensitive and difficult to protect. Also, striking them requires very little force. The eyes can be poked, scratched, and gouged from a variety of angles and vantages. Depending on the force of your strike, it can cause numerous injuries, including watering of the eyes, hemorrhaging, blurred vision, temporary or permanent blindness, severe pain, rupture, shock, and even unconsciousness.

### 445. ATTACK HIS THROAT.

In a life-and-death situation, attacking your assailant's throat can save your life. The throat is considered a lethal target because it is only protected by a thin layer of skin. This region consists of the thyroid, hyaline cartilage, cricoid cartilage, trachea, and larynx. The trachea, or windpipe, is a cartilaginous cylindrical tube that measures four and a half inches in length and approximately one inch in diameter. A direct and powerful strike to this target may result in unconsciousness, blood drowning, massive hemorrhaging, strangulation, and death. If the thyroid cartilage is crushed, hemorrhaging will occur, the windpipe will quickly swell shut, and the assailant will die of suffocation. You can effectively strike the assailant's throat with knives, hands, and elbow strikes.

### 446. STRIKE HIS TEMPLE.

The temple or sphenoid bone is a thin, weak bone located on either side of the skull approximately one inch from the eye. Because of its inherently weak structure and close proximity to the brain, a very powerful strike to this anatomical target can be deadly. Other possible injuries include unconsciousness, hemorrhaging, concussion, shock, and coma. You can use the following body weapons to strike the assailant's temple: elbow strikes, hook punches, and, in some cases, the knee strike.

## 447. STRIKE HIS NOSE.

The nose is made up of a thin bone, cartilage, numerous blood vessels, and many nerves. It is a particularly good impact target because it stands out from the assailant's face and can be struck in three different directions (up, straight, and down). A moderate blow can cause stunning pain, eye-watering, temporary blindness, and hemorrhaging. A powerful strike can result in shock and unconsciousness. Lead straights, rear crosses, palm heels, uppercuts, hammer fists, elbow strikes, and knee strikes can be delivered effectively to the assailant's nose.

## 448. HAMMER FIST HIS NOSE.

The vertical hammer fist can also be delivered to the bridge of the assailant's nose. To deliver this deceptive and painful strike, apply the following steps: (1) assume a de-escalation stance with both hands open and facing your assailant; (2) while conversing and distracting your adversary, quickly whip your rear hammer fist down the bridge of his nose. Be certain not to retract or chamber your strike prior to its execution. Follow up with either a vertical knee strike or uppercut to the assailant's face.

## 449. HIT HIS CHIN.

In Western boxing, the chin is considered a "knockout button," responsible for retiring many boxers. The chin is also a good target for street fighting. When the chin is struck at a 45-degree angle, shock waves are transmitted to the cerebellum and cerebral hemispheres of the brain, resulting in paralysis and immediate unconsciousness. Depending on the force of your blow, other possible injuries include broken jaw, concussion, and whiplash to the assailant's neck. Some of the best body weapons to strike the chin are uppercuts, elbow strikes, knee strikes, palm heels, and even head butts.

## 450. STRIKE HIS CERVICAL VERTEBRAE.

The back of the assailant's neck consists of the first seven vertebrae of the spinal column. They function as a circuit board for nerve impulses from the brain to the body. The back of the neck is a lethal target because the vertebrae are poorly protected. A very powerful strike to the back of the assailant's neck can cause shock, unconsciousness, a broken neck, complete paralysis, coma, and death. Two of the best body weapons with which to strike the cervical vertebrae are hammer fists and elbow strikes.

## 451. ATTACK HIS RIBS.

There are 12 pairs of ribs in the human body. Excluding the 11th and 12th ribs, they are long and slender bones that are joined by the vertebral column in the back and the sternum and costal cartilage in the front. Since there are no 11th and 12th ribs (floating ribs) in the front, you should direct your strikes to the 9th and 10th ribs.

A moderate strike to the anterior region of the ribs may cause severe pain and shortness of breath. An extremely powerful 45-degree blow could break the assailant's rib and force it into a lung, resulting in the lung's collapse, internal hemorrhaging, air starvation, unconsciousness, excruciating pain, and possible death. Some of the best offensive tools to deliver to the ribs are shovel hooks, uppercuts, elbow strikes, and knee strikes.

## 452. HIT HIS SOLAR PLEXUS.

The solar plexus is a large collection of nerves situated below the sternum in the upper abdomen. A moderate blow to this area can cause nausea, pain, and shock, making it difficult for the adversary to breathe properly. A powerful strike to the solar plexus can result in severe abdominal pain and cramping, air starvation, and shock.

## 453. STRIKE HIS GROIN.

Just about every person will agree that the groin is an extremely sensitive target. The testes can be kicked, punched, or crushed. A moderate kick or strike to an assailant's groin can cause a variety of possible reactions, including severe pain, nausea, vomiting, shortness of breath, and possible sterility. A powerful strike to the groin may crush the scrotum and the testes against the pubic bones, causing shock and unconsciousness.

## 454. STRIKE HIS THIGHS.

Many good fighters overlook the thighs as an impact target. As a matter of fact, because the thighs are large and difficult to protect, they make excellent striking targets in a fight. Although you can kick the thighs at a variety of different angles, the ideal location is the assailant's common peroneal nerve located on the side of the thigh, approximately four inches above the knee. Striking this area can result in extreme pain and immediate immobility of the afflicted leg. An extremely hard kick to the thigh may result in a fracture of the femur, internal bleeding, severe pain, intense cramping, and long-term immobility.

## 455. ATTACK HIS KNEES.

The knees are relatively weak joints that are held together by a number of supporting ligaments. When the assailant's leg is locked or fixed in position and a forceful strike is delivered to the front of the joint, the crucial ligaments will tear, resulting in excruciating pain, swelling, and immobility. Located on the front of the knee joint is the kneecap, or patella, which is made of a small, loose piece of bone. The patella is also vulnerable to possible dislocation by a direct, forceful kick. Severe pain, swelling, and immobility may also result.

### 456. KICK HIS SHINS.

Like the thighs, the shins are excellent striking targets because they are very difficult to protect. The shins are also very sensitive because they are only protected by a thin layer of skin. A powerful kick delivered to this target may fracture it easily, resulting in extreme pain, hemorrhaging, and immobility of the afflicted leg.

### 457. BREAK HIS FINGERS.

The fingers are exceptionally weak and vulnerable. They can easily be jammed, sprained, broken, torn, and bitten. While a broken finger might not stop a determined fighter, it will certainly force him to release his hold. A broken finger will also make it very difficult for the assailant to clench his fist or hold a knife or bludgeon. When attempting to break the fingers, it's best to grab the finger securely and then forcefully tear backward against the knuckle.

### 458. STOMP HIS TOES.

In grappling range, a powerful stomp of your heel can break the small bones of the assailant's toes, causing severe pain and immediate immobility. Stomping on the assailant's toes is also one of the best ways for escaping many holds. Keep in mind that you should avoid attacking the toes if the attacker is wearing hard leather boots (e.g., combat, hiking, or motorcycle boots).

## TACTICS & STRATEGY

# FIGHTING MULTIPLE ATTACKERS

### 459. PREPARE FOR TWO TYPES OF SCENARIOS.

Because many street punks characteristically attack in groups, it's important to learn how to defend against multiple attackers. Since power lies in their numbers, the odds are heavily stacked against you. Nevertheless, you can survive this type of threat by applying the knowledge and skill featured in this section.

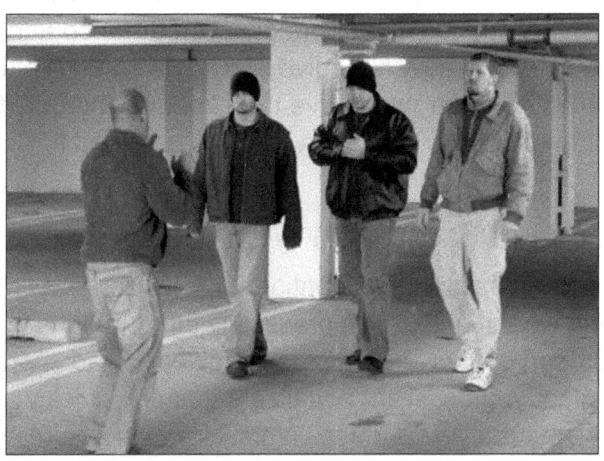

To begin, there are two different types of multiple attacker scenarios you need to be aware of, and they include: (1) The Ambush - The victim is caught off guard and ambushed by his attackers. One of the best defenses for this type of attack is developing a strong sense of situational awareness, (2) The Set-Up - The victim is first approached by the attackers and *set-up* for the attack. Usually there is some brief dialogue between the attackers and the victim. The set-up differs from the ambush because it offers you greater control of the situation. In fact, your survivability improves significantly because you have more options, tactics, techniques, and strategies at your disposal.

## 460. LOOK FOR ESCAPE ROUTES OR BARRIERS.

When faced with multiple attackers, quickly scan your environment and look for any possible escape routes. Look for windows, doors, fire escapes, staircases, fences, escalators, or any other avenue that will allow you to flee quickly and safely from this situation. If the opportunity presents itself for you to run and escape safely, take it. Don't let your ego get in the way. *WARNING: Make sure that your version of an escape route doesn't lead you into a worse situation.*

A *barrier* is any object that obstructs the attacker's path of attack. At the very least, barriers give you distance and some precious time, and they may give you some safety—at least temporarily. A barrier must have the structural integrity to perform the particular function you have assigned it.

## 461. LOOK FOR MAKESHIFT WEAPONS.

If you can't escape the situation, look for any possible *makeshift weapons* that can drastically turn the odds in your favor. Broken bottles, sticks, pipes, crowbars, and shards of broken glass are excellent equalizers that can quickly and effectively neutralize your assailants. However, make certain that you are proficient with these different types of weapons before attempting to use them against your attackers. Otherwise, they may use them against you and make matters worse. (More information about makeshift weapons is discussed in the next section).

## 462. KEEP MOVING.

Whenever faced with multiple attackers, always keep moving. Mobility makes you a difficult target to hit and prevents your assailants from surrounding you. Mobility also enhances the power of your blows and makes your attackers misjudge your range. Most importantly, mobility may help you locate an open area in which to safely escape.

## TACTICS & STRATEGY

### 463. NEVER LET YOURSELF BE SURROUNDED.

Never, ever let yourself be surrounded by your attackers. It is impossible to defend yourself in every possible direction all at once. Mobility can help prevent you from being trapped. Constantly angle your body so there is always one assailant between you and the rest of them. Take advantage of your environment by trying to maneuver yourself in strategic positions, such as between parked cars or doorways. This prevents them from utilizing their full strength and can permit you to fight them one at a time.

Some instructors advise you to keep your back to the wall to prevent being surrounded. I strongly disagree with this because it inhibits your mobility and limits the body mechanics of your fighting techniques. The wall will also provide a possible striking surface for your assailant to smash your head or body.

### 464. DETERMINE WHO IS THE IMMEDIATE THREAT

When unarmed and faced with multiple attackers, you must divide them and attack the assailant who presents the most immediate threat to you. Usually the armed assailant is your most immediate threat. If none of the attackers are armed with a weapon, then go for the one closest to you. If more than one attacker is of equal distance from you, then the assailant who is blocking your escape route is the most immediate threat.

Finally, if more than one assailant is blocking your escape route, go for leader or *alpha* of the group. He's the ringleader who fuels the "spirit of the group" which motivates the others to attack. Also, he's often the one with the biggest mouth.

### 465. ATTACK THE IMMEDIATE THREAT.

Once you've determined which assailant is the greatest threat, attack him immediately. Quickly move to the flank of the assailant and attack with a barrage of swift blows. Your tactical objective is to injure him as quickly and as efficiently as possible. Remember to strike first, strike fast, strike with authority, and keep the pressure on.

Because of the extreme threat and danger posed by multiple attackers, it's imperative that you make an example of your first assailant. Attack him with extreme prejudice. For example, if the other assailants see their partner violently choking from a brutal throat strike, it might kill their spirit to continue their assault on you.

## 466. ATTACK THE EYES OR THROAT.

Assuming range isn't an issue, the two primary anatomical targets to strike in a multiple attacker situation are the *eyes* and *throat.* This is not to say that other targets don't matter – they certainly do! However, you should focus your strikes at the eyes and throat because they can instantly disable your attackers. *Warning! Always be certain your self-defense actions are legally and morally justified in the eyes of the law!*

## 467. EMPLOY THE ASSEMBLY LINE PRINCIPLE.

When attacking the immediate threat, try to maneuver yourself so a straight line is created between you and all of the attackers. I call this the *assembly line principle* because it temporarily forces assailant number one to be a natural barrier between you and the other attackers. Once again, this will only buy you a couple of seconds, but a few precious seconds can make all the difference between life and death in the streets.

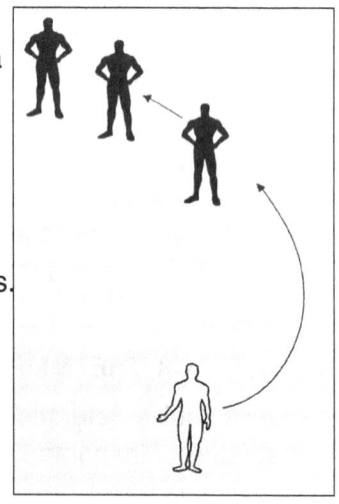

## TACTICS & STRATEGY

### 468. APPLY THE HUMAN SHIELD PRINCIPLE.

Once you've injured the first attacker, use him as an obstacle or *human shield* to the help prevent the other attackers from reaching or attacking you. For example, try pushing or swinging him into the other attackers. This will momentarily slow down the other assailants and give you a few seconds to either escape or attack again.

*Here, the author demonstrates the human shield principle.*

# MAKESHIFT WEAPONS

### 469. USE MAKESHIFT WEAPONS.

*Makeshift weapons* or *Improvised weapons* are common, everyday objects that can be converted into either offensive or defensive weapons. There are four makeshift weapon classifications you should be aware of: (1) cutting weapons - objects or implements used to stab or slash your assailant; (2) shielding weapons - objects used to shield yourself from attack; (3) distracting weapons - objects that can be thrown into your assailant's face, torso, or legs to temporarily distract him; and (4) striking weapons - objects used to strike the assailant.

## 470. USE "DISTRACTING" MAKESHIFT WEAPONS.

*Distracting makeshift weapons* are various items and objects that can be thrown at your assailant to distract him temporarily. Distracting makeshift weapons offer the following strategic advantages in a fight: (1) surprise - you can catch the assailant off guard and launch the rest of your offensive attack, (2) visual impairments - certain objects can impair the assailant's vision temporarily or permanently, (3) time - distracting makeshift weapons will also buy you a little time from the adversary, (4) windows of opportunity - throwing objects into the assailant's face almost always causes a reaction dynamic that permits you to exploit his targets, and (5) defensive flow - distracting makeshift weapons put the assailant into a defensive flow.

Generally, distracting makeshift weapons are thrown into your assailant's face. Some examples include sunglasses, magazines, ashtrays, books, salt shakers, alarm clocks, coins, bottles, bars of soap, shoes, dirt, sand, gravel, rocks, videotapes, small figurines, cassette tapes, hot liquids, paperweights, pesticide sprays, and oven cleaner spray.

## TACTICS & STRATEGY

### 471. USE "STRIKING" MAKESHIFT WEAPONS.

*Striking makeshift weapons* are common, everyday objects that you can use to strike an assailant. When selecting a striking makeshift weapon, make certain that it is appropriate to the tactical function you have assigned it.

Examples of striking makeshift weapons include sticks, bricks, crowbars, baseball bats, shovels, golf clubs, lamps, books, light chairs, pool cues, pipes, heavy flashlights, hammers, binoculars, glass bottles, beer mugs, tool boxes, briefcases, car doors, canes, walking sticks, an automobile, light dumbbells, 2 x 4s, etc.

### 472. USE "SHIELDING" MAKESHIFT WEAPONS.

In some self-defense situations, a *shielding makeshift weapon* may be the only thing that stands between you and death. Shielding makeshift weapons are ubiquitous items that can shield you effectively and temporarily from the assailant's punch, kick, or strike. However, in most cases, shielding makeshift weapons are used to protect against knife and bludgeon attacks. Examples include briefcases, trash-can lids, bicycles, thick sofa cushions, backpacks, barstools, lawn chairs, drawers, cafeteria trays, suitcases, thick pillows, leather jackets/coats, motorcycle helmets, small end tables, etc. Once again, be certain that your makeshift weapon has the structural integrity to get the job done effectively.

### 473. USE "CUTTING" MAKESHIFT WEAPONS.

*Cutting makeshift weapons* are objects that can be used to cut the assailant by either stabbing or slashing him. Examples include most kitchen cutlery, screwdrivers, broken bottles, broken glass, scissors, car keys, pitch forks, ice scrapers, pointed sticks, crowbars, letter openers, pens, sharp pencils, razor blades, sharp rocks, shovels, pitchforks, axes, intrenching tool, etc.

## 474. CARRY A PEN WITH YOU.

Pens and pencils are ubiquitous. They are also very effective stabbing makeshift weapons that can puncture and seriously wound your assailant. A pen or pencil can be thrust into the following anatomical targets: (1) eye socket, (2) ear cavity, (3) under the chin, (4) the base of the skull, (5) throat, (6) groin, (7) top of the hands, and (8) solar plexus. As the saying goes, "The pen is mightier than the sword."

## 475. AVOID USING FLEXIBLE WEAPONS.

Chains, belts, and other flexible weapons are ineffective in a street fight for the following reasons: (1) they are generally difficult to control, (2) they lack neutralizing force, (3) they lack quick retraction, (4) they must follow through the complete range of motion to be re-executed, (5) they open up your body targets to a variety of possible counters, and (6) they can get snagged on your assailant's body or limbs.

## 476. AVOID DEPENDENCY.

Far too many people assume that the mere possession of a weapon (e.g., firearm, knife, bludgeon, pepper spray, makeshift weapon) will save them from peril. This faulty logic forms the delusion of dependency. *Dependency* is the sole reliance on a particular tool or weapon for self-defense. Although a .45 semiautomatic can stop just about anyone, no single weapon, tool, or technique is the absolute answer. Every weapon has its combat limitations. Guns can jam, knives can be dropped accidentally, sticks can break, and pepper spray canisters can clog. Further, not all street fights justify the use of a weapon. Consider, for example, that a hostile scuffle with your unarmed brother-in-law won't justify self-defense with a weapon.

## TACTICS & STRATEGY

**477. LEARN WEAPON-RETENTION SKILLS.**

Learn retention skills for the following hand-held weapons: (1) handguns, (2) rifles, (3) shotguns, (4) knives/edged weapons, (5) sticks/bludgeons, (6) makeshift weapons, and (7) pepper spray canisters.

# PEPPER SPRAY

**478. USE PEPPER SPRAY.**

*Oleoresin capsicum* or *Pepper Spray* is a resin extracted from finely ground, dried chili peppers of the botanical group capsicum, which is then converted into an oil. Pepper spray is an inflammatory agent that affects the assailant's mucus membranes (eyes, nose, throat, and lungs). When OC is sprayed in the assailant's face, it causes the eyes to swell shut immediately, restricts breathing, and severely burns the entire face. The assailant's vision is impaired for approximately 10 minutes, and breathing is inhibited for about 30 minutes.

Pepper spray is considered the best spray for self-defense because it is potent and works almost immediately on your assailant. Unlike Mace or choking gas, pepper spray will incapacitate an adversary regardless of his tolerance to pain. When used properly, pepper spray can neutralize large and powerful assailants, psychotics, drug users, and violent drunks. Depending on the model you purchase, spraying distances will vary from 8 to 10 feet. Some models will even shoot up to 40 feet. *WARNING: If you intend to use pepper spray for self-defense, get training from a qualified instructor. You must learn several essential tactics before using this tool on the streets. Before you purchase or carry OC, check with your local and state laws regarding its possession and use.*

If you are going to use pepper spray, remember the following guidelines: (1) in order to ensure that the aerosol unit is functioning properly, make sure it is shaken and tested before initial use; (2) spray from an upright position; (3) spray from a 4 to 6 foot distance or as recommended by the manufacturer; (4) spray directly into the assailant's face with a 1 or 2 second burst depending on his distance, speed of movement, and wind conditions; (5) if the assailant is holding his breath, use multiple short bursts; and (6) use lateral movement when spraying.

### 479. KNOW WHICH WAY THE WIND IS BLOWING.

Don't be the victim of your own pepper spray. When using OC it is critical that you know which way the wind is blowing so that you can position yourself accordingly. Be especially careful of breezeways, hallways, and dead-end alleys since the air flow in these environments tends to be unpredictable.

### 480. ASSUME THE PROPER STANCE WHEN USING OC.

Your stance is very important when using pepper spray. A proper stance will put you in a position of tactical advantage. Remember to apply the following: (1) position your body at a 45-degree angle to your adversary, (2) keep your weak side to the front of your adversary and your strong side to the rear, (3) hold the OC unit in your strong hand between the weak hand and the center of your body, (4) keep your feet shoulder-width apart with your weight evenly distributed, and (5) keep your weak hand open and slightly bent.

### 481. KNOW THE PRD OF PEPPER SPRAY.

When using pepper spray for self-defense, make certain

## TACTICS & STRATEGY

you are aware of the assailant's *probable reaction dynamics* (PRD), which can include the following: (1) his hands will cover his face, (2) he will drop whatever is in his hands, (3) his upper body will bend forward, (4) he will shake uncontrollably, (5) he will blindly grope around, (6) he will drop to his knees for stability, and (7) his body will become rigid and he will not respond to your voice commands.

### 482. SCORCH HIM.

In my *Feral Fighting Program, Scorching* is the process of inconspicuously applying oleoresin capsicum (hot pepper extract) to your fingers tips and then *razing* the adversary. This devastating self-defense tactic is the most excruciating form of hand-to-hand combat. It's especially useful for people who frequent dangerous, high-risk environments and who want to amplify the power of their *razing* techniques. However, to really appreciate the painful nature of scorching, you need a fundamental understanding of oleoresin capsicum and it's effects on the human body.

### 483. DON'T USE MACE.

Mace is a chemical tear gas that causes tearing, burning of the eyes, and minor difficulty in breathing. Mace, however, won't work on crazed assailants who have high tolerances to pain, such as psychotics, drug abusers, and violent drunks. In many cases, Mace can make aggressors angrier and more violent.

### 484. DON'T RELY ON PEPPER SPRAY.

Never forget that all self-defense sprays have their

limitations. First, you must always have the unit in your hand and ready to fire. It won't do you any good if the canister is in your car when you are suddenly jumped by an attacker. Second, if there is a strong or unpredictable wind, the spray can be useless. Aerosol canisters can also jam, and you cannot spray someone in a confined area like a car.

# DEALING WITH THE POLICE

### 485. KNOW HOW TO DEAL WITH THE POLICE.

After a street fight, there is always the possibility that you will have to talk to the police. Here are a few important suggestions: (1) be polite and respectful - don't ever talk back to police officers, and always address them as either "sir" or "ma'am"; (2) watch what you say - speak slowly and clearly, avoid using profanity, sarcasm, and racial or derogatory remarks, and realize that what you say can be used against you; (3) identify yourself - identify yourself as the victim and be prepared to show identification, but carefully avoid quick or sudden movements when reaching for your wallet, and always try to keep your hands in plain view; (4) explain what happened - clearly describe the sequence of events that led to the fight, and if the assailant used a weapon in the fight or said anything to you, report it; (5) follow orders - if the officer orders you to wait at a particular spot while he sorts out the matter, obey him; and finally, (6) don't get angry - if you get angry or hostile with the police officers, you will land in jail for the night.

## TACTICS & STRATEGY

### 486. USE "REST GESTE" STATEMENTS.

After a street fight, be very careful about what you say to a police officer. If you must speak, consider using *rest geste* statements. Rest geste statements are defined as statements that you couldn't control something. Such statements will help you establish a legal defense if you have to go to court. They include the following: (1) "I didn't mean to" - this establishes that you did not mean to hurt your adversary, (2) "He wouldn't stop" - this establishes that your adversary was the predator and you were the victim, (3) "I was just trying to defend myself" - this establishes that you possessed a self-defense mind-set, (4) "I thought he was going to kill me" - this establishes that you were in fear for your life. *NOTE: Keep in mind that all rest geste statements should be repeated several times in a distraught and remorseful manner.*

### 487. KNOW YOUR RIGHTS.

Whenever you are involved in a self-defense situation, there is always the possibility that you will be arrested by the police. If you are taken into police custody, you have the right to remain silent, obtain a lawyer, be informed of the charges against you, and have a judge decide whether you should be released on bail until your trial.

### 488. COPS CAN APPROACH YOU.

Police officers are permitted to approach you in a public place and request information. If a cop reasonably suspects that you are committing, have committed, or are about to commit a crime, he may detain you briefly for questioning.

If a police officer reasonably suspects that you are armed and dangerous, he or she is permitted to frisk you without making an arrest. If while frisking you for weapons or evidence the officer finds anything illegal, he can confiscate it and arrest you.

# THE AFTERMATH OF A FIGHT

### 489. CHECK YOURSELF OUT.

Once the fight is over and you have fled the scene safely, conduct a quick inventory of your body. Quickly scan your torso, hands, arms, legs, and feet for any possible signs of injury. Run both hands down your face and over your head and neck to check for blood. This is important because many times fighters are seriously injured after a fight and don't even know it because the adrenaline rush from the fight-or-flight response shuts off the pain.

### 490. KNOW HOW TO TREAT BATTLE WOUNDS.

It is important that you know how to treat some of the most common injuries that occur in a fight. Here are five injuries you should be aware of: (1) Sprained thumb - this is caused by connecting improperly with your target. A sprained thumb is  usually accompanied by swelling and aching pain due to ruptured capillaries and torn ligaments. First, apply a large bandage, then apply ice to the area and keep your thumb immobilized. See your family physician as soon as possible. (2) Split lip - this is caused by a blow that forces the soft tissue of your lip against your teeth. Place a gauze bandage against the cut. Keep pressure on the cut until the bleeding stops. (3) Abrasions - these are caused by blows that remove the top layer of the skin. Apply antiseptic to the area and cover with a sterile pad. (4) Nosebleed - this is caused by a blow that ruptures the small capillaries in the septum. To stop the bleeding, compress the nostrils together for a few minutes until the bleeding stops. (5) Black eye - this is caused by a blow that ruptures the small capillaries around the eye. Apply ice directly to the injured area and then use heat packs once the swelling has stopped.

### 491. GET MEDICAL TREATMENT IMMEDIATELY.

If you find that you are seriously injured after a fight, seek medical assistance immediately. Have a good friend drive you to the hospital or dial 911 and request an ambulance. Try to stay calm, breathe slowly, and tell the emergency dispatcher your exact location. If you are bleeding heavily, apply direct pressure to the wound site. If the wound is on a limb, elevate the extremity above the level of the heart. This will slow down the loss of blood. If you get cut or shot in the leg, do not try to stand up or walk. This will worsen the injury and increase the loss of blood.

### 492. PREPARE FOR REVENGE.

No one likes to lose. In fact, whenever you defeat an assailant in a fight, there's always the possibility that he will seek revenge. Some assailants are direct. They'll wait a few days and launch a surprise attack. I know of one street fighter who sought revenge by hiding behind a tree with a baseball bat. When his victim walked by, he turned him into a bloody pulp. Other assailants are more twisted and indirect. Some get tremendous satisfaction by attacking or terrorizing your family, blowing up your car, harassing you at work, breaking into your home, or mutilating your pet. The best advice to avoid revenge or retaliation is to avoid disclosing any information about yourself or your family. If the fight occurs next to your car, avoid letting your assailant see your license plate.

Once the assailant is out of the fight, leave the scene immediately. You don't want him to remember what you look like. If the fight was newsworthy, stay clear of the press. You don't want your name or face in the news.

### 493. PREPARE FOR A LEGAL BATTLE.

You should prepare yourself for a possible legal battle. Not all combat situations end in a desolate alley. Many are dragged into the courtroom. In America, anybody can sue anybody for anything. Maybe your assailant can find a legal basis for a lawsuit.

Martial artists, self-defense experts, and firearms instructors should be particularly careful when fighting. If you're not careful, you can be ruined financially or thrown into jail. Now is a good time to find an attorney who can represent you if a situation arises. Make certain that your attorney specializes in criminal law. Find out his or her exact credentials and record. More importantly, you want an attorney who can be reached when you may need him or her the most.

# CHAPTER FIVE
## Grappling & Ground Fighting

*"A great majority of all street fights go to the ground. Need I say more?"*

# THE BASICS

**494. KNOW YOUR ODDS.**

Regardless of how proficient your striking arsenal may be, there is still a strong possibility that the fight will go to the ground. As a matter of fact, most street fights go to the ground. Make certain that you are equipped with the knowledge and skills necessary to handle a ground fight.

**495. MASTER BOTH GRAPPLING PLANES.**

If you want to be truly prepared for the street, make certain that you can fight in both the vertical and horizontal grappling planes. Many fighters assume that grappling can only take place on the ground. To the contrary, it often occurs while two fighters are standing toe-to-toe with one another.

**496. MASTER THE GROUND.**

Though there are many strategic reasons to master ground fighting, range proficiency is one of the most important. *Ground fighting mastery* means possessing the knowledge, skills, and attitude necessary to fight your adversary efficiently and effectively on the ground.

To master the ground fight, you must study and ultimately possess a wide variety of skills and tactics. Here is a brief list: (1) using anatomical handles; (2) establishing and maintaining the mounted position; (3) applying submission holds from the mounted position; (4) striking from the mounted position; (5) defending against the mounted assailant; (6) establishing and maintaining the leg guard position; (7) applying submission holds from the leg guard position; (8) striking from the leg guard position; (9) defending against the leg guard position;

(10) escaping various submission holds from a variety of angles and vantages; (11) possessing a variety of conventional ground fighting tactics that can be employed in nonlethal situations; and (12) possessing a variety of nuclear ground fighting tactics that can be used in lethal force situations.

### 497. BE PREPARED FOR THE GROUND FIGHT.

If you're not prepared for a potential ground fight, you may be subjected to (1) premature exhaustion (to the untrained, ground fighting is the most exhausting form of fighting), (2) panic, (3) injury or possible death, (4) humiliation, (5) defeat, and (6) suffocation.

### 498. UNDERSTAND THE NATURE OF TAKEDOWNS.

A *takedown* is a staple technique found in every MMA fighter's arsenal. Simply put, a takedown is defined as a technique or maneuver that immediately forces a standing fighter to the floor. Your adversary might attempt a takedown for one of three reasons: (1) strategic attack - a deliberate and planned method of attack, (2) desperation move - he realizes his stand up fighting skills are grossly deficient and in an act of desperation he grabs hold of you and takes you to the ground. (3) practitioner error - he accidentally slips or trips during the course of the stand up fight, grabs hold of you to stabilize his balance, and ends up taking you to the ground with him.

### 499. KNOW THE LIMITATIONS OF GROUND FIGHTING.

Never forget the following tactical limitations of ground fighting: (1) multiple assailants - since ground fighting requires maximal body entanglement, it's virtually impossible to fight multiple attackers; (2) edged weapons - it is often difficult to defend against knives and edged weapons when locked up with your assailant; (3) spectator intervention - spectator intervention can occur when you are locked up in a ground fight; (4) positional asphyxia - when ground fighting a heavier assailant, a position that inhibits your breathing, causing unconsciousness or death, can occur; (5) terrain - the type of terrain you're ground fighting on can be dangerous (e.g., broken glass, sharp metal, broken wood, etc.); (6) environmental dangers - your environment and immediate surroundings can harm you (i.e., heavy traffic, a cliff, a street curb, etc.); (7) limited vision - ground fighting can significantly inhibit your peripheral vision; and (8) limited mobility - you cannot move quickly when you are locked in a ground fight.

## 500. KNOW THE RISKS OF SUBMISSION HOLDS.

Although submission holds are a necessary component of your combat cache, never forget their inherent risks and limitations. Here are a few: (1) somatotypes - many ground fighting maneuvers and techniques will not work effectively against large or hyper flexible assailants; (2) assailant's size and strength - these factors can often negate the effectiveness of certain submission holds; (3) psychoactive drugs - their effects will often nullify your control and restraint techniques; (4) exact anatomical positioning - this is crucial to any submission technique's working effectively; (5) frenetic movements - it is often difficult to apply precise submission holds because of your assailant's frenetic movements; and (6) clothing - you can't employ certain submission holds effectively when wearing thick or cumbersome clothing (i.e., rain slickers, down jackets, snow suits, etc.).

## 501. KNOW THE FOUR SUBMISSION CLASSIFICATIONS.

There are four submission hold classifications that you must be aware of. They include (1) pain-compliance submission holds; (2) asphyxiation submission holds involving

a) air - the air supply is temporarily cut off and b) blood - oxygenated blood is cut off temporarily; (3) joint-manipulation submission holds involving a) counter-joint movement - pressure is applied against the motion of the joint and b) hyperextension - the joint is forced beyond its natural range of motion; and (4) immobilization submission holds.

### 502. KNOW THE FIVE GROUND FIGHTING POSITIONS.

Although ground fighting is a very dynamic form of unarmed combat, these are the five general positions that you will find yourself in: (1) mounted position - when you're sitting on top of your assailant's torso or chest; (2) perpendicular mount - when both of your legs are on one side of your assailant's body, and your body runs perpendicular to your assailant's body; (3) guard position - when your assailant's torso is held between your legs; (4) chest to back position - when your chest is on the assailant's back (it does not matter if you are on top of him, he is on top of you, or you are both on your sides); and (5) opposite poles - when both you and your assailant are facing opposite directions (this often occurs when sprawling against your adversary).

### 503. KNOW THE VARIATIONS.

In grappling range, there's a variety of postures from which you can engage your assailant. They include the following: (1) both you and your assailant are prone, (2) you are kneeling and your assailant is prone, (3) your assailant is kneeling and you are prone, (4) both you and your assailant are kneeling, (5) you are standing and your assailant is prone, (6) your assailant is standing and you are prone, (7) you are standing and your assailant is kneeling, (8) your assailant is standing and you are kneeling, and (9) both you and your assailant are standing.

## THE FIVE GROUND FIGHTING POSITIONS

*Mount Position.*

*Guard Position.*

*Chest to Back.*

*Perpendicular Mount.*

*Opposite Pole.*

# GRIPS

### 504. KNOW THE DIFFERENT HAND GRIPS.

The foundation of most submission holds are predicated on your hand grip. There are many different types of hand grips. Here are four that you should know: (1) Three-finger grip - join your hands together and place your thumb between the index and middle finger of your other hand, then clasp your hands together; (2) Knife-hand grip - join your hands together by grasping the knife edge of your other hand; and (3) Wrist grip - join your hands together by grasping the wrist of your other hand; (4) Indian grip - join your hands together, locking and curling your fingers into both palms.

*Three Finger Grip.*

*Knife-Hand Grip.*

*Wrist Grip.*

*Indian Grip.*

## 505. NEVER INTERLACE YOUR FINGERS.

The finger interlace grip is one of the most common and ineffective hand grips. Under no circumstances should you ever interlace your fingers to establish a grip. The finger interlace grip is dangerous for the following reasons: (1) it dramatically inhibits your ability to switch to another grip or hold, (2) it provides poor structural integrity, and (3) if your assailant can reach your fingers, he can squeeze them together, causing extreme pain and a possible finger dislocation.

## 506. NEVER USE A FULL-HAND GRIP.

When ground fighting with your adversary, never use a full-hand grip. This feckless grip is combatively deficient because it separates your thumb too much from your other four fingers. This weakens the structural integrity of your grip, thus allowing your assailant to escape your hold. Consider using the Indian grip instead.

# CONVENTIONAL SUBMISSION TECHNIQUES

## 507. GO CONVENTIONAL.

In fighting situations where lethal force is unwarranted (i.e., schoolyard fight, feud between relatives, unarmed scuffle with drunk friend, etc.), conventional ground fighting tactics are in order. Conventional ground fighting techniques are not designed to maim or terminate your assailant. However, when applied properly, they will put him out of commission. Some conventional tactics include (1) all submission holds and locks, (2) certain choking techniques, and (3) certain striking techniques.

## 508. LEARN BY FEELING.

The only real way to learn ground fighting skills is to experience them. *"Feeling"* every movement is your first step to grappling mastery.

## 509. MASTER THE SCISSORS HOLD.

When you're on your back, one of the best methods of preventing the assailant from establishing the mounted position is to employ the *scissors hold* (leg guard). To apply the scissors hold, wrap both of your legs around the assailant's waist and hook your ankles together. Be certain to keep both of your legs tightly secured around his waist. You inflict pain on the assailant by straightening your legs and simultaneously squeezing them together. Keep in mind that strong adductor (inner thigh) muscles play an important role in solidifying the hold.

## 510. TAILSPIN.

In a street fight, there is always the possibility that you may slip and fall to the ground. While your assailant does have the tactical advantage, you can use the tailspin technique to get yourself out of trouble. The *tailspin* technique is executed by first chambering one of your legs back (to launch a kick) and then pivoting and rotating your body in the direction of your assailant. Quick pivoting can be accomplished by spinning on your butt while your elbows maintain your balance.

The tailspin technique will allow you to accomplish the following objectives: (1) temporarily prevent your assailant from either rushing, jumping, or kicking you; (2) keep your assailant back; (3) injure your assailant if he moves in your range; and (4) buy you a little time to further assess your situation.

## GRAPPLING & GROUND FIGHTING

### 511. SPRAWL.

*Sprawling* is one of the best methods of countering an assailant who attempts an appendage takedown (e.g., double-leg takedown). The sprawl is accomplished by lowering your hips to the ground while simultaneously shooting both of your legs back. The primary objective of sprawling is to get your legs back and force your body weight onto your assailant's shoulders and head.

*Pictured here, Sprawling against a double leg takedown.*

### 512. COMPRESS HIM

The *chest compression* is one of the most effective methods of throwing your assailant into a state of panic. To execute this hold, apply the following steps: (1) from the mounted position, drop down and pull your assailant's face deep into your chest cavity; (2) let your body weight sink into your assailant's nose and mouth; (3) stabilize your assailant's head by grasping the nape of his neck with both hands; (4) make certain to keep both of your elbows in, close to your body; (5) keep your head down and your entire body low to the ground; and (6) spread both of your legs wide apart or maintain a tight grapevine on both of your assailant's legs.

## 513. GRAPEVINE HIM.

A *grapevine* is a stabilizing technique used when your assailant is on his back. The grapevine is applied when you have either one (single-leg grapevine) or both (double-leg grapevine) of your feet hooked around the assailant's legs.

The grapevine serves several strategic purposes, including the following: (1) it can stabilize or immobilize your assailant's movement, (2) it causes your assailant to panic, (3) it causes pain for your assailant, and (4) it prevents your assailant from bumping you from the mounted position.

## 514. CHOKE HIM OUT.

There are several chokes that can be applied in the grappling range. However, one of the most effective chokes you can employ is the *rear naked choke*. The naked choke is known for putting an assailant to sleep in a matter of seconds.

To apply the naked choke effectively, follow these important steps: (1) be certain to apply the choke from behind your assailant, (2) begin the naked choke by positioning your right arm around your assailant's neck with your palm facing down, (3) make certain the assailant's windpipe is positioned in the crook of your right elbow, (4) put your right hand on your left shoulder, (5) place the blade side of your left forearm on the back of the assailant's neck, and (6) with your right arm, slowly squeeze the lateral sides of the assailant's neck.

## 515. CRANK HIS SHOULDER.

The *shoulder crank* is applied when your assailant is held

inside your scissors hold. To apply the shoulder crank, do the following: (1) with your assailant lying on top of you, uncross your scissors hold and grab the assailant's right wrist with your left hand; (2) quickly reach over his right arm (triceps region) with your right arm and grab your left wrist; (3) elevate the assailant's elbow and crank his right arm backward as he falls onto the floor; and (4) shuffle and turn your body sideways so the assailant's face and chest are flat against the floor; (5) once again, scissors both of your legs around the assailant's waist; and (6) maintain pressure on his shoulder joint.

*The Shoulder Crank.*

## 516. KNOW THE LEG GUARD STRATEGY.

There is much more to the leg guard (scissors hold) than simply wrapping your legs around your assailant's waist and holding him in place. The leg guard is an excellent grappling hold that will permit you to execute a variety of techniques and maneuvers. Some include the following: (1) reverse and turn your assailant onto his back, (2) apply joint locks, (3) squeeze your assailant into submission, and (4) choke your assailant out.

Here's a few more reasons why the leg guard should be employed in a ground fight: (1) it prevents your assailant from mounting you, (2) it causes extreme pain for your assailant, (3) it restricts your assailant's breathing, (4) it bruises and injures your assailant's internal organs, (5) it restricts your assailant's mobility, and (6) it controls your assailant for submission manipulation. *WARNING: Be careful when applying the leg guard. If you don't embrace the range and tie up his hands and arms, he might be able to strike you.*

## 517. APPLY THE BOX.

*The box* technique is a painful submission hold that can be applied when you have perpendicularly or vertically mounted the assailant. To apply this hold, follow these steps: (1) with your assailant on his back, let your bodyweight rest on his chest; (2) grab the assailant's left wrist with your left hand (make certain your left hand is held in the thumb-over position); (3) insert your right hand underneath the assailant's left arm and on top of your left wrist and hold it securely (also make certain your right hand is held in the thumb-over position); and (4) raise the assailant's left elbow slightly and drag his hand down toward his legs (be certain to keep the assailant's wrist on the floor as you drag his arm downward).

*The Box.*

## 518. MASTER THE JAPANESE ARM BAR.

The *Japanese arm bar* is a versatile submission hold that can be used in a variety of different positions. One of the best positions is when you have mounted your assailant and he unknowingly offers you an outstretched arm.

To execute the Japanese arm bar from this position, follow these important steps: (1) place both of your palms on the assailant's chest (make certain that the assailant's right arm is between both of your arms); (2) without telegraphing your movements, push off the assailant's chest and lift your entire body up and around the assailant's torso; (3) simultaneously grab hold of the assailant's right wrist with both of your hands, stretching it out as you fall onto your buttocks; (4) once you're on the floor, your body should lie perpendicular to the assailant's body, and his right arm should be between your legs (try to keep your groin region close to the assailant's right shoulder); (5) to guarantee proper arm alignment, make certain your assailant's right thumb is pointing upward and your inner thighs are close together; and (6) to inflict pain on the assailant's elbow, simultaneously arch your back and pull his right wrist toward your chest.

*The Japanese Arm Bar.*

## 519. COME TO A BASE.

One of the fundamental elements of ground fighting is learning how to correctly "come to a base." Coming to a base means getting up to your hands and knees from the prone position. This is important for the following reasons: (1) it conserves energy, (2) it provides quick defensive capability, (3) it minimizes appendage exposure, and (4) it provides powerful body lift. The proper method of coming to a base consists of first bringing your left knee up to your side and then simultaneously bringing your left elbow into your knee and pushing yourself over that knee.

## 520. ESCAPE THE LEG GUARD.

Getting out of an assailant's leg guard (scissors hold) is not an easy task. Many well-known grappling arts have attempted to address this issue, yet failed. Basically, there are two effective methods: (1) striking method - attacking the assailant with a flurry of hammer fists to the groin region until the scissors hold is released and (2) submission hold method - strategically twisting and torquing the assailant's ankle and knee.

*Escaping the Leg Guard.*

## 521. LEAN BACK.

Once you have successfully bumped your assailant out of the mounted position and he has placed you into his leg guard, be certain to lean back. Leaning back is important for the following reasons: (1) it prevents your assailant from embracing you, (2) it offers you the range and angle to strike his groin repeatedly, (3) it will allow you to strike his face effectively if he decides to reach and grab you, and (4) it puts you in a position to escape from his leg guard.

## 522. MASTER THE BICEPS CHOKE.

The *biceps choke* is another effective method of controlling your assailant. To apply the biceps choke, take the following steps: (1) with your assailant lying on his back, place your left arm around his neck; (2) with your right hand, push the assailant's left arm across his own neck; (3) use your head to press his left arm against his neck; (4) grab your left arm with your right hand to secure the choke; and (5) drag your right elbow down toward your waist (this will tighten the choke on your assailant).

## 523. MAINTAIN A LOW BASE.

Whenever you are mounted on your assailant, it is equally important to maintain this position. Here are some important points to remember: (1) relax - a tense or rigid torso makes it easier for the assailant to throw you off; (2) keep your center of gravity low and close to the assailant - when applying submission holds from the mounted position, always keep your chest married against the assailant's chest; (3) be cognizant of where you place your arms - they can be grabbed by the assailant and used as levers to bump you; (4) if possible, keep your feet tucked under his thighs - this creates a "crazy glue" effect between you and the assailant; and (5) be patient - wait for him to make the move that will lead to his demise.

## 524. MASTER THE FOREARM CHOKE.

You can choke your assailant from the mounted position by using the *forearm choke*. To apply this technique, follow these important steps: (1) from the mounted position, place your left forearm behind the assailant's neck; (2) insert the web of your right hand into the crook of your left forearm and place the blade side of your right forearm into the assailant's windpipe; (3) compress and scissors both of your forearms into one another; and (4) keep your base as low as possible and tuck your face away from the assailant (be sure to employ the double-leg grapevine, because this will prevent your adversary from bumping you out of the mounted position). *WARNING: The forearm choke can crush the assailant's windpipe, causing death, and should be used only in life-and-death situations when lethal force is warranted.*

*The Forearm Choke.*

## 525. LEVER HIS WRIST.

To apply the *wrist lever*, do the following: (1) from the mounted position, drop your body weight onto the assailant and grab the back of his left hand (his palm facing upward) with your right hand; (2) place your left elbow and forearm against the left side of the assailant's head; (3) place the left side of your head on the outside of the assailant's left elbow; (4) pull the assailant's left wrist away from the side of his head.

## 526. MASTER THE STRAIGHT ARM BAR.

The *straight arm bar* is a versatile submission hold that can be applied in a variety of different positions. To apply the straight arm bar from a perpendicular mounted position, apply the following: (1) with the assailant on his back and his right arm extended straight out, grab the assailant's right wrist with your left hand; (2) insert your right forearm under the assailant's right elbow and grab hold of your left forearm; and (3) while making certain the assailant's right thumb is pointing up, force his right wrist down while forcing his right elbow up with your right forearm (pressure is on his right elbow).

*The Straight Arm Bar.*

## 527. USE THE ANKLE HOLD.

Contrary to what some fighters might think, there is a time and place for ankle holds. To apply the ankle hold, execute the following: (1) with the assailant on his back, wrap your left arm around his left ankle (make certain the blade of your left forearm is against his left Achilles tendon); (2) with the assailant's left instep tucked in your left armpit, grab your left wrist with your right hand; (3) place your left leg over his left thigh; (4) place your right leg over your left instep and scissor your legs together; and (5) slowly arch your body back while stretching your legs out (pressure is on the assailant's left Achilles tendon).

**528. MASTER THE PARTY FLEX.**

The *party flex* has a wide variety of applications and can be applied while standing or ground fighting. To apply the party flex from the mounted position, apply the following steps: (1) stabilize the assailant's elbow by grabbing his left elbow with your left hand, with your left elbow placed against the left side of his head and (2) use your right hand to flex the assailant's left wrist toward the ground.

*The Party Flex.*

**529. PULL HIM IN AND CONTROL HIS ARMS.**

When applying the leg guard position (scissors hold) on your assailant, be certain to pull him close to your body (embrace the range) and try to control his arms. This is

## GRAPPLING & GROUND FIGHTING

important for the following reasons: (1) it prevents your adversary from effectively striking your groin, (2) it restricts your assailant's ability to strike your face and stomach accurately, (3) it negates the necessary leverage for your assailant to apply locks and chokes, and (4) it allows you the opportunity to apply a variety of submission holds and maneuvers.

### 530. COUNTER BEAR HUGS SWIFTLY.

Bear hugs are used primarily to immobilize your body and throw you to the ground. Nevertheless, it's a feckless hold that can be countered readily. There are four effective counters to various types of bear hugs.

(1) If you're attacked from the rear (arms are free), immediately lower your weight and simultaneously widen your feet; thrust your hips and buttocks backward, throwing your attacker backward; then counter with powerful knuckle raps to your assailant's hand. Once his grip is loosened, finger peel your way out of the hug and neutralize him.

(2) If you're attacked from the rear (arms are pinned to your sides), immediately lower your weight and simultaneously widen your feet, then thrust your hips and buttocks backward, throwing your attacker backward. Counter with multiple hammer fists to the assailant's groin, followed by elbow strikes to his solar plexus.

(3) If you're attacked from the front (your arms are free), you should counter with either hammer fists to the attacker's nose or attack with eye rakes or thumb gouges to his eyes until he releases his hold.

(4) If you're attacked from the front (arms are pinned to your sides), immediately head butt your attacker's nose and bite if possible, or try to crush his testicles until he releases his hold.

# STRATEGIES

### 531. DON'T LET HIM BREAK YOUR BALANCE.

If your assailant is to take you down to the ground, he must first disrupt or "break" your balance. Here are the four primary ways he can accomplish this: (1) redirection of force - when your adversary exploits your energy or dynamic pressure; (2) strength manipulation - when your adversary uses his raw power and strength to disrupt your balance; (3) striking - when your assailant hits you and then throws you off balance; and (4) feinting/faking - when your assailant feints and draws a defensive reaction from you and takes you down to the ground.

### 532. BEWARE OF POSITIONAL ASPHYXIA.

*Positional asphyxia* is a position that causes a lack of oxygen or excess of carbon dioxide in the body that is usually caused by interruption of breathing and that causes unconsciousness or death. Make it your mission to avoid the dangers of "positional asphyxia."

*Positional asphyxia is one of your biggest concerns when ground fighting a larger and heavier adversary. Here, the man on the bottom is in serious trouble.*

## 533. SIT ABOVE HIS HIPS.

When mounting your assailant, always try to sit above his hips and as close to his chest as possible. This is important for the following reasons: (1) it prevents the assailant from bumping you; (2) it places you closer to the assailant's facial targets so you can effectively strike them; (3) it brings you closer to the assailant's arms and throat for instantaneous submission holds and chokes; and (4) it helps marry his back to the floor.

## 534. MOVE ON THE GROUND.

One of the foundational elements of effective ground fighting is being able to move well on the floor. Ground fighting mobility is just as important as standing mobility.

## 535. KNOW YOUR GROUND FIGHTING WEAPONS.

When ground fighting, you have a wide variety of weapons at your disposal. Your ground fighting arsenal is divided into the following five categories: (1) immobilization techniques - various techniques designed to immobilize your adversary; (2) locks - various submission holds designed to manipulate and injure your assailant's limbs; (3) chokes - various techniques designed to restrict your assailant's air or blood supply; (4) natural body weapons - various natural body weapons designed to inflict severe damage (i.e., tight punches, hammer fists, biting, gouging, tearing, etc.); and (5) pain-compliance holds - various techniques that create extreme pain for your adversary.

## 536. SEIZE THE OPPORTUNITY.

In any grappling situation, you must know how to take advantage of an opportunity. To accomplish this, three elements must be present: (1) you must recognize the opportunity immediately, (2) you must know the proper technique or maneuver that should be applied, and (3) you must be capable of applying the appropriate technique with precision, finesse, and proper timing.

### 537. MASTER 3 GROUND FIGHTING OBJECTIVES.

When engaged in a ground fight, there are three primary objectives that must be acquired. They include (1) controlling or maintaining your position, (2) changing your position (if necessary), (3) acquiring submission (either through striking, joint locks, or chokes).

### 538. USE ALL THREE CONTROL ELEMENTS.

There are three primary elements that can be used to control or trap your adversary during a ground fight: (1) your body, (2) your assailant's body, and (3) the ground.

### 539. NEVER, EVER ROLL ONTO YOUR STOMACH.

One of the cardinal rules for ground fighting is that under no circumstances should you ever roll over onto your stomach. This is dangerous for the following reasons: (1) the assailant can easily choke you out; (2) your assailant can deliver a barrage of blows to your head, neck, and back; (3) it's virtually impossible to defend against your assailant from this position; and (4) you cannot effectively counterstrike from this position.

### 540. UTILIZE DEAD WEIGHT.

When in the mounted position or in a perpendicular mount, always relax your body and rest your dead weight on the assailant's chest, ribs, and diaphragm. This makes your adversary work for every breath.

## 541. EMPLOY ANTI-GRAPPLER STRATEGIES.

When standing toe-to-toe with a grappler, apply the following strategies: (1) stay mobile by moving on the balls of your feet; (2) strike first and try to inflict as much damage on him as you can before he locks up with you; (3) never kick at a charging attacker, as this will throw you off balance, allowing your assailant to control the takedown; (4) when your assailant locks up with you, embrace him and attack with a variety of close-quarter tools; (5) when the fight goes to the ground, immediately go for the mounted position and try to maintain it; and (6) once the mounted position is established, attack the assailant with a barrage of vicious strikes to his facial targets until he is neutralized.

## 542. DON'T GET DUPED BY A SUCKER PUNCHER.

Since conventional ground fighting tactics can be applied in non–life threatening situations (squabble with a relative, drunk friend, or in a schoolyard fight, etc.), you must be aware of the sucker puncher. The sucker puncher is a deceptive assailant who usually feigns submission or compliance in order to be released from a submission hold. Once he is free he will cold cock you. *CAUTION: Be exceptionally careful when releasing your adversary from a submission hold.*

## 543. MASTER TRANSITIONAL HOLDS.

To minimize your chances of being sucker-punched when releasing a submission hold, you will have to employ a transitional hold. A *transitional hold* is a sequence of moves that allows you to progressively abort your position in order to safely disengage your assailant.

## 544. GRAB ANATOMICAL HANDLES.

Effective grappling requires a thorough understanding of the assailant's anatomical handles. *Anatomical handles* are various body parts (i.e., appendages, joints, and, in some cases, organs) that can be grabbed, held, pulled, or otherwise manipulated during a ground fight. Anatomical handles should be utilized for the following strategic reasons: (1) to temporarily control or immobilize your adversary; (2) for leverage; (3) to injure your assailant; (4) to maintain your balance; (5) to throw, lift, or direct your adversary in a particular direction; and (6) to throw your adversary off balance.

There are numerous anatomical handles, including hair, eye sockets, nose, chin, jaw, ears, throat, neck, elbows, wrists, arms, back of knees, ankles, and hip region.

## 545. AVOID THROWS.

Avoid utilizing throwing techniques in a street fight. Throwing techniques are generally used for one of two reasons. (1) To use an impact surface to injure your assailant. (This violates the economy of motion principle. Instead, use a natural body weapon as your impact surface.) (2) To take the fight to the ground. (Remember, the ground is the last place you want to be in a street fight.)

Throwing techniques are risky and inherently dangerous. For example, they require you to place one or both hands on the assailant to lift or lever him into the desired throwing position. This can open you up to a variety of counterstrikes.

## GRAPPLING & GROUND FIGHTING

### 546. RELY ON FEEL, NOT SIGHT.

A good ground fighter can control and dominate his assailant by tactile feeling. *Tactile sight* is a critical attribute that will permit you to excel in the ground fight.

### 547. DON'T OFFER YOUR ARMS.

If your assailant has established the mounted position during the ground fight, be certain NOT to offer him an extended arm. This can be dangerous for the following reasons: (1) your elbows will lose strategic placement on his thighs, thus allowing him the opportunity to ride higher in the mounted position, which will give him the ability to force you over and onto your stomach; (2) your assailant can perform a variety of holds and chokes, including the biceps choke and the Japanese arm bar.

### 548. WORK QUICKLY AND PRUDENTLY.

The longer a fight lasts, the greater your chances of injury or death. This is especially true in a ground fight. When grappling with an assailant, it's essential that you don't rush a movement or technique.

If you work too quickly, you will be subjecting yourself to the following potential risks and dangers: (1) you can lose your positional advantage, (2) you can lose your balance, (3) you can lose your leverage and expose yourself to a variety of counter holds by the assailant, and (4) the strategic timing to the application of a technique will be compromised, and the technique will not work.

### 549. SHOOT YOUR LEGS BACK.

When riding on top of your assailant's back, it is important to get him flat on his stomach as quickly as possible. The best method of accomplishing this task is by leg shooting. Leg shooting is applied as follows: (1) maintain your position by grabbing hold of your assailant's neck; (2) when the assailant attempts to stand up, let the weight of your entire body drop onto his back and then insert both of your legs inside his legs; (3) quickly drive both of your legs down and into his inner thighs while simultaneously thrusting your hips and upper body forward, forcing your legs to stretch out; (4) this will force the assailant to drop flat on the ground where you can proceed with a variety of techniques.

### 550. FORGET TAKEDOWNS.

*Takedowns* are various maneuvers designed to take your assailant down to the ground. Takedown techniques can be applied to either the assailant's upper or lower body, and they can be initiated from a variety of positions.

Although takedowns may sound effective, they present significant dangers and should be eliminated from your repertoire of street combat techniques. Here are the reasons why: (1) they provoke a ground fight, (2) they require significant energy expenditure, (3) they bring your facial targets within knee- and elbow- strike range, (4) they can be negated with effective sprawling maneuvers, and (5) they present the risk of your being suffocated.

### 551. EXPLOIT YOUR ENVIRONMENT.

Once you've established the mounted position, you can take advantage of your environment and use it to your advantage. Here are a few examples: (1) drive or smash the assailant's head or face into the pavement or street curb; (2) force your assailant's head under water, sand, snow, thick mud, or a pile of wet leaves for a prolonged period of time; (3) shove your adversary's head or eyes into broken glass; (4) thrust your assailant's eyes or head into barbed or razor wire; and (5) maneuver your assailant's entire head into the pathway of moving machinery. *WARNING: This type of environmental exploitation should only be used in life and death encounters where lethal force is warranted and justified in the eyes of the law.*

## 552. KICK FROM THE GROUND.

There are some instances during a ground fight when you'll have the opportunity to launch a quick kick at your adversary. For example, if the assailant attempts an ankle hold, a quick kick to his face or throat may be in order. Depending on his angle and vantage, some targets may include the assailant's thighs, shins, knees, groin, face, or throat. *WARNING: Be prudent when kicking during a ground fight. Avoid full chambering positions prior to delivering your kick. Not only will this telegraph your movements, but it will also allow the assailant to trap and control your lower body.*

## 553. KEEP YOUR KNEES UP.

Whenever your assailant mounts you, it's important to instinctively keep your knees raised up. This is important for the following reasons: (1) it brings your foot closer to the trapping foot position necessary to bump the assailant off you; (2) it offers greater leverage and thrusting power than straight legs; (3) raised knees facilitate mobility on the ground.

### 554. EMBRACE THE RANGE.

*Embracing the range* is a ground fighting strategy that is often used when your assailant has mounted you and you cannot escape immediately. Embracing the range means pulling or embracing your assailant. This is often accomplished by securing his neck with a hooked arm.

Embracing the range is important for the following reasons: (1) it negates the assailant's reach and angle to deliver accurate blows; (2) it negates the assailant's gravitational advantage to deliver powerful blows; (3) it brings your assailant closer to you so you can execute an escape technique effectively; and (4) it temporarily prevents your assailant from applying various locks and chokes. The best hand grip for embracing the range is the Indian grip. *NOTE: Embracing the range can also be applied when your assailant is inside your leg guard.*

### 555. MOUNT IMMEDIATELY.

When a street fight goes down to the ground, it behooves you to acquire the mounted position immediately. The fighter who establishes the mounted position has a tremendous tactical advantage in the ground fight. In many ways, the mounted position is the "cockpit" from which to ground fight effectively. The most important aspect of the mounted position is that it facilitates your delivering of a variety of blows and submission holds while making it very difficult for your assailant to counter or escape effectively.

### 556. HIDE YOUR FACE.

When applying various submission holds and chokes from the mounted position (i.e., box, party flex, wrist levers, forearm or biceps chokes), make it a habit to keep your face and head tucked away. Tucking your face into your shoulders will lower your base and also reduce the possibility of your assailant striking you.

*Get into the habit of keeping your head tucked away.*

## 557. KEEP YOUR HEAD.

Panicking during a ground fight can cost you your life. The following are various reasons why you must keep your cool during the course of a ground fight: (1) it conserves your energy, (2) it keeps your mind focused on the task at hand, (3) it keeps your psychomotor skills sharp, (4) it enhances your combat perceptions, (5) it enhances your killer instinct, (6) it aids in accurate assessment skills, (7) it significantly reduces your target exposure, and (8) it psyches out your adversary.

## 558. CHOOSE THE APPROPRIATE BLOW.

Depending on the "use-of-force" justification, you must choose the appropriate blow when sitting in the mounted position. Generally, linear punches (e.g., lead straights, rear crosses) are much more destructive than circular blows, because the assailant's head is married to the floor and he is forced to absorb the force of your blow completely.

### 559. MOVE CORRECTLY IN THE GRAPPLING RANGE.

When grappling in the vertical plane, it's important to move correctly. Improper footwork can subject you to a wide variety of dangers and risks. Here are a few key points that apply: (1) keep your weight equally distributed on both legs, (2) stay flat-footed and avoid moving on the balls of your feet, (3) always take short, deliberate steps, (4) don't cross- step, and (5) apply the step-and-drag footwork.

### 560. STAND UP CORRECTLY.

Strategic standing from the ground is essential for the following reasons: (1) it minimizes target exposure, (2) it facilitates balance, (3) your counterstrike ability is established quickly, and (4) mobility can be employed immediately. It is also important to be able to stand up correctly and efficiently from both the right and left sides.

### 561. DON'T FORCE IT.

Avoid forcing a lock, choke, or hold. If you have to "force" the technique, chances are it's tactically inappropriate. The correct application of a submission technique can only be found within a window of opportunity.

Generally, six elements must be present for a submission technique to be applied effectively: (1) the assailant's appendage is exposed and free from obstruction, (2) you are in the proper range to apply the technique, (3) you are in the correct position to apply the technique, (4) you have the most efficient angle of application, (5) your submission technique does not place you in harm's way, and (6) you have the necessary leverage to apply the technique effectively.

### 562. KNOW THE SIX WAYS TO GO TO THE GROUND.

There are six ways that your adversary can take you down

to the ground. They include (1) throwing techniques - your assailant arcs your body through the air before it impacts with the floor (i.e., hip throws or fireman's carry); (2) tripping techniques - your adversary strategically plants his leg and pushes you over it; (3) sweeping techniques - your assailant sweeps your foot, or feet, off the ground through a dynamic motion of his leg; (4) appendage takedowns - your assailant applies pressure or dynamic force to your appendage to take you down (i.e., double-leg takedown); (5) locking throws - your assailant locks your joint so he can take you down or throw you; and (6) striking takedowns - your assailant strikes you and causes you to fall to the ground (this is the most indirect form of a grappling takedown).

## 563. IT'S DIFFICULT TO RECOVER FROM A THROW.

Since one of the primary objectives of a grappler is to take you off your feet and slam you onto the ground, you'd better know how to break your fall. Keep in mind that it's often difficult to recover from a violent throw onto the concrete or asphalt. There are no mats in a real ground fight.

## 564. FALL SAFELY.

The importance of learning how to fall safely cannot be overstated. It is an invaluable skill that can greatly reduce the possibility of injury. Here are some important principles to employ when falling: (1) keep your body relaxed, (2) roll with the force, (3) protect your head and neck as you fall, (4) at impact, a forceful exhalation should be made to reduce shock and help control your breathing, (5) slap the ground with your palms to lessen the shock and then return your arms back to a defensive position, (6) do not fall "flat" on the ground, and (7) do not break your fall with your arms or wrists.

There are many types of falls that you can practice. Here's one: (1) standing rear fall - from a standing position, bend your knees to a full squatting position. Roll back while maintaining a tucked position, and as your diaphragm area (middle of back, lower edge of shoulder blades) makes contact, extend your arm (slightly bent at the elbow), slap the ground and exhale, and automatically return your arms to a defensive position. Keep in mind that when learning how to fall for the first time, begin from the ground (in a squatting position) and gradually work your way up to a standing position.

# NUCLEAR TACTICS

### 565. NUKE HIM.

When faced with a life-and-death encounter where lethal force is warranted and justified (i.e., criminal assault with intent to kill), prudence demands using nuclear ground fighting tactics. *Nuclear ground fighting techniques* are designed to inflict immediate and irreversible damage, rendering the criminal assailant helpless. Some nuclear tools and tactics include: (1) biting, (2) tearing, (3) crushing, (4) long-term choking, (5) gouging, (6) raking, and (7) all striking techniques.

### 566. CRUSH IT.

When faced with a deadly force situation, you must employ nuclear ground fighting tactics to ensure your survival. These techniques are the quickest and most efficient method of terminating the fight. One brutal technique is crushing, which can be employed when standing in grappling range or lying in the prone position. The two primary crushing targets are the assailant's throat and testicles, although crushing the assailant's throat is not an easy task. It requires quick and exact digit placement and sufficient leverage accompanied by the vicious determination to destroy your assailant.

## GRAPPLING & GROUND FIGHTING

**567. TEAR IT.**

Another nuclear ground fighting tactic is tearing. Tearing tactics are quick, efficient, and can be employed while standing, kneeling, and lying in the prone position. They are applied primarily with your fingers. Viable targets include the eyelids, ears, and fingers. Like crushing techniques, tearing requires a vicious determination to destroy your adversary.

**568. PUMMEL HIM.**

Know how to pummel your assailant into submission. The *pummel tactic* is generally applied when you have mounted your assailant and your hands are free to strike. Once your balance is established in the mounted position, proceed with a vicious flurry of offensive strikes designed to take your assailant out of the fight. The power of your blows is not such a critical concern because you have the gravitational advantage and your assailant's head is flush against the floor (the ground functions as a stabilizer that concentrates your impact). The best blows for the pummel assault are tight linear punches, tight hooks, hammer fists, and, in some cases, elbow strikes. *WARNING: Because of the vicious characteristics of the pummel tactic, spectator intervention is a strong possibility. Be aware of your surroundings!*

**569. BE A SAVAGE.**

*Tactical biting* is a game changer during a ground fight. At first glance, it may seem a bit unexceptional, basic and simple.

However, when it comes to the *Savage Street Fighting* methodology, nothing could be further from the truth. Tactical biting is one of the most effective and destructive self-defense methods known to mankind. Most importantly, it works against any opponent of any size! This is especially helpful for men and women who don't have the physical size and strength to defend against large and powerful criminal attackers.

### 570. MANIPULATE HIS HAND GUARD.

When sitting in the mounted position and employing the pummel technique, you can manipulate your assailant's hand guard in one of two different ways: (1) narrowing the hand guard - by employing linear blows directly into his face you will draw his hand guard inward (narrowing) and create openings for circular or hooking blows and (2) widening the hand guard - by employing circular blows to the assailant's face, you will draw his hand guard outward (widening) and create openings for linear blows.

### 571. USE THE FLUID SHOCK STRIKE.

If you want to maximize the damage during your pummel

assault, employ the *fluid shock strike*. The fluid shock strike is performed by allowing your fist to remain on and pressed into the target area for a brief but definite period of time. This action prevents the target tissue from immediately bouncing back (due to its elastic nature), therefore causing the force of the strike to penetrate deeply. By penetrating the muscle and affecting the nerves within, the effect on your adversary will be greatly multiplied in comparison to a jabbing strike, which only affects the surface of the target. *WARNING: This technique can cause permanent brain damage and even death. Be absolutely certain your actions are legally justified.*

# GROUND TRAINING

### 572. GROUND FIGHTING REGULARLY.

To be truly prepared for a violent street fight, you must engage in rigorous and frequent ground fighting with a competent instructor. Strive to train at least three times a week for a minimum of one hour per session. Take your time and work slowly through the various techniques.

Here are some important techniques to work on: (1) maintaining ground fighting mobility, (2) maintaining the mounted position, (3) escaping the assailant's guard, (4) escaping the assailant's mounted position, (5) defending against the pummel, (6) escaping from the side headlock, (6) escaping from various submission holds and chokes, (7) establishing the mounted position, (8) executing the pummel assault from the mounted position, (9) establishing the perpendicular mount, (10) maintaining the perpendicular mount, (11) switching from the guard position back to the mounted position, (12) grapevine techniques, (13) utilizing anatomical handles, and (14) body shielding.

## 573. GROUND FIGHT TWO PEOPLE AT ONCE.

The unfortunate fact about grappling is that you may be faced with more than one adversary. Therefore, it's imperative that you experience what it's like to ground fight two assailants at the same time. This type of training can be conducted while you and your training partners are either standing, kneeling, or lying in the prone position. *REMEMBER: It's important that your training partners work slowly with you through the training session.*

## 574. FOLLOW SAFETY GUIDELINE WHEN PRACTICING.

Considerable attention must be given to safety when ground fighting. Here are a few rules and guidelines you should follow: (1) always warm up prior to ground fighting sessions; (2) keep your fingernails well trimmed; (3) don't wear jewelry, including rings, earrings, necklaces, and bracelets, during training sessions; (4) avoid ground fighting next to walls, mirrors, windows, or doors; (5) practice with a training partner who is trustworthy and can control his techniques; (6) keep your training mats clean and disinfected; and (7) avoid training with someone who is sick or has an infection.

## 575. DON'T INJURE YOUR PARTNER.

When conducted properly, ground fighting training can be an injury-free activity. Nevertheless, because of its dynamic nature, there is always the possibility of injuries. Here are some: (1) cauliflower ear - a deformity caused by repeated injury to the ear, which results in the irregular buildup of scar tissue; (2) impetigo, boils, herpes, or ringworm - caused by unsanitary mats or by a training partner who has a virus or infection; (3) torn cartilage, bone fracture, or dislocations - primarily caused by submission holds; and (4) general sprains - caused by improper falling or by forcing a joint beyond its normal range of movement.

# GRAPPLING & GROUND FIGHTING

**576. GROUND FIGHT WITH DIFFERENT WEAPONS.**

Experience what it is like to ground fight with different types of weapons. Experiment and see what it's like to grapple with edged weapons (use rubber training knives only), sticks and bludgeons, and various types of makeshift weapons.

**577. PEPPER SPRAY AND GROUND FIGHT.**

Experience what it's like to ground fight when you've been exposed to a chemical irritant such as pepper spray.

**578. GROUND FIGHT WITH ONE ARM.**

If you want to be exceptionally prepared for the ground fight, you'll need to experience what it's like to fight with only one arm. Find a trustworthy partner with whom you can work (he can use both arms but you can only use one). This type of training is important for the following reasons: (1) it prepares you both physically and psychologically to fight while handicapped, (2) it enhances your awareness of your arm when ground fighting, (3) it reinforces good tactics, and (4) it builds ground fighting confidence.

## 579. PRACTICE HEADLOCK COUNTERS.

Although the side headlock is a feckless submission hold that exposes a fighter to a variety of openings, it's also one of the most common locks. Therefore, it's important for you to know its various counters and escapes.

Here are the two different types of side headlocks that you must know how to escape from: (1) standing position - your assailant applies the side headlock when you're both standing and (2) prone position - your assailant applies the side headlock when you are lying on the floor ground fighting.

## 580. GROUND FIGHT WHILE BLINDFOLDED.

In the course of your training, you should regularly experience what it's like to ground fight while blindfolded. This is important for the following reasons: (1) it helps you develop a keen sense of kinesthetic awareness, (2) it helps prepare you to ground fight while visually handicapped, (3) it develops anatomical orientation, (4) it reinforces proper body mechanic skills, and (5) it cultivates your tactile "sight."

# CHAPTER SIX
## Bludgeons & Stick Fighting

*"Sticks and bludgeons are ubiquitous.
Make certain you know how to use them."*

# THE BASICS

**581. MASTER STICK FIGHTING.**

A prepared fighter must master the entire hierarchy of weapons, including sticks and bludgeons. Stick-fighting skills are important for several reasons, including: (1) in order to defeat a stick-wielding assailant, you must know and understand his weapon's strengths and limitations; (2) you may be required to use a stick or bludgeon in a self-defense situation; and (3) sticks and bludgeons are ubiquitous.

**582. GRIP IT CORRECTLY.**

When holding your stick or bludgeon, allow enough room (one fist length) on the bottom portion of your weapon. When you hold your stick in this fashion, it offers you the following advantages: (1) one stick becomes two weapons - the end portion can be used for butting techniques at close-quarter range, (2) it offers greater leverage for striking, and (3) it promotes enhanced weapon retention.

**583. DON'T HOLD IT TOO TIGHTLY.**

Grasping your stick too tightly can be problematic for the following reasons: (1) it will tire your hands and cause unnecessary cramping, (2) it may telegraph your strikes, (3) it will significantly reduce the speed of your strikes, (4) it will reduce the power of your strikes, and (5) it will throw off your offensive and defensive timing.

**584. MASTER THESE GRIPS.**

While there are many different types of stick/bludgeon grips out there, there are four essential ones that you should master, including: (1) hammer grip, (2) ice-pick grip, (3) baseball-bat grip, (4) quarter-staff grip.

*Hammer Grip.*   *Ice Pick Grip.*   *Baseball-Bat Grip.*

*Quarter-Staff Grip.*

## 585. STICK FIGHT FROM EVERY POSITION.

There are nine general positions in which you and your adversary can stick fight. They include the following: (1) both you and your assailant are prone; (2) you are kneeling and your assailant is prone; (3) your assailant is kneeling and you are prone; (4) both you and your assailant are kneeling; (5) you are standing and your assailant is prone; (6) your assailant is standing and you are prone; (7) you are standing and your assailant is kneeling; (8) your assailant is standing and you are kneeling; and (9) both you and your assailant are standing.

# TECHNIQUES AND ANGLES

### 586. MASTER THE AMERICAN STICK STRANGLE.

The *American stick strangle* is a brutal strangle hold that should only be used in life-or-death self-defense situations. To apply the strangle, perform the following steps: (1) with your right hand, hold the stick in front of your assailant, parallel to the floor and against his throat; (2) place your left arm (triceps area) over your adversary's left shoulder while making certain that the end of your stick rests in the crook of your left elbow; (3) place the palm of your left hand against the back of your assailant's neck, and (4) in one fluid motion, apply pressure with your left hand against the back of your adversary's neck while simultaneously pulling your stick toward yourself with your right hand. *WARNING: Prolonged lack of oxygen to the brain may cause permanent injury or death. Stick strangles can be lethal and should only be used in situations that legally warrant their use.*

### 587. MASTER THE ICE-PICK STRANGLE.

The *ice-pick strangle* is another vicious strangle hold that can be applied with minimal effort. To apply the ice-pick strangle, follow these important steps: (1) standing behind your assailant with your stick in your right hand and in the ice-pick grip, insert the bottom portion of your stick around the front of your assailant's neck from your left side; (2) make certain that your stick rests against the front of your assailant's throat and is parallel to the floor; (3) cross your left arm over your right forearm and grasp the stick on the right side of your assailant's neck; and (4) while making certain that both of your hands are close to the assailant's neck, apply immediate pressure by pulling both of your hands backward.

## 588. FOLLOW THROUGH WITH IT.

When striking at your adversary with a stick or bludgeon, always use a *follow-through* strike. The follow-through strike is the most effective strike for stick combat because it creates the maximum amount of force to incapacitate your adversary.

## 589. MASTER THE NINE ANGLES OF ATTACK.

Knowledge of the basic striking angles is essential for effective stick fighting. Make certain that you can efficiently deliver the following nine angles:

(1) Angle one is a diagonal forehand strike traveling from right to left. Targets include your assailant's temple, clavicle, elbow, ribs, thigh, and knee joint.

(2) Angle two is a diagonal backhand strike traveling from left to right. Targets include your assailant's temple, clavicle, elbow, ribs, thigh, and knee joint.

(3) Angle three is a horizontal forehand strike traveling from right to left. Targets include your assailant's temple, clavicle, elbow, ribs, thigh, and knee joint.

(4) Angle four is a horizontal backhand strike traveling from left to right. Targets include your assailant's temple, clavicle, elbow, ribs, thigh, and knee joint.

(5) Angle five is an upward diagonal forehand moving from right to left. Targets include your assailant's temple, clavicle, elbow, ribs, thigh, and knee joint.

(6) Angle six is an upward diagonal backhand strike moving from left to right. Targets include your assailant's temple, clavicle, elbow, ribs, thigh, and knee joint.

(7) Angle seven is a linear thrust delivered anywhere on the assailant's centerline. Targets include your assailant's face, throat, torso, back, and groin.

(8) Angle eight is a downward vertical strike. Targets include the head, clavicle, elbow, ribs, thigh, and knee joint.

BLUDGEONS & STICK FIGHTING

(9) Angle nine is an upward vertical strike. Targets include your assailant's head, elbow, ribs, groin, thigh, and knee joint.

## 590. BEND YOUR ELBOW.

When delivering a blow with your stick, keep your elbow bent and attack with a short-arc strike. This is important for the following reasons: (1) it prevents hyperextension of your elbow, (2) it enhances the speed of your strike, (3) it enhances the power of your blow, (4) it reduces telegraphic movement, (5) it promotes a short-arc strike, (6) it makes it difficult for your assailant to defend against your strike, and (6) it minimizes your target exposure.

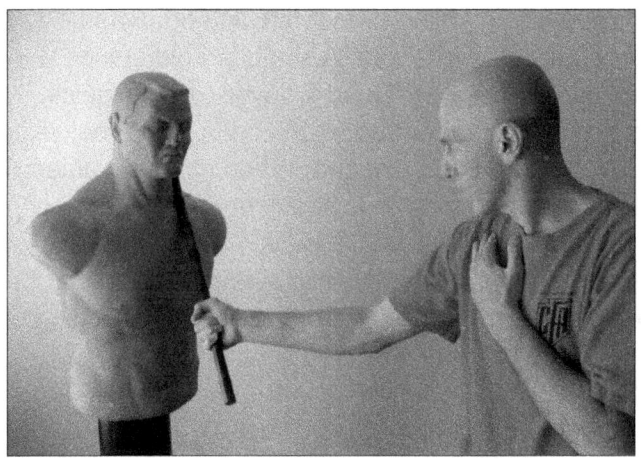

*Pictured here, a short-arc angle one strike.*

## 591. AVOID LONG ARC STRIKES.

The long-arc strike is ineffective in combat for the following reasons: (1) it's easier for your assailant to defend against, (2) it is a relatively slow strike, (3) you can possibly hyperextend your elbow when you impact with your target, (4) it lacks sufficient neutralizing power, (5) it promotes telegraphic movement, (6) your adversary can zone your strike, and (7) it maximizes your target exposure.

## 592. DON'T THRUST IT.

Avoid executing thrusting motions when stick fighting. Thrusting your stick or bludgeon can be risky for the following reasons: (1) your assailant can avoid your weapon easily, (2) thrusting motions place tremendous strain on the side of your wrist, (3) you can lose your weapon when impacting with a strong surface area, and (4) thrusting motions lack neutralizing power. *NOTE: Thrusting motions with a stick or bludgeon should be used sparingly. Generally, thrusting motions should be used with knives and other pointed weapons.*

## 593. APPLY DYNAMIC AND EXPLOSIVE FOOTWORK.

Effective stick fighting requires you to be dynamic and explosive with your footwork. A static or rigid stance will almost certainly get you injured. Good footwork means quick, economical steps performed on the balls of the feet while you are relaxed, alert, and balanced. When moving, remember to keep your arms up, your legs shoulder-width apart, and your weight evenly distributed. *WARNING: Avoid cross-stepping when stick fighting. Remember to apply the standard footwork rule of thumb - first move the foot closest to the direction that you want to go and the other leg should follow an equal distance. This applies to both linear (advance and retreat) and lateral (right and left) movement.*

## 594. BE COGNIZANT OF YOUR CENTERLINE.

When stick fighting, avoid exposing your centerline unnecessarily. Not only does this expose your vital targets, it also diminishes your balance and inhibits efficient footwork. During stick combat, try to maintain a 45-degree stance in relation to your adversary.

## 595. MAKE IT FAST.

There are several ways to increase the speed of your stick strike, including the following: (1) minimize follow-through - don't allow your strike to completely "settle" in the selected target; (2) step with the strike - step in the direction of your blow; (3) use repetition - practice various angles of attack thousands of times to sharpen the movement; (4) visualize regularly - visualize the strike being delivered at great speed; (5) relax - avoid unnecessarily tensing your body and relax your muscles prior to the execution of your strike; (6) breathe - exhale during the execution of your strike; (7) act - learn to act rather than react to a self-defense situation; (8) kinesthetic perception - develop and refine your kinesthetic perception; (9) moderate grip - try to maintain a moderate stick grip; (10) wrist snap - snap your wrist prior to impact with your target.

## 596. USE YOUR SECONDARY HAND.

The *secondary hand* is a close-quarter technique that permits you to move from defense back to offense. The primary function of your secondary hand is to hold your assailant's weapon hand in place after you have employed a defensive maneuver. In this way, you can prevent him from returning with another strike. When you are fighting with a single stick, your secondary hand is the one not holding the weapon. *NOTE: When engaged in either the mid or long range, your secondary hand is kept close to your face and body.*

## 597. KEEP IT MOVING.

When squared off with your assailant, always keep your stick moving. This is important for the following reasons: (1) it prevents inertia from setting in, (2) it enhances the overall velocity of your strikes, (3) it minimizes telegraphing prior to striking, (4) it enhances your defensive reaction time, (5) it minimizes your hand and digit exposure, (6) it significantly enhances your offensive flow, and (7) it causes your assailant to misjudge your weapon's range.

## 598. MASTER ALL STICK-FIGHTING RANGES.

The following are three separate distances of stick fighting that you must master: (1) long range combat - the farthest distance at which you can strike only your assailant's hand with your stick; (2) mid-range combat - the distance at which you can strike your assailant's head, arms, and body with your stick; (3) close-quarter-range combat - the third and final distance at which you can strike your assailant with the butt of your weapon and employ a variety of elbow, knee, and head butt strikes.

## 599. ATTACK HIS WEAPON HAND.

When using a stick to protect yourself against an armed assailant (non ballistic, of course), try to strike your assailant's weapon hand. In most combat situations, if your assailant loses his weapon, he will lose the fight.

## 600. GET BEHIND IT.

When stick fighting, keep your stick in front of your face and torso. Learn to "hide behind your weapon."

## 601. KNOW YOUR FOUR OPTIONS.

When a stick attack comes your way, you only have four options: (1) evade - you can move out of the angle of attack, (2) deflect - you can deflect the attack, (3) block - you can block the oncoming attack, and (4) strike - you can strike the assailant's weapon hand. Make certain you can execute all four of these options with ease and efficiency.

## 602. DON'T FAN YOUR STRIKES.

Some fighters advocate fanning strikes during combat. The fanning strike or *abaniko* is simply a snap-back strike that rapidly changes the angle of attack. Fanning techniques can be executed vertically, horizontally, and diagonally, and they are often used to fake out or set up an assailant.

Nevertheless, fanning strikes are risky and ineffective for real combat. Here are some important reasons why they should not be employed: (1) they lack the significant follow-through necessary to incapacitate a powerful and formidable assailant, (2) they unnecessarily prolong a combat encounter, and (3) in most cases, they will simply agitate your assailant.

## 603. DEFLECT IT.

You must be proficient with stick deflections. Unlike the stick block, a stick deflection is used to redirect your assailant's stick strike. Generally, deflections will flow into a counterstrike, and they are used most commonly when you're attacked with a light stick.

## 604. BLOCK IT.

Know the difference between a deflection and a block. A stick block is performed by meeting your assailant's stick with direct force. Blocks generally do not flow naturally into a counterstrike. Generally, the weight of your assailant's stick will determine whether you need to block or deflect it. If your assailant's stick is heavier than yours, you will most likely have to block his attack.

## 605. ZONING HAS LIMITATIONS.

*Zoning* is a defensive maneuver designed to evade or block your assailant's strike through strategic movement and precise timing. Zoning can be accomplished by either moving in the direction of your assailant's strike (before it generates significant force) or by moving completely out of the stick's arc. While this may sound prudent and effective from a theoretical perspective, zoning does not always work.

Zoning prior to or after your assailant's swing will only work against an unskilled assailant who is wielding a heavy bludgeon (e.g., baseball bat). However, it won't work against a formidable stick fighter who's wielding a light bludgeon. Light bludgeons move with minimal telegraphing and can travel at speeds in excess of 100 miles per hour. The bottom line is that you can't zone against a light bludgeon, even if you have the luxury of knowing where it's coming from.

## 606. HOLD ON TO IT.

When engaged in stick fighting, avoid dropping your weapon. Here's some important reasons why: (1) if your assailant is armed with a weapon he will now have the tactical advantage; (2) if your assailant is unarmed, he can pick up your weapon and use it against you; (3) spectators can attack you with it; (3) you can possibly trip over it and lose your balance. *NOTE: There are some combat situations that will require you to drop your weapon to defeat your adversary.*

A well-trained stick fighter is trained adequately in stick- and bludgeon-retention skills. He knows effective counters to various types of grabs. Don't engage in a stick fight unless you're certain you can maintain complete control over your weapon. And remember to practice stick and bludgeon retention skills on a frequent basis.

### 607. THE ANGLE OF ATTACK IS CRITICAL.

When defending against a bludgeon attack, your primary tactical concern should be your assailant's angle of attack.

### 608. DON'T UNDERESTIMATE THE SPEED OF A STICK.

When defending against a stick, don't underestimate its blistering speed. Many strikes can travel in excess of 100 miles per hour and be delivered in two-tenths of a second.

### 609. KNOW WHEN TO MOVE IN.

When you are unarmed and defending against a bludgeon attack, it's critical that you know when to move in on your adversary. Ideally, the best time to "choke" your assailant's weapon is either during the initiation or completion phase of his bludgeon swing.

### 610. KNOW THE CHARACTERISTICS OF A BLUDGEON.

Like all weapons of combat, there are unique characteristics to different types of bludgeons. For example, a light bludgeon will usually have the following attributes: (1) fast moving, (2) less telegraphic, (3) faster on recoil, (4) difficult for your adversary to zone against, (5) conducive to snapping impact, (6) less deadly, (7) conducive to a short arc, (8) easier to manipulate in close-quarter range, (9) less intimidating looking, and (10) superior with regard to weapon retention.

A heavy bludgeon will usually have the following characteristics: (1) slower moving, (2) more telegraphic, (3) slower on recoil, (4) easier to zone against, (5) conducive to breaking impact, (6) more deadly, (7) conducive to a longer arc, (8) more difficult to manipulate in close-quarter range, (9) more intimidating looking, and (10) weaker with regard to weapon retention.

### 611. MASTER THE BLUDGEON-DEFENSE STANCE.

The *bludgeon-defense stance* is a strategic posture used when confronted by a bludgeon-wielding attacker. To assume this stance, execute the following: (1) keep your stronger side forward, facing your adversary; (2) blade your feet and torso at approximately a 45-degree angle to the attacker; (3) keep both of your hands up (beside each other); (4) keep your hands, arms, and elbows close to your body; (5) keep your head behind your hands and stay relaxed and vigilant; (6) keep your knees slightly bent and flexible with both legs approximately shoulder-width apart; (7) keep your body weight equally distributed on each leg; and (8) keep your chin angled slightly down. When assuming a bludgeon-defense stance, avoid tightening your shoulders or arms.

### 612. STICK DISARMS ARE DIFFICULT TO APPLY.

Because a light stick can travel in excess of 100 miles per hour, it's very difficult to counter by attempting a lock or disarming technique. However, disarming techniques can be effective when defending against a slow and heavy bludgeon.

## 613. BLUDGEON DISARMS DO WORK.

Since a heavy bludgeon usually cannot generate a high retraction speed, disarm techniques can be applied. There are three primary principles that must be employed to disarm a heavy bludgeon successfully: (1) move out of the weapon's line of attack, (2) control the assailant's weapon, and (3) neutralize your assailant.

## 614. MASTER BLUDGEON DEFENSE SKILLS.

When you are unarmed and faced with a potential bludgeon attack, you should adhere to the following 14 principles: (1) become familiar with different types of bludgeons and sticks; (2) always respect the bludgeon; (3) try to determine your assailant's intent; (4) keep your cool; (5) try to escape safely or run if possible; (6) create distance between you and the bludgeon; (7) stay balanced and mobile; (8) try to utilize makeshift weapons; (9) maintain a strategic stance; (10) assess the bludgeon grip; (11) determine the bludgeon's range of impact; (12) determine the bludgeon's angle of attack; (13) attack your adversary first, engage, and control the bludgeon; and (14) neutralize your assailant.

## 615. BECOME FAMILIAR WITH THEM.

One of the fundamental principles of bludgeon disarms is familiarity. Take the time to familiarize yourself with as many types of bludgeons as possible. Learn the different types of grips, stances, chamber positions, weights, and materials. Try to find a knowledgeable instructor who can teach you about bludgeons, stick fighting concepts, and effective defenses. Familiarity is critical because it will help eliminate some of the fear associated with this weapon and will better prepare you to protect yourself if faced with a bludgeon attack.

### 616. BEWARE OF THE REVERBERATION PATH.

When blocking or deflecting your assailant's blow, stay clear of your stick's reverberation path. Stick reverberation occurs when your weapon (usually a light bludgeon) absorbs the assailant's force, causing it to bounce back at you.

### 617. DETERMINE THE INTENT.

It's critical to make an accurate threat assessment when confronted by a bludgeon-wielding assailant. Use split-second judgment to determine exactly what your adversary wants to accomplish. Some assailants might not want to harm you if they can avoid it. Others may be dead set on smashing your skull to pieces. If you have determined that your assailant plans to harm you, you must resort to aggressive disarming tactics immediately.

### 618. MASTER THE CENTER, LEFT, AND RIGHT HIGH BLOCK.

The center high block is used to defend against a powerful bludgeon strike directed toward the top section of your head and shoulders. The left high block is used to defend against a powerful bludgeon strike directed toward the left side of your head and shoulders. The right high block is used to defend against a powerful bludgeon strike directed toward the right side of your head and shoulders. Each block is performed by raising your stick up to meet the assailant's descending strike while your free hand grips the other end of your stick.

## 619. MASTER THE LEFT AND RIGHT MID BLOCK.

The left mid block is used to defend against a powerful bludgeon strike directed toward the left side of your chest and torso. The right mid block is used to defend against a powerful bludgeon strike directed toward the right side of your chest and torso. Each block is performed by moving your stick across your body to meet the assailant's strike while your free hand grips the other end of your stick.

## 620. MASTER THE LEFT AND RIGHT LOW BLOCK.

The left low block is used to defend against a powerful bludgeon strike directed toward the lower left section of your torso. The right low block is used to defend against a powerful bludgeon strike directed toward the lower right section of your torso. Each block is performed by lowering your stick to meet your assailant's swing while your free hand grips the other end of your stick.

## 621. MASTER THE CENTER LOW BLOCK.

The center low block is used to defend against a powerful bludgeon strike directed toward the lower section of your torso and groin. The block is performed by lowering your stick to meet your assailant's upward swing while your free hand grips the other end of your stick.

## 622. KNOW THE THREE STAGES OF A STICK SWING.

There are three stages or phases to a stick or bludgeon strike. They include (1) initiation phase, (2) mid phase - the contact or impact point of your swing, and (3) completion phase.

# TRAINING

### 623. TRAIN WITH RATTAN STICKS.

For a good portion of your training, use rattan sticks. These training sticks are preferred over others because rattan is generally inexpensive and safe to work with.

### 624. CHOOSE THE PROPER LENGTH.

Though rattan sticks come in a variety of lengths (anywhere from 21 to 26 inches), the most preferred length for training is approximately 26 inches. If your stick is too short, it will negate your weapon's range capability; if it is too long, it will be difficult to manipulate in close-quarter combat.

### 625. OCCASIONALLY TRAIN WITH AX HANDLES.

To strengthen your wrists, hands, arms, and shoulders, occasionally train with oak ax handles. Ax handles can be purchased at your local hardware store.

### 626. WARM UP YOUR WRISTS.

To develop a flexible and strong wrist, hold your stick in its center and rapidly twist it back and forth. This warm-up movement should be performed before and after your training routine.

### 627. TWIRL IT.

The *stick twirl* is an excellent dexterity exercise that should be performed on a regular basis. To perform the forward stick twirl, hold your stick tightly between your thumb and index finger and then forcefully twirl the entire weapon forward at your side, allowing your other three fingers to move freely. To perform the backward stick twirl, hold your stick tightly between your thumb and index finger, then forcefully twirl the entire weapon backward at your side, allowing your other three fingers to move freely. You can also twirl two sticks at the same time.

### 628. GEAR UP.

Before engaging in full-contact stick fighting be certain you are donned with the right gear. This includes the following items: (1) fencing mask, (2) mouth piece, (3) digit gloves or street hockey gloves, (5) elbow pads, (6) shin guards.

### 629. PRACTICE WITH DIFFERENT BLUDGEONS.

When preparing to defend against bludgeon attacks, it's important to have your training partner attack you with a wide variety of sticks, including the following: (1) long, (2) short, (3) light, (4) heavy, (5) balanced, (6) unbalanced, (7) makeshift, (8) wooden, and (9) metal.

## 630. PREPARE FOR ALL THE ANGLES OF ATTACK.

If you want to be completely prepared for a bludgeon attack, make certain that you are trained to defend against the following angles of attack (in both long and short arcs): (1) vertical plane, (2) horizontal plane, (3) diagonal plane, and (4) longitudinal plane.

## 631. AVOID PREMATURE STICK SPARRING.

While full-contact stick sparring is essential, it's important to integrate this training methodology at the proper time. Never introduce students to full-contact stick sparring until they've acquired the following skills: (1) a variety of offensive and defensive stick techniques that can be readily applied, (2) the ability to control the force of their stick strikes, (3) the fundamental attributes of combat (i.e., speed, timing, coordination, accuracy, balance, and the ability not to telegraph), and (4) a safe attitude toward stick training.

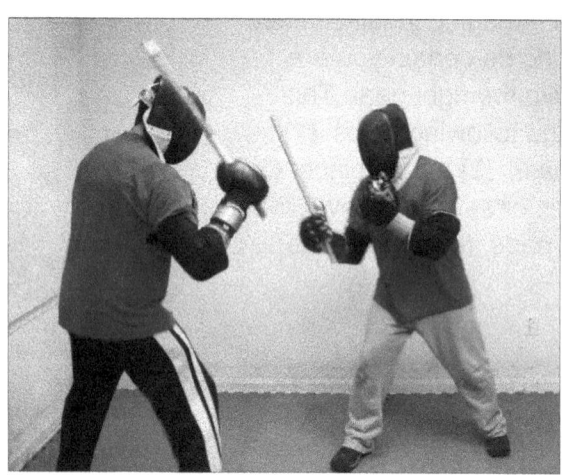

## 632. OCCASIONALLY SHUT YOUR EYES.

When performing stick fighting drills with your partner, occasionally close your eyes and feel the movements. This type of training will enhance your kinesthetic perception.

### 633. PERFORM PENALTY PUSH-UPS.

To show respect for your stick (or any weapon, for that matter), if you ever drop it accidentally during training, immediately drop to the ground and perform 25 penalty push-ups. This is ideal for instilling weapon retention skill with your students.

### 634. UTILIZE FIGURE-EIGHT DRILLS.

Utilize figure-eight drills to develop speed, coordination, and fluidity with your stick strikes. Figure-eight movements will also sharpen and refine overhand strikes, backhand strikes, and upward strikes. Remember when executing figure-eight movements to keep your arcs short and tight.

### 635. STICK FIGHTING EVERYWHERE.

Practice your stick fighting techniques in a variety of different environments, terrains, locations, and positions, including in doorways, in hallways, on the stairs, ascending a hill, descending a hill, on top of a car, in a ditch, in an elevator, on an escalator, on a bridge, under a bridge, standing in the water, in the snow, in the mud, in the sand, in tall grass, in between shrubbery, between trees and branches, in the kneeling position, and in the prone position.

### 636. PRACTICE SINGLE AND DOUBLE-STICK DRILLS.

The only real way to be prepared for stick fighting is to engage in a variety of different drills regularly. Stick fighting drills can be performed with either one or two weapons and will provide the following benefits: (1) improved confidence, (2) increased speed, (3) more powerful blows, (4) minimized telegraphic movements, (5) improved eye-hand coordination,

(6) improved ability to adapt to unpredictable angles of attack, (7) reinforced good habits, (8) refined and enhanced mobility, (9) sharpened sense of timing, (10) learned range specificity, and (11) reinforced target recognition.

# CHAPTER SEVEN
## Knife Defense & Knife Fighting

*"The knife is a fierce weapon. Depending on who wields it, it can be your best friend - or your worst enemy."*

# FACTS

### 637. RESPECT THE KNIFE.

Too few people realize just how deadly knives and other edged weapons are. Even a child becomes dangerous with a knife in hand. The entertainment industry has done us a great disservice by making everyone believe that a knife-wielding assailant can be neutralized with one swift kick, shoulder throw, or punch. It's not like that in the real world. In fact, the odds are strongly stacked against your survival if you're unarmed and attacked by an assailant with a knife.

### 638. KNIVES ARE UBIQUITOUS.

Street criminals can hide knives or edged weapons just about anywhere. Here are just a few possible locations: in newspapers, magazines, books, shopping bags, briefcases, pockets, tote bags, wallets, purses, hats, sleeves, shoes, socks, belts, automobiles, and motorcycles; under their arms; and behind their forearms.

### 639. KNOW WHY CRIMINALS PREFER KNIVES.

Street criminals prefer knives to commit crimes for some of the following reasons: (1) they're silent, (2) they don't misfire or jam, (3) they do not require reloading, (4) they're easy to conceal, (5) they're easy to dispose of, (6) they're symbolic to psychopaths, (7) they leave no ballistic clues, (8) the courts tend to be more lenient with knives than guns, (9) they're ubiquitous, (10) they're inexpensive, and (11) makeshift knives are easy to create.

### 640. IT'S A GREAT EQUALIZER.

Armed with a knife, a small person can easily dispatch a vicious 200-pound killer, provided that the knife wielder has the proper mental and physical training and a razor-sharp blade. Unlike in unarmed combat, when you're armed with a knife, physical strength is no longer a necessary consideration. It takes little real strength to stab into one of the assailant's vital organs or slash a major artery.

### 641. FAMILIARIZE YOURSELF.

There are seven different classifications of knives: (1) gravity blades, (2) spring blades, (3) lock blades, (4) folding blades, (5) fixed blades, (6) ballistic blades, and (7) makeshift/improvised blades.

# KNIFE DEFENSE

### 642. DON'T JUDGE HIS SKILL LEVEL.

When unarmed and confronted by a knife-wielding assailant, don't assume you can judge his proficiency with the way he holds his weapon. Always assume that anyone holding a knife (or any weapon for that matter) knows how to use it and will do just that. Besides, even if your assailant is unskilled as a knife fighter, he can still kill you.

### 643. MASTER KNIFE-DEFENSE SKILLS.

When you're unarmed and faced with an edged-weapon attack, here are 12 principles you should follow: (1) become familiar with all types of knives and edged weapons, (2) always respect the knife, (3) try to determine your assailant's intent, (4) keep your cool, (5) try to escape safely or run if possible, (6) create distance between you and the blade, (7) stay balanced and mobile, (8) utilize makeshift weapons, (9) maintain a strategic knife-defense stance, (10) focus on the knife, (11) attack your adversary first and control the knife, and (12) neutralize your assailant with extreme prejudice.

### 644. MASTER THE KNIFE-DEFENSE STANCE.

Surviving a knife attack requires mastery of the knife-defense stance. This stance ensures maximal mobility, minimal target exposure, and facilitates immediate counterstrike ability.

To assume the knife-defense stance, apply the following steps: (1) angle your body (internal organs) approximately 45 degrees to your assailant; (2) slightly hunch your shoulders forward and let your stomach sink in; (3) keep your head and face back and away from random slashes or stabs; (4) keep your hands, forearms, and elbows close to your body to diminish target opportunities for your assailant; (5) cup your hands with your palms facing you, which will turn soft tissue, veins, and arteries in the arms away from the blade; (6) keep your knees slightly bent and flexible, your feet shoulder-width apart, and your weight equally distributed on each leg; and (7) don't tense up - always stay relaxed and alert.

### 645. DON'T CLENCH TOO TIGHTLY.

When assuming a knife-defense stance, make certain that your fingers are semi clenched. Also, avoid clenching your fists too tightly. This may cause your veins to protrude from your arms, and retard hand speed.

**646. MASTER THE V-GRIP.**

When defending against a knife attack, the only effective method of controlling the assailant's knife hand is to use the *V-grip*. The V-grip is applied by grabbing the assailant's wrist with both of your hands (make certain that the webs of your hands completely envelope your assailant's wrist). Once you have made contact, squeeze hard and hold on with all your might. When applied correctly, the V-grip allows you to redirect the knife away from your body and counter attack.

*Pictured here, the V-grip.*

**647. MOBILITY AND BALANCE ARE PARAMOUNT.**

Two of the most important aspects of knife defense are mobility and balance. Mobility is important for the following reasons: (1) it allows you to quickly move in and out of the range from various slashes and stabs, (2) it makes you a more evasive target, and (3) in some cases it helps minimize your assailant's complete blade penetration.

Balance is critical for these reasons: (1) it permits you to change your direction of movement quickly and efficiently, (2) it enhances your general reaction time, (3) it aids your ability to be mobile, and (4) it allows you to recover quickly from a committed movement.

# KNIFE DEFENSE & KNIFE FIGHTING

**648. ATTACK THE ATTACKER.**

If you're unarmed and faced with a knife-wielding assailant with nowhere to escape, *attack him first*. This is important for the following reasons: (1) it psyches him out - nothing is more shocking than an unarmed person attacking first, even though the assailant holds all of the cards; (2) it prevents the defensive flow - since you're initiating the attack, it doesn't give your assailant sufficient time to force you into the defensive flow; and (3) it's conclusive - regardless of the outcome, such an act quickly formulates a conclusion to your emergency situation; you have no time to be tormented by despair and fear.

**649. ATTACK WITH EXTREME PREJUDICE.**

Once you have gained solid control over your knife attacker's knife hand (via V-grip), it is critical that you attack him as viciously as possible. Drive your knee repeatedly into his groin, stomp on his instep, head-butt his nose, and bite into his jugular if necessary. Attack him repeatedly with cold determination. Your goal is to kill him. As you start to gain the advantage, you can consider releasing one of your hands to gouge or rake his eyes, crush his windpipe, or strike the front of his throat with the edge of your hand. Don't stop until your adversary is out of commission. Remember, he attacked you with a knife, and that's deadly force - as deadly as it gets!

**650. DON'T GET DUPED.**

If a knife fighter ever throws his weapon to the floor and challenges you to get it, don't! Chances are that he has another one and he's going to use it when you bend down to the ground.

## 651. WEAR LOOSE-FITTING CLOTHES.

The clothing that you wear on the street can play an important role when defending against a knife attack. Clothing that hugs your body will allow your assailant's slashing movement to pass through the material easily. Loose-fitting shirts and jeans will not only make your assailant misjudge the exact target distance, but they will also make it more difficult for his knife to penetrate your flesh.

## 652. PROTECT YOUR FLEXORS AND BLOOD VESSELS.

When unarmed and faced with a knife attack, avoid exposing the belly of your forearms. To accomplish this, keep both of your hands, forearms, and elbows close to your body to diminish target opportunities. Cup both of your hands with your palms facing you to protect your flexors and blood vessels from your assailant's blade.

## 653. CREATE DISTANCE BETWEEN YOU AND THE KNIFE.

When unarmed and defending against an edged-weapon attack, try to create as much distance as you can between you and the knife. Distance is critical because it enhances your defensive reaction time and allows you to control your options.

Obviously, running away is a great way to put distance between you and the blade, but you can also use different types of objects in the environment to create barriers between you and your adversary. Cars, trucks, couches, large chairs, tall fences, park benches, and large tables are only a few examples. Remember, though, that these objects are only buying you a little precious time; they don't negate the threat. The bottom line is to stay as far away from the knife as possible. Keep in mind that the only time you want to be close to a knife is for disarming purposes, and then only if the situation is absolutely unavoidable.

## 654. DON'T PANIC.

When unarmed and faced with a knife attack, do not panic. This may seem difficult, but with proper training and crisis rehearsal, it can be done. People naturally freeze up when they are faced with a knife attack. This only makes it easier for your assailant to accomplish his nefarious mission. You must rise to the occasion and summon all of your spirit and courage to ward off the deleterious effects of fear, anxiety, and stress. You must be determined to fight your adversary to the death if necessary.

## 655. EXPECT TO GET CUT.

Whether you're unarmed and defending against a knife attack or knife fighting with your adversary, *expect to get cut*. This frame of mind is critical for the following reasons: (1) it prepares you for the harsh reality of knife combat, (2) it helps prevent you from going into mental shock if you do get cut, and (3) it frees you from the mental concern of your well-being.

## 656. NEVER KICK AT THE ASSAILANT'S KNIFE HAND.

When unarmed and defending against a knife-wielding assailant, never attempt to kick the knife out of his hand. This is asinine and hazardous for the following reasons: (1) the speed of your kick is no match for the speed of a knife; (2) to successfully hit your assailant's knife hand, you will be required to execute a high-line kick, which is suicide in any type of physical confrontation; (3) you run the risk of losing your balance and falling on the ground; (4) it unnecessarily exposes your vital targets to the knife-wielding assailant; (5) it temporarily inhibits your ability to execute quick and evasive footwork; and (6) your assailant can cut your ankle, foot, or calf when you deliver the kick.

## 657. SCAN FOR MAKESHIFT WEAPONS.

When unarmed and confronted by a knife-wielding assailant, scan your environment for any makeshift weapons, especially ones that can shield against knife stabs and slashes. A strong briefcase makes a great shield. So are metal trash can lids, sofa and chair cushions, and even small chairs and tables. Also look for makeshift weapons with which you can strike your assailant. If you can get hold of a striking weapon, use it to strike quickly at your adversary's hand — the one holding the knife. Effective striking weapons are hardwood limbs, metal pipes, and long sticks.

## 658. RECOGNIZE KNIFE PALMING.

Don't be caught off guard! Learn to recognize *knife palming*. Knife palming is a strategic method of concealing a knife or other edged weapon behind one's forearm. It is probably one of the most deceptive forms of knife concealment and can surprise even the most seasoned street fighter. Therefore, when confronted by a potential adversary, always be aware of his hands. If you can't see his fingertips, beware - he could be palming a knife.

## 659. DETERMINE HIS INTENT.

It's critical to make an accurate threat assessment when confronted by a knife attacker. Use split-second judgment to determine exactly what your adversary wants to accomplish. Some might not want to harm you if they can avoid it. Others may be dead-set on cutting you from limb to limb. If you have determined that your assailant plans to harm you, you must resort to aggressive disarming tactics.

### 660. DON'T RECOVER HIS KNIFE... YET

Once you have disarmed your assailant, don't become obsessed with recovering the blade. This will distract you from neutralizing your assailant and possibly lead to a renewed attack.

## KNIFE FIGHTING SKILLS

### 661. AVOID A KNIFE FIGHT AT ALL COSTS.

A knife fight should always be avoided at all costs. It is a desperate situation that should only be undertaken when all other means of avoiding the situation have been thoroughly exhausted. Always attempt to escape or run from a knife fight.

### 662. OBEY THE LAW.

If you are going to carry a knife for self-defense, you must assume the legal and social responsibilities that go along with it. Before you purchase a knife, check your state and local laws. In some states, certain knives are prohibited altogether. If you are going to carry a knife, make certain that you do so in a manner consistent with applicable laws.

### 663. BUY A GOOD BLADE.

Here are a few important points to consider when purchasing a knife for self-defense: (1) make certain the knife fits comfortably in both your right and left hands; (2) choose a knife that is designed for slashing as well as stabbing; (3) choose a blade that is sharp and large enough to penetrate the assailant's vital arteries and organs; (4) choose a knife that is light enough for you to manipulate easily and quickly; (5) use either a lock blade or fixed blade made of high-carbon stainless steel; and (6) try to purchase a knife that has a hand guard, which will prevent your hand from slipping onto the blade when you thrust it (the hand guard will also offer some protection from the assailant's blade).

### 664. GET A TACTICAL FOLDING KNIFE.

While a fixed blade is ideal for knife fighting, it's size and weight will often makes it impractical as a daily carry weapon for most people. Luckily, there is the *tactical fighting folder* that can be carried on your person or concealed in your everyday carry bag. Best of all, it can be used in a wide range of survival situations and environments.

*Pictured here, a tactical folding knife.*

### 665. GET A KINETIC OPENER.

Under the spontaneous and stressful conditions of a knife fight, your tactical folder knife must be opened quickly and positively. Therefore, a good tactical folder should have dual thumb studs that allow one-handed opening. At the same time, you should also be able to open the knife kinetically - meaning it can be opened with one hand and with a quick flick of the wrist. I often refer to this as a *kinetic opener* because it functions kinetically due to a particular tension where the knife connects.

## KNIFE DEFENSE & KNIFE FIGHTING

### 666. USE A PARTIALLY SERRATED BLADE.

Your tactical folder should have a partially serrated edge, also called a *combo blade*. A serration is simply a sharpened recessed curve along the edge of the blade. Serrations act like micro teeth that will saw through tough clothing (especially leather and thick denim).

The serrations should also be located on the lower portion of the blade. For knife fighting, I would avoid using a tactical folder that only has a straight edge. Straight edge blades might not slice through thick fabric like leather jackets.

### 667. SIZE MATTERS.

If you're going to use a knife as a daily carry weapon, you must be able to conceal it from the public eye. However, it must be large enough to penetrate the assailant's vital arteries and organs. Therefore, I recommend a blade of at least 3.75 inches that is light enough for you to manipulate quickly and easily. *WARNING! It's your responsibility to research and comply with all local, state, and federal laws and regulations pertaining to the possession, carry, and use of a knife.*

### 668. CHOOSE RUBBER GRIPS.

Avoid using a knife that has a wood or metal grip. Wood and metal grips provide poor gripping, especially when your hands are wet with blood. Rubberized "sure grips" are essential for edged-weapon combat. Remember, puncture wounds will make your blade and grip bloody and slippery.

### 669. MASTER KNIFE FIGHTING SKILLS.

It's important to master knife fighting skills for the following reasons: (1) you must understand the nature of the beast - the best way to defeat a knife attacker is to first become a knife fighter, (2) knowledge conquers fear - the more you know about knives and other edged weapons, the less you will fear them, (3) knives are a component of the hierarchy of weapons, and (4) knife fighting skills complement unarmed combat skills.

### 670. MASTER THE KNIFE FIGHTING STANCE.

The *knife fighting stance* is used when both you and your adversary are armed with a knife or similar edged weapon, such as a shard of glass, broken bottle, shank, tactical pen, etc. When assuming this stance, drop your head down and keep your neck and throat behind both of your arms at all times. This diminishes target size and reduces the likelihood of a quick kill slash or stab to either your neck or subclavian artery.

Deeply crouch your body, with your shoulders and stomach sunk inward. This unusual posture brings your chest and internal organs away from dangerous puncture wounds. Both of your arms are held up, with your hands, forearms, and elbows close to your body to diminish target opportunities.

### 671. AVOID SPRING BLADES.

Avoid using spring blades (i.e., switchblades, stilettos) in a knife fight. They are inherently dangerous for the following reasons: (1) the internal spring can malfunction, (2) the structural integrity of the knife is usually poor, (3) the hand grips are usually too thin and often slippery, and (4) they look menacing and have a criminal stigma attached to them. Remember, if you are later taken to court, the jury will look unfavorably at you, even though you may have been justified in killing your adversary.

## 672. MAKE IT CONCEALABLE.

A good tactical fighting folder should be convenient, concealable, and easy to carry on your person. It's size and weight should not be cumbersome if you were to carry it with you throughout the day. Moreover, it should be something that is easily concealed in an EDC or survival bag.

## 673. MASTER THE TWO PRIMARY KNIFE GRIPS.

One of the foundational elements of effective knife fighting is the grip. The two primary knife grips that you must master are as follows: (1) hammer grip (2) ice-pick grip.

*The Hammer Grip.*     *The Ice Pick Grip.*

## 674. CHOOSE THE CORRECT KNIFE GRIP.

When knife fighting, select the grip appropriate for your range. To accomplish this there are three knife fighting ranges you must be aware of: (1) long range - the hammer grip is ideal for this range and can be used to apply both slashing and linear thrusting movements, (2) mid range - the hammer grip is also the most preferred grip for this distance of engagement, and (3) close quarter - the ice-pick grip or modified-ice-pick grip is preferred in this particular range and can be used to apply tight slashing and angular stabbing movements.

### 675. LOW PORTION OF THE BLADE GOES FIRST.

The *contact point* of the blade is important when performing slashing movements. When slashing, be certain to make contact with the low portion of the blade first (also called the low point), and then pull the remainder of the knife (mid and high points) through the target. This will create a much deeper cut and produce the greatest amount of damage to the target.

This is when the serrated portion of the blade comes into play during a knife fight. For example, if the serration portion of the blade is located at the lowest point of the blade, you'll be able to penetrate thick protective clothing, allowing the remainder of the blade to make contact with a vital target.

## BLADE CONTACT POINTS

### 676. IGNORE YOUR WOUND.

If you're cut in a knife fight, don't look at your wound until the encounter is over. Doing so can be dangerous for the following four reasons: (1) it takes your eyes off the immediate threat, (2) it can psyche you out, (3) it may cause you to go into shock, and (4) it empowers your assailant.

### 677. DON'T THROW IT.

Contrary to what you see in movies or video games, throwing your knife at your assailant asinine for the following reasons: (1) few knives are designed and balanced for throwing, (2) it's extremely difficult to hit a moving target when throwing any type of knife, (3) if your knife misses its target, it will automatically arm your adversary with your weapon.

### 678. USE YOUR SECONDARY WEAPONS.

When engaged in a knife fight, never forget that you have numerous *secondary weapons* at your disposal. Some include: (1) head - used for butting your adversary, (2) teeth - used for biting your assailant, (3) elbows - used for striking your assailant, (4) knees - also used for striking your adversary, (5) legs - used for kicking your assailant at the mid range of knife combat, and (6) hands - used for striking your assailant at the mid range of knife fighting.

### 679. MEET THE THREE ESSENTIAL REQUIREMENTS.

Never carry a knife unless you meet the three essential requirements to facilitate effective deployment: (1) knowledge - this means knowing and understanding the elements, nature, and characteristics of edged-weapon combat and how to apply them to any combat situation; (2) skills - this means possessing the proficiency, aptitude, and dexterity to knife fight, developed through training and experience and perfected through consistent practice; and (3) attitude - refers to your immediate state of mind or disposition toward edged weapon combat.

## 680. NEVER THREATEN WITH A KNIFE.

A knife is a tool of destruction that's intended to injure or kill, not intimidate. Never pull a knife unless you're legally and morally justified to use it. A knife should only be displayed when you have no other choice but to use justifiable deadly force.

## 681. MASTER KNIFE RETENTION SKILLS.

A well-trained knife fighter is adequately trained in knife retention skills. He knows effective counters to various types of grabs. Never pick up a knife unless you are absolutely confident that you can maintain complete control over it. Remember, if you drop your knife, you might lose your life.

## 682. STRONG SIDE FORWARD.

If you ever have the option or luxury of assuming a knife fighting stance, try to position your stronger and more coordinated side forward. For example, if you are right-handed, your right side is generally your stronger and more coordinated side. This strong-side stance is important for knife combat because it maximizes the speed, power, dexterity, and accuracy of your blade movement.

## 683. HOLD YOUR KNIFE IN FRONT OF YOU.

When knife fighting, hold your knife in your front hand. This knife-forward stance is critical for the following reasons: (1) it brings your closest weapon (your knife) to the assailant's closest targets, and (2) the unprotected (or unarmed) side of your body is kept back and away from your assailant's stabs and slashes. Generally, a lead-hand knife fighter will have a tactical advantage over a rear-hand knife fighter.

## 684. USE THE SWORD AND SHIELD PRINCIPLE.

If you have the luxury of acquiring a shielding makeshift weapon during a knife fight, place it in your rear hand so that it may protect you from various cuts and slashes. Your lead hand should then be holding your knife. This is known as the *sword and shield principle*.

## 685. KNOW WHY SOME PREFER A REAR HAND STANCE.

The following are four general reasons why some people will hold a knife in the rear hand: (1) protection - their front hand is free to block or deflect any strikes launched against them; (2) grabbing - their front hand is free to grab and pull victims off balance, thereby exposing vital targets; (3) distracting - their front hand is free to cause feints or other distractions; and (4) striking - their front hand is used as a secondary weapon that can punch or strike at will.

## 686. ALLOW AN AVENUE OF ESCAPE.

During a knife fight, always allow your assailant an avenue of escape. Many people will choose to run once they catch the sight of their own blood. Avoid making the tragic mistake of forcing your assailant into a corner.

## 687. DRIVE IT TO THE HILT.

When going for a quick-kill move, drive your weapon deep into your assailant until the surface of his body makes contact with the hilt of the knife. Once you have acquired deep penetration, twist and pump the blade repeatedly to maximize organ and tissue damage and accelerate blood loss.

## 688. KEEP YOUR KNIFE CLOSE TO YOUR BODY.

When knife fighting, avoid overextending your knife hand.

This is dangerous for the following reasons: (1) it inhibits your balance, (2) it leaves you vulnerable to attack, and (3) it significantly reduces your ability to attack your assailant. When holding a knife, keep it in your front hand and hold it close to your body. Keep your rear hand in with your elbow close to your body while keeping the belly of your forearm and palm facing your chest. This will keep the flexors and blood vessels of your "secondary hand" away from random slashes from your assailant. The only time your knife should be away from your body is when you are executing an attack.

### 689. LOOK SEASONED.

When assuming a knife-fighting stance, it's important that you appear like a *seasoned* knife fighter. When your opponent observes your tactical stance, he should immediately perceive an experienced knife fighter who is no stranger to blade fighting. This visual might, hopefully, make your opponent second guess his skills and turn the other way and run.

### 690. STAB, DON'T JAB.

Don't jab at your assailant with your knife. If you're going to commit yourself to a linear attack, deliver a quick, forceful thrust. Stabbing should always be used as a fully committed move.

### 691. MASTER KNIFE TARGETING.

*Knife targeting* is classified into three distinct categories: (1) Bleeders - anatomical targets that directly impact the enemy's cardiovascular system. (2) Immobilizers - targets that hinder or immobilize the assailant's limbs. It can be muscle and nerve tissue, tendons, ligaments, and connective tissue. (3) Quick kills - are lethal knife fighting targets. In most cases, one cut to a quick kill target will immediately end the knife fight.

## 692. CUT AT A 45-DEGREE ANGLE.

When cutting your assailant, try to direct your blade at a 45-degree angle. This cutting angle is important for the following reasons: (1) it's an efficient cutting angle, (2) it creates a larger arterial wound, and (3) it's more difficult for arteries to clot when severed at 45 degrees.

*When slashing your adversary, try to cut at a 45-degree angle.*

## 693. KNOW THE TWO WAYS OF GETTING CUT.

Sound knife fighting training requires that you acquire a basic understanding of how you get wounded by a knife. There are two ways in which to get cut. (1) Stabbing - there is a stabbing motion that punctures tissue and is more likely to be fatal. Stab wounds produce internal damage and bleeding. (2) Slashing - unless the slash severs a major artery, it is not as immediately threatening as a stab wound. Keep in mind that both stabbing and slashing motions can be executed from a variety of grips and postures.

## 694. ANTICIPATE IMPACT SHOCK.

Despite your best efforts to cut soft tissue targets, there's always the good possibility that you'll make contact with something hard and resistant. Essentially, this means that each and every time you attempt to cut a target, you run the risk of hitting bone and possibly dislodging your knife from your hand. It's just a fact that you have to accept when knife fighting.

*Impact shock* is the resistance your hand receives when your knife makes contact with a hard surface. So, if you want to maintain your grip and hold on to your weapon, you must anticipate this and train for it.

### 695. MASTER THE 9 ANGLE NUMBERING SYSTEM.

If you're truly concerned about surviving a knife fight, you'll want to steer clear of complex numbering systems and use something that is simple, practical and easy to remember under the extreme duress of a deadly knife fight.

Over the years, I've designed a *nine angle numbering system* that is efficient, effective, and safe for both stick and knife fighting applications. They include:

*Angle One* is a diagonal slash or stab traveling from right to left. Targets can include your assailant's ear canal, back of neck, carotid artery, subclavian artery, throat, brachial, radial or ulnar arteries, triceps, femoral artery, back of knee, and wrist flexor.

*Angle Two* is a diagonal slash or stab traveling from left to right. Targets can include your assailant's ear canal, back of neck, carotid artery, subclavian artery, throat, brachial, radial or ulnar arteries, triceps, femoral artery, back of knee, and wrist flexor.

*Angle Three* is a horizontal slash or stab traveling from right to left. Targets can include your assailant's ear canal, lateral side of the head, back of neck, carotid artery, throat, brachial, radial and ulnar arteries, triceps, femoral artery, back of knee, and wrist flexor.

*Angle Four* is a horizontal slash or stab traveling from left to right. Targets can include your assailant's ear canal, lateral side of the head, back of neck, carotid artery, throat, brachial, radial and ulnar arteries, triceps, femoral artery, back of knee, and wrist flexor.

*Angle Five* is an upward diagonal slash or stab moving from right to left. Targets can include your assailant's carotid artery, axillary artery, brachial, radial or ulnar arteries, triceps, femoral artery, back of knee, and wrist flexor.

*Angle Six* is an upward diagonal slash or stab moving from left to right. Targets can include your assailant's carotid artery, axillary artery, brachial, radial or ulnar arteries, triceps, femoral artery, back of knee, and wrist flexor.

*Angle Seven* is a linear stab. Anatomical targets include the assailant's eyes, ear canal, lateral side of the head, throat, heart, back of neck, and groin.

*Angle Eight* is a downward vertical slash or stab. Targets can include your assailant's eyes, back of neck, carotid artery, subclavian artery, throat, brachial, radial or ulnar arteries, triceps, femoral artery, back of knee, and wrist flexor.

*Angle Nine* is an upward vertical slash or stab. Targets can include your assailant's throat, heart, carotid artery, axillary artery, brachial, radial or ulnar arteries, triceps, femoral artery, groin, back of knee, and wrist flexor.

## 696. WEAR LEATHER.

Leather is a knife fighter's armor because it is surprisingly resistant to cuts. When on the town, wear a thick and loose-fitting leather jacket.

## 697. PUSH-OFF.

Stabbing is not just a matter of thrusting and retracting your knife. You must be aware potential problems that come with stabbing your adversary in a knife fight. More specifically, you must be cognizant of retracting the blade after penetrating your target.

To remedy many retraction problems, use the *push-off technique* - simply push your assailant away with your free hand as you pull out your blade. This permits a quick withdrawal and throws the assailant off balance, making his counterattack difficult. For maximum power and leverage, apply the push off with your palm up.

## 698. SPEED IS MORE IMPORTANT THAN POWER.

In knife combat, speed is much more important than power. Remember, a razor-sharp blade does not require a lot of power to cut effectively.

## 699. DON'T SHIFT YOUR WEIGHT TO YOUR REAR LEG.

When advancing in a knife fight, never shift your weight to the rear leg prior to moving forward. Shifting your weight back prior to moving forward will telegraph your movement, waste time, and propel you upward rather than forward.

## 700. MASTER ANGULAR THRUSTS.

Master angular thrusts with your knife. Angular thrusts can be delivered using either the ice-pick or hammer grip.

## 701. PULL IT THROUGH.

When slashing with your knife, always pull the blade of your knife through the target. This will maximize the penetration depth of your cut. When slashing, allow the base or *low portion* of the knife edge to make contact with the target first and then pull (draw) the rest of the blade through.

## 702. EMPLOY THE SAFETY CHECK AFTER THE MEET.

*The meet* is a defensive technique applied in both the mid and close-quarter knife ranges. Its primary function is to intercept your assailant's line of attack with a slash to his wrist. Since you are still positioned in your assailant's line of attack, be certain to use a safety check to prevent the assailant's knife from following through.

## 703. TRY TO ESCAPE IF POSSIBLE.

If you have the chance to run and escape during the course of a knife fight, do it immediately! Quickly try to scan your environment for possible escape routes. Look for doors, windows, stairwells, or other avenues of safe escape. Under no circumstances should you engage in a knife fight unless it is absolutely necessary. Don't let your ego or pride trap you into believing that it's cowardly to run. *WARNING: If you attempt to outrun your adversary, be certain that you have the athletic ability to really move - and don't offer him target opportunities in your flight.*

## 704. USE THE MODIFIED ICE-PICK GRIP.

If your knife is not designed with a protective hilt, then the *modified ice-pick grip* should be the preferred grip when violently stabbing into your assailant. The thumb positioning on the modified ice-pick grip helps prevent your hand from accidentally slipping onto your blade.

## 705. NEVER FORGET WHAT A KNIFE FIGHT REALLY IS.

There are many words that accurately describe the nature and characteristics of a knife fight. Here are a few: brutal, vicious, unpredictable, unfair, hazardous, menacing, precarious, treacherous, uncertain, unsafe, quick, swift, nonstop, variable, cruel, deadly, fierce, barbarous, exhausting, difficult, ugly, graceless, grisly, and gruesome.

## 706. THROW HIM OFF BALANCE.

One of the other strategic benefits behind the "secondary hand" is that it can throw your assailant off balance.

## 707. MASTER THE PASS.

*The pass* is a defensive technique that can be executed in the mid and long knife range. Like the meet, the function of the pass is to intercept your assailant's line of attack with a cut to his wrist. When employing this defensive maneuver, be certain to lean back and angle your torso away from your assailant's strike. Generally, when employing the pass (at long- knife range), there is no need for a safety check.

## 708. MASTER THE FOLLOW.

Another defensive technique used in the mid to long range of knife combat is *the follow*. Like the pass, the follow requires you to lean back and angle your torso away from your assailant's strike. However, instead of cutting your adversary's wrist, you execute a backhand cut to his hand.

## 709. CUT AND MOVE.

As in unarmed combat, you must be able to cut your adversary and move at the same time without any preliminary movements.

## KNIFE DEFENSE & KNIFE FIGHTING

### 710. KNIFE FIGHTING IS A SCIENCE.

There is much more to knife fighting than simply slashing and stabbing. There are correct and incorrect methods of cutting an assailant.

### 711. CUT TIGHT AND FAST.

When executing an inward slash with your knife, avoid wide and long arcing movements. Always keep your arc tight and make your movements quick.

### 712. MASTER THE FIVE KNIFE FIGHTING PRINCIPLES.

To minimize your chances of injury and maximize your chances of survival, here are five knife fighting principles that you should follow: (1) maintain a 45-degree stance to minimize target exposure; (2) remain mobile, agile, and hostile; (3) keep your knife or edged weapon in your front hand; (4) keep your knife close to your body; (5) when your adversary attacks, try to angle yourself away from his line of attack and simultaneously cut his weapon hand.

### 713. DON'T LOCK YOUR ELBOW.

Never lock your elbow when delivering type of slashing motion. This is critical for the following reasons: (1) it makes your elbow susceptible to a dislocation, (2) the arc of your

will be longer and thus slower, (3) the arc of your slash will be telegraphic, (4) the arc of your slash will lack power and economy of motion, and (5) it offers your assailant the opportunity to counter effectively.

### 714. DON'T SLASH THE TORSO.

Slashing movements are best delivered to the assailant's arms, eyes, neck, and knee region. Avoid slashing your assailant's torso, which is best suited for thrusts and stabs.

## 715. MASTER THE INWARD SLASH.

The inward slash can be delivered at various heights and planes. It can also be employed vertically, horizontally, and diagonally.

## 716. KNOW THE DIFFERENCE.

There is a clear difference between jabbing and thrusting a knife. While both movements can puncture your assailant's body, jabbing with a knife is a quick "darting" motion that lacks the necessary force to penetrate the assailant's vital organs.

Although the thrust requires a 100-percent follow-through and deep penetration into the target, it is generally the coup de grace. When attempting to thrust your knife, be exceptionally quick about it. And don't forget that thrusting movements can be delivered at various angles to the assailant's body.

## 717. BE CAREFUL WHEN PULLING OUT.

Although thrusting motions are an essential part of a knife fighter's arsenal, beware of the following potential problems when withdrawing your knife: (1) your knife can become extremely slippery from the assailant's blood, (2) suction generates around the wound area, which can make it difficult to withdraw the blade from the assailant's body, (3) your knife can get lodged between the assailant's bones or joints, and (4) your knife can get tangled in the assailant's clothes.

To remedy many of these inherent problems, use the push-off technique - simply push your assailant away with your free hand as you pull out your blade. This permits a quick withdrawal and throws the assailant off balance, making a counterattack difficult. For maximum power and leverage, apply the push off with your palm up.

## 718. TWIST YOUR BLADE CORRECTLY.

*Blade twisting* is used after the knife is plunged into its target. This knife fighting technique is used to increase the size of the wound channel, which will result in faster blood loss and greater structural damage.

The direction that you twist your blade upon withdrawal is dependent upon the type of thrust that you deliver. For example, when delivering direct thrusts with your palm up, turn the knife counterclockwise. When delivering an inward thrust with your palm down, turn your knife clockwise.

## 719. BE CAREFUL WHEN ATTACKING HIS RIBS.

Be especially careful when thrusting your knife into your assailant's ribs. There is a distinct possibility that your blade may get lodged.

## 720. MASTER STRATEGIC LEANING.

Strategic leaning is a maneuver that permits you to evade your assailant's knife while allowing you to remain in range to counter his attack. This is particularly important when your environment won't permit you to be mobile. When performed at the proper time, strategic leaning can also increase the power of your counter cut. *WARNING: When performing the strategic lean maneuver, be especially careful not to "over lean," which will cause you to lose your balance.*

## 721. KNOW THE INSERTION POINTS.

There are specific *insertion points* on your assailant's anatomy that can be used for stabbing. Here are a few to remember: (1) ear cavities, (2) eye sockets, (3) temples, (4) base of skull, (5) cervical vertebrae, (6) jugular vein, (7) underside of the chin, (8) carotid artery, (9) subclavian artery, (10) heart, (11) lungs, (12) brachial arteries, (13) radial arteries, (14) third and fourth rib regions, (15) solar plexus, (16) groin, and (17) femoral arteries.

## 722. GRIP YOUR KNIFE PROPERLY.

A powerful and secure grip is essential for knife fighting. When gripping your knife, always make certain that the cutting edge faces your assailant. Also, be very careful not to wrap your fingers too tightly around the handle. This can be dangerous for the following reasons: (1) it restricts wrist mobility, (2) it reduces your slashing speed, (3) it weakens your forearm muscles, and (3) it creates greater target exposure by forcing your veins to protrude from your hands and forearms.

## 723. DEVELOP THESE IMPORTANT SKILLS.

There is a lot more to knife fighting than just the knife itself. The best combat knife in the world is no substitute for skill and training. A well-trained knife fighter can stab and gouge you to death with a sharp pencil. Here is just a brief list of some important skills that must be practiced with a qualified instructor: (1) concealment strategies, (2) grips and stance, (3) target orientation, (4) target selection, (5) drawing techniques, (6) target exploitation, (7) safe handling procedures, (8) footwork, (9) weapon control and retention, (10) range manipulation, (11) withdrawing skills, (12) secondary weapon training, (13) insertion points, and (14) strategic leaning.

# KNIFE DEFENSE & KNIFE FIGHTING

# TRAINING

### 724. USE REALISTIC TRAINING KNIVES.

The only effective method of developing knife fighting skills is to practice safely with a training partner. When looking to purchase training knives, avoid buying flimsy rubber knives that *wiggle* when you move them. These knives are cheap and very unrealistic. *CAUTION: Be exceptionally careful when slashing at your partner's face with a training knife. To prevent eye injuries, wear some form of eye protection.*

### 725. PRACTICE WITH YOUR WEAK HAND.

When practicing knife fighting skills, always devote sufficient time to your weak hand. As in unarmed combat, ambidexterity is an invaluable skill. Here are just a few reasons why it should be developed: (1) there is a possibility that your strong hand might be injured in a knife fight, (2) it enhances your overall combat confidence, (3) it reinforces good combat skills, and (4) your strong hand might be occupied during the fight.

### 726. PRACTICE IN FRONT OF A MIRROR.

In front of a mirror, practice linear and lateral footwork movements with a training knife in your hand. This should be performed in both your right and left stances. Be aware of your stance as you move, keep your weight evenly distributed, keep your balance, and stay relaxed. This should be practiced on all different types of terrain (wet grass, mud, ice, wet pavement, snow, gravel, and sand).

*Hard rubber knives are ideal for fixed blade training.*

### 727. PRACTICE KNIFE FIGHTING ON THE GROUND.

Practice knife fighting skills while ground fighting with your training partner. Practice from a variety of postures and positions.

### 728. MAKE IT INSTINCTUAL.

You must practice the knife fighting stance until it becomes instinctual. This means that you will have to practice in front of a full-length mirror. Scrutinize yourself and pick out the strategic deficiencies. For example, what targets are exposed? Is your balance sacrificed? Are your knees bent?

### 729. MASTER DRAWING SKILLS.

Spend adequate time learning how to draw your knife quickly and efficiently from both the standing and seated position. When standing, avoid using the cross-draw technique, which allows your adversary the opportunity to immobilize your drawing arm temporarily.

# KNIFE DEFENSE & KNIFE FIGHTING

## 730. DEVELOP SECONDARY HAND SKILLS.

You must learn to practice quick slashing movements with your secondary hand closely trailing your blade. This can be practiced and refined in front of a full-length mirror.

## 731. TIME YOURSELF.

Occasionally use a stopwatch to see how quickly you can open a lock blade. Time yourself with both your right and left hands.

## 732. PRACTICE IN CLOSE QUARTERS.

Learn how to use your knife in close-quarter environments. Here are just a few examples: (1) in your car, (2) in an elevator, (3) on a bridge, (4) in a narrow hallway, (5) in a doorway, (6) in a bathroom stall, (7) in a crowd, (8) in a cluttered garage, (9) on a narrow stairwell, and (10) between shrubbery.

### 733. USE PETROLEUM JELLY

If you want to replicate the sweat, blood and grim that often accompanies a knife fight, rub a liberal amount of petroleum jelly on your hands prior to knife training. Not only will this test the integrity of your grip, it will also teach you how to improvise your knife fighting skills when faced with adverse conditions.

Just remember, this type of knife fighting training is very challenging and should only be used by experienced practitioners who possess a strong foundation in edged weapon combat.

### 734. TAKE CARE OF YOUR KNIFE.

Like any tool used for combat, your knife will require a bit of care and maintenance. Proper maintenance of your knife will ensure that it will work effectively when needed. Here are four important guidelines: (1) keep your blade clean at all times, (2) don't use your knife as a pry bar or chisel, (3) keep your knife lubricated if it's a lock blade, and (4) always keep your knife razor sharp.

# CHAPTER EIGHT
## Firearms & Combat Shooting

*"A firearm places you in the position of judge, jury, and executioner, all in a matter of seconds."*

FIREARMS & COMBAT SHOOTING

# OWNERSHIP

### 735. SUPPORT THE SECOND AMENDMENT.

The Second Amendment reads, *"A well regulated militia, being necessary to the security of a free state, the right of the people to keep and bear arms, shall not be infringed."* Each and every American citizen has a responsibility to protect and defend the Constitution of the United States, especially the Second Amendment right of the individual to keep and bear arms.

### 736. THINK SERIOUSLY ABOUT IT.

The decision to own a firearm warrants considerable thought and honest reflection. Here are some important questions to ask yourself: (1) Do you abuse alcohol or use drugs? (2) Are you hot tempered? (3) Could you take the life of another person? (4) Do you experience long periods of depression? (5) Do you live alone? (6) Do children live in your household? (7) Why do you want to own a firearm? (8) Have you ever shot a gun? (9) Are you a disorganized person? (10) Are you clumsy or accident-prone? (11) Are you willing to take the time to obtain the knowledge, skills, and attitude needed to handle firearms safely?

### 737. DO YOUR HOMEWORK.

Before you purchase a firearm, it's important that you do your homework. With so many firearms on the market, it is difficult to make a choice. Nevertheless, there are some questions that you should ask yourself that will help you with your selection. What purpose will the gun serve? Will it be used for hunting, collecting, target practice, or self-defense? Are you interested in purchasing a shotgun, autoloader, or revolver? How much money are you willing to spend? Will you be carrying the firearm, and how will you carry it?

Also consider the following tips before purchasing a gun for self-defense: (1) get advice from firearm experts, knowledgeable police officers, and reputable dealers; (2) familiarize yourself with the various models on the market; (3) read gun magazines, books, and articles and find out which guns have the greatest practicality for your use; (4) read the warranty or guarantee that comes with the firearm; (5) look for high-quality brand-name firearms; (6) be aware of the gun's recoil before you buy it; (7) buy the firearm from a reputable dealer; (8) be certain the gun fits comfortably in your hand; (9) look for a gun that is easy to clean and operate; and (10) be certain the caliber of the weapon has sufficient stopping power.

### 738. KNOW THE FIREARM LAWS.

Before you purchase a firearm, it's your responsibility to understand and obey the various laws governing its use, possession, and transportation. Such laws vary from state to state and city to city, so learn the ones that apply to you and your community. Your local police or sheriff's department can help you.

### 739. CHOOSE YOUR RESIDENCE CAREFULLY.

If at all possible, try to avoid living in a country, state, or city that prohibits firearm ownership. Move if you can.

# GUN SAFETY

### 740. DON'T BE CARELESS

Never forget that the two major causes of firearm accidents are ignorance and carelessness. *Ignorance* means that you are unaware of the firearm safety rules, and *carelessness* means that you are knowledgeable of firearm safety rules but fail to apply them.

### 741. TAKE A FIREARM SAFETY COURSE.

Don't even think about owning a gun unless you have successfully completed a firearm safety course, been extensively trained in its use, and have developed the necessary confidence and proficiency.

### 742. KNOW THE FIREARM SAFETY RULES.

Safe gun handling is your responsibility, and safety must always be your concern. To ensure the safe use of any firearm, always follow these four primary safety rules: (1) take a firearm safety course before you acquire a firearm, (2) always assume that a firearm is loaded, (3) always point a firearm in a safe direction, (4) always be certain of your target, and (5) never put your finger on the trigger until you are ready to shoot. Other gun safety rules include the following:

- Read the owner's manual that comes with your firearm.
- Be sure the barrel of your gun is clear of obstructions.
- Use clean, factory-made ammunition of the proper caliber.
- Wear ear protection and safety glasses when practicing.
- Do not leave a loaded gun unattended.
- Never trust a safety.
- Never use alcohol or drugs before or while shooting.
- Never allow your firearm to be used by anyone who is not knowledgeable of the safety rules.
- Before cleaning your firearm, make sure that the chamber is empty and be absolutely certain it's unloaded.
- Always keep ammunition away from the cleaning area.

- Store guns so they're not accessible to others.
- Be certain your firearm is safe to operate.
- Comply with the safety regulations of your firing range.

### 743. KNOW THE MOST IMPORTANT SAFETY RULE.

Although all of the firearm safety rules are important, never forget the most important rule: *Always point a firearm in a safe direction.* This way, if the firearm is discharged unintentionally, it will not cause injury or death.

### 744. OBEY THE FIRING RANGE SAFETY COMMANDS.

A properly supervised firing range is essential. Every shooter is personally responsible for understanding and obeying all of the range commands. The standard range commands include the following: (1) load - when the shooter is on the firing line, he may load his weapon; (2) commence fire - the shooter may begin firing the weapon when he is ready; (3) cease fire - the shooter must stop firing the firearm immediately.

### 745. DON'T MAKE GUNS A TABOO SUBJECT.

If you own a gun and have kids, then it's your responsibility to be a positive role model for your children. You should talk openly about guns with your children. Making guns a taboo subject can elicit children's curiosity and possibly lead them to investigate guns on their own. Even if you're not a gun owner, your son or daughter may one day come in contact with a firearm at a relative or friend's house.

The best time to talk about firearms is when your child begins to show interest, e.g., when your child begins to act out gun scenes or ask questions. The amount of information and training that you give your child will depend upon the following factors: (1) the child's age, (2) the child's level of maturity, and (3) the child's ability to reason. When discussing guns with your child, be certain to answer all questions. If you don't know the answers to particular questions, speak with a qualified firearms instructor.

### 746. KEEP IT CLEAN.

Always keep your weapon clean. Cleaning your firearm is important for the following reasons: (1) it will ensure that your weapon will operate properly and safely when fired, (2) it will help maintain the weapon's value, (3) it will help extend the life of the weapon, and (4) it will allow you the opportunity to inspect your gun for proper functioning.

You will need the following materials to clean your gun properly: cleaning rod, cleaning rod attachment, bore brush, cleaning patch, bore cleaner solvent, gun oil, cleaning cloth, old toothbrush, and Q-tips. *WARNING: Before cleaning your firearm, be certain that it is unloaded, the action is open, and there is no ammunition present. After cleaning the firearm, always check to make sure that no cleaning patch or other obstruction is in the bore or chamber.*

# FACTS

### 747. IF IT'S UNLOADED, IT'S USELESS.

When it comes to personal protection, never forget that an unloaded firearm is a useless firearm.

### 748. DON'T BLAME GUNS, BLAME PEOPLE.

Guns are neither good nor evil. They are simply neutral tools that can either be abused or used to protect property and lives.

## 749. ABILITY OVERRIDES THE WEAPON.

Most people don't understand that it is really not the firearm that is important, but the skill and ability of the person operating the weapon. *Remember, a firearm is only as effective as the person who uses it.*

## 750. LOOKOUT FOR CONCEALED WEAPON CARRY.

Criminals do not usually carry their guns in holsters. Train yourself to immediately spot unusual bulges and people who seem to be performing security body pats.

## 751. THEY SHOOT BACK.

Combat is often very disjointed, hard to understand, and confusing. A gunfight is nothing like what you see in the movies or video games. It is not romantic or antiseptic. It is horrifying, brutal, confusing, rapid, bloody, and final. And although practice is essential, never forget that training at a firing range has little to do with the explosive dynamics of a lethal gunfight. And, most important, in a real encounter, the targets move and shoot back.

## 752. HANDGUNS ARE SUPERIOR.

In most armed self-defense situations, the handgun (autoloader and revolver) is superior to a long gun. Here are just a few reasons why: (1) unlike rifles and shotguns, handguns can be drawn and fired more quickly with practice and training; (2) handguns can be transported more easily; (3) handguns are smaller and can be concealed better; (4) in a close-quarter struggle, long guns can be disarmed more easily than handguns; (5) handguns can, if necessary, be shot with just one hand; and (6) handguns can be holstered, allowing you to utilize other "use-of-force" options and tactics on your adversary.

# NOMENCLATURE AND MECHANICS

### 753. KNOW WHAT YOU'RE TALKING ABOUT.

Understand the nomenclature of your firearm. The following are some basic terms that you should understand clearly: (1) for the revolver - muzzle, barrel, front and rear sights, ejector rod, cylinder, trigger and trigger guard, frame, grip, cylinder release latch, hammer spur, hammer, firing pin, and chambers; (2) for the autoloader - magazine, cartridge ejection port, slide, grip, frame, front and rear sights, hammer, trigger, trigger guard, recoil spring, slide catch lever, and magazine floor plate.

### 754. KNOW THE DIFFERENCE BETWEEN A SEMIAUTOMATIC AND A REVOLVER.

A true combatant must understand the mechanical difference between a revolver and a semiautomatic pistol. The semiautomatic, or autoloader, differs from the revolver in many ways. They are called *semiautomatics* because when fired, they automatically feed a fresh round and eject the spent casing. All you have to do is keep squeezing the trigger. With the autoloader, rounds of ammunition are loaded vertically in a metal container called the *magazine*. The magazine is then inserted into the grip of the gun. Generally, autoloaders are slightly more complicated to operate than their revolver cousins.

Although the revolver is not the most efficient handgun for an armed encounter with a criminal assailant, it still has its place in the world of self-defense. This type of handgun is called a revolver because its cylinder revolves when the trigger is pulled. Revolvers can hold anywhere from five to nine cartridges, depending on the type of cylinder. They also come in single-action (you have to cock the hammer before it can be fired) or double-action (you just squeeze the trigger). Loading a revolver is generally safe and simple, and you can easily tell when it is loaded. They almost never jam, and they can be trusted to fire effectively.

*Pictured here, the revolver.*

### 755. CHOOSE THE SEMIAUTOMATIC.

When compared to the revolver, the *semiautomatic pistol* is the superior weapon for armed combat for several reasons: (1) it has a larger ammunition capacity, (2) it is faster firing (because of the single-action trigger pull), (3) it is faster reloading, (4) it has greater hit potential, (5) it is more accurate, (6) it has greater control, (7) it has lighter trigger pull, (8) it has less kick or recoil than revolvers of equal stopping power, (9) it is more comfortable—the hand grip designs on most semiautomatic pistols tend to fit more comfortably in the hand, and (10) clearing malfunctions are quicker to remedy than with revolvers.

# FIREARMS & COMBAT SHOOTING

*Pictured here, the semiautomatic.*

## 756. GET A BENELLI M4.

If you're looking to own a combat shotgun and money isn't an issue, consider the *Benelli M4 tactical shotgun*. This semi-automatic shotgun is a beast of a weapon, and considered by many (including myself) to be the "king of shotguns". It's no surprise the Benelli M4 was adopted by the armed forces of the United States, Italy, and United Kingdom, and has proved itself in numerous military conflicts.

*Pictured here, the Benelli M4 Combat Shotgun.*

## 757. LEARN CARTRIDGE COMPONENTS.

The more you know about firearms, the better. For example, know the component parts of a pistol *cartridge*. A pistol cartridge consists of the following four components: (1) case - a metal cylinder that is closed at one end, (2) primer - an impact- sensitive chemical compound, (3) powder charge -

a quick-burning chemical compound used as a propellant, and (4) bullet - a projectile that travels at great velocity.

### 758. UNDERSTAND FIREARM MECHANICS.

Understanding the various mechanics of a firearm can go a long way. For example, is there a safety on the assailant's weapon? Is his weapon cocked to single-action, or is it in the double-action mode? Are cartridges visible in the cylinder of his revolver? Is the slide of his autoloader locked back to the rear? What do the different types of autoloader malfunctions look like? How many rounds did he fire versus the number of rounds that are available? How can you induce a malfunction in his weapon (e.g., by pushing back on the slide and stopping the cylinder from turning, etc.)?

### 759. DON'T TRUST YOUR SAFETY.

Never trust the safety on your gun. Like any mechanical device, a safety can fail.

# AMMUNITION

### 760. AMMUNITION CRITERIA MATTERS.

When selecting a self-defense cartridge for your gun, make certain that your ammunition fulfills these five requirements: (1) stopping power - it must be able to stop your assailant immediately from any further action; (2) controlled recoil - it should allow you to recover quickly from the recoil of your shot; (3) limited ricochet - it should reduce the bullet's ability to ricochet off hard surfaces; (4) maximum penetration - it must be able to go through objects (e.g., car doors, furniture, etc.); (5) reliability - it must be free from various cartridge malfunctions (e.g., hang fire, misfire, or squib loads).

## 761. STORE IT SAFELY.

When storing ammunition, please take the following factors into consideration: (1) always store your cartridges in a cool, dry place that is free from extremely high temperatures; (2) never submerge your cartridges in water or expose them to ammonia, bore cleaner, acids, salts, or petroleum products (including gun oil) - all solvents that can deteriorate the primer or power in your cartridge; and (3) for safety reasons, store ammunition so that it is inaccessible to unauthorized persons, especially children.

## 762. ROTATE SPARE MAGAZINES.

Long-term compression of the magazine spring in your autoloader can prevent proper cartridge feeding. This is otherwise known as *spring set.* Here are two suggestions that will help prevent unnecessary magazine spring stress in your semiautomatic pistol: (1) get into the habit of rotating your spare magazines every three months and (2) don't load your magazine to full capacity; leave at least one round out.

*Remember to rotate your spare magazine every three months.*

## 763. CHOOSE YOUR CALIBER CAREFULLY.

Don't use a .38 or .22 caliber pistol for personal protection.

Its stopping power is questionable. Generally, when selecting a handgun for self-defense, choose a 9mm or higher caliber.

### 764. KNOW THE CARTRIDGE FIRING SEQUENCE.

Although it is critical to know how a firearm operates, it's also important to understand the cartridge firing sequence, which is as follows: (1) the firing pin strikes the cartridge primer, (2) the cartridge primer ignites, (3) the primer flame ignites the powder charge, (4) the powder charge burns quickly and produces a large volume of gas, and (5) the expanding gases push the bullet out of the cartridge case and sends it out of the barrel at a high rate of speed.

## MALFUNCTIONS

### 765. CARTRIDGES CAN MALFUNCTION.

There are three different types of cartridge malfunctions that you need to be aware of. They include (1) misfire - the cartridge fails to fire after the primer has been struck by the firing pin; (2) hang fire - there is a delay in the ignition of the cartridge when the primer is struck; (3) squib load - there is less than normal pressure/velocity after the ignition of the cartridge.

### 766. TAP-RACK-BANG.

There may come a time when you will be faced with a malfunction caused by either a defective cartridge or a magazine that isn't inserted completely. When this problem occurs, you can solve it with the following *tap-rack-bang* technique: (1) tap - with your weak hand, tap the floor plate of the magazine back into the grip; (2) rack - with your weak hand, rack or cycle the slide, ejecting the defective cartridge and reloading a fresh one; (3) bang - resume firing your weapon.

### 767. PREPARE FOR AUTOLOADER MALFUNCTIONS.

Although the semiautomatic pistol is an extremely reliable tool, there is always the possibility of a malfunction. You must therefore be aware of the different types of autoloader malfunctions and know their remedies.

(1) Out of battery - occurs when the slide fails to go into battery after firing. To clear this malfunction, apply the following steps: a) maintain your position on your target; b) take your finger off the trigger; c) with your weak hand, slam the back of the slide with the heel of your palm; and d) resume firing.

(2) Smokestack - occurs when a spent casing is caught in the ejection port. To clear this malfunction, apply the following steps: a) maintain your position on your target; b) take your finger off the trigger; c) with your weak hand, rake the heel of your palm along the slide and the empty casing; d) knock the casing out of the breech; e) once the casing is clear, the slide should move forward, cycling a fresh round; and f) resume firing.

# FUNDAMENTALS

### 768. MASTER FIREARM FUNDAMENTALS.

If you intend to rely on a firearm for self-defense, be certain to develop proficiency in each of the following aspects of marksmanship: (1) grip, (2) stance, (3) sight alignment, (4) trigger squeeze, (5) breath control, and (6) follow-through.

## 769. IT ISN'T EASY.

It's difficult to apply the fundamentals consciously in a gunfight. Firearm fundamentals must be instinctive and automatic. Keep in mind that if you have to think about them, you may lose the opportunity to fire in a timely manner.

## 770. AIM WITH YOUR DOMINANT EYE.

When shooting a firearm, always aim with your dominant eye. To determine which is your dominant eye, perform the following exercise: (1) extend both of your arms in front of you; (2) place your hands together, forming a small hole between them; (3) keep both of your eyes open and look through the hole at a distant object; (4) while looking at the distant object, slowly move your hands back until they touch your face; and (5) the hole between both of your hands will be over one eye - this will be your dominant eye for shooting.

## 771. LEARN SIGHT ALIGNMENT.

*Sight alignment* is another critical aspect of marksmanship. It is achieved by correctly aligning your dominant eye with both the front and rear sights. To achieve proper sight alignment, first align the top of your front sight so that it is even with the top of your rear sight, and then make certain that the top of your front sight is centered in the notch of your rear sight. *REMEMBER: Correct sight alignment is the key to accuracy. Misalignment of the front and rear sights will produce an angular error that will be multiplied with distance.*

## 772. ACCEPT THE ARC OF MOVEMENT.

It's practically impossible to hold a perfect sight picture. There will always be some motion. Accept the fact that you will never eliminate this "arc of movement" when aiming.

# FIREARMS & COMBAT SHOOTING

### 773. UTILIZE FOLLOW-THROUGH.

*Follow-through*, an important element of marksmanship, simply means continuing to employ the shooting fundamentals throughout the delivery of your shot. This is critical because it aids in preventing any unnecessary movement before the bullet exits the barrel. Moreover, it enhances recoil recovery and provides for effective follow-up shots, if needed.

### 774. DON'T PULL, SQUEEZE.

Another important component of marksmanship is the *trigger squeeze*. The trigger squeeze is achieved by squeezing the trigger of your gun straight to the rear in a smooth and fluid manner without disturbing the sight alignment. *REMEMBER: Finger placement is a critical element of trigger squeeze. Prior to taking your shot, make sure the trigger rests halfway between the tip of your index finger and the first joint.*

### 775. CONCENTRATE ON THE FRONT SIGHT.

The human eye is only capable of focusing on one object at a time. With your dominant eye properly focused, you should see the following: (1) the front sight should be clear and sharp, (2) the rear sight should appear less sharp, and (3) your target should look blurred. *REMEMBER: If you want an accurate shot, it's critical to concentrate primarily on the front sight.*

### 776. THE TWO MOST IMPORTANT FUNDAMENTALS.

Never forget that the two most important fundamentals of marksmanship are sight alignment and trigger squeeze.

### 777. GOOD SURVIVAL TACTICS ARE CRITICAL.

Although marksmanship skills are the key to surviving armed encounters, they cannot replace good survival tactics.

Marksmanship ability degenerates under the stress of combat, but good tactics compensate for this.

# POSITIONS, STANCES, & GRIPS

### 778. MASTER THE STANDING TWO-HAND STANCE.

Work on perfecting the *standing two-hand firearm stance* until it is quick and natural. This stance is ideal because it's comfortable and balanced, and it controls the weapon's recoil, minimizes target exposure, and allows you to move in a 180-degree traverse.

There are several important elements to this two-handed firearm stance: (1) keep your feet approximately shoulder-width apart, with both knees slightly bent; (2) blade your stance with your strong side behind; (3) aggressively lean your body weight forward; (4) slightly bend your gun hand, pushing it forward; (5) bend your supporting arm, pulling inward with the elbow pointing to the ground; and (6) grip your handgun tightly with the thumb-to-thumb, knuckle-to-knuckle placement.

### 779. USE THE AGGRESSIVE FORWARD LEAN.

When shooting with a two-handed combat stance, adopt an *aggressive forward lean*. This type of body posture aids in controlling the weapon's recoil and helps maintain target acquisition and sight alignment.

## 780. SHOOT FROM THE KNEELING POSITION.

Shooting from the *kneeling position* gives you a strong advantage in a gunfight. Here are just a few reasons why: (1) it minimizes excessive muscle tremors, (2) it allows you to fire your weapon from behind a low or high barricade position, (3) it reduces your target exposure, and (4) it is one of the most secure combat shooting positions and can be maintained for a prolonged period.

The kneeling position can be executed by applying the following: (1) drop your strong knee to the ground with your weak knee pointed upward; (2) keep your weak foot flat on the ground and the ball of your strong foot on the ground; (3) keep your torso and head erect; (4) keep your gun arm slightly bent and pushed forward; (5) keep your supporting arm bent, pulling inward with the elbow pointing to the ground; (6) grip your handgun tightly with the thumb-to-thumb, knuckle-to-knuckle placement; and (7) to minimize recoil, lean your torso slightly forward. Develop the combat kneeling position until it's quick and natural. *WARNING: When assuming the kneeling position, avoid touching your supporting elbow to your knee. This elbow-to-knee placement hinders your ability to traverse to your flanks, and limits your shot angle.*

## 781. SHOOT AT VARIOUS LEVELS.

Combat shooting should be practiced from the following four levels: (1) hip level - one and two hand grip, (2) chest level - one and two hand grip, (3) point shoulder level - one and two hand grip, and (4) sighted level (point shoulder level) - two hand grip.

## 782. SHOOT FROM THE PRONE POSITION.

Learning to shoot from the *prone position* is important for the following reasons: (1) it dramatically minimizes target exposure, (2) it provides the most stable firing position, (3) it provides practice in seeking cover (e.g., when faced with suppression fire), (4) it gets you accustomed to situations where you might be injured and forced to the ground, and (5) it provides the best protection when there is no cover.

To shoot from the prone position, do the following: (1) roll onto the strong side of your body while positioning your body at 45 degrees; (2) if you're right-handed, bring your weak knee up and to the left; (3) extend your gun hand straight to your target and use your weak hand for support (the knife- hand edge of both hands should be flush with the ground); (4) place your cheek on the shoulder/biceps region of your arm; and (5) relax your body and get a secure grip on your weapon.

*Pictured here, the prone position.*

## 783. THUMB-TO-THUMB, KNUCKLE-TO-KNUCKLE GRIP.

Learn the proper way to grip your firearm. To achieve a proper two-hand grip, follow these guidelines: (1) fit the web of your dominant hand as high as possible on the back strap area of the frame, (2) align your wrist and forearm with the back strap of the frame, (3) control the pressure of the grip with your thumb and the lower three fingers of your shooting hand, (4) overlap your non dominant hand over your shooting hand (thumb-to-thumb and knuckle-to-knuckle), and grip your weapon tightly.

*Pictured here, the thumb-to-thumb, knuckle-to-knuckle grip.*

## 784. GRIP IT TIGHTLY.

When holding your autoloader, always grip the weapon tightly. This is important for the following reasons: (1) it helps to control the action of the weapon, (2) it aids in controlling the recoil of the firearm, (3) it helps prevent inaccurate shooting, and (4) it prevents "limp wrist" malfunctions.

## 785. DON'T EXTEND YOUR INDEX FINGER.

When holding your handgun in a stalking situation, avoid extending your index finger along the frame of the weapon. This is dangerous for the following reasons: (1) the extended index finger usually catches the trigger guard, slowing down finger-to-trigger placement; (2) it can cause an accidental discharge of your weapon; (3) the extended finger has been known to depress the slide stop stud accidentally on some autoloaders, causing possible malfunctions; (4) the anatomical placement of the index finger lacks overall economy of motion when firing becomes necessary; and (5) if your assailant attempts to disarm you by twisting the weapon out of your hand, he can easily break your index finger.

To remedy the problem of the extended index finger, employ the bent-finger position. This finger placement permits quick and accurate finger-to-trigger placement, minimizes unintentional weapon discharge, and reduces the possibility of injury if a struggle ensues between you and your adversary.

*The bent-finger placement is ideal because it permits quick and accurate finger-to-trigger placement, minimizes unintentional weapon discharge, and reduces the possibility of injury if a struggle ensues between you and your adversary.*

### 786. UNIFORMITY IS CRITICAL.

One of the most important and often neglected components of a proper pistol grip is *uniformity*, which means that you grip your firearm the same way every time. This ensures consistent accuracy.

# FIREARMS & COMBAT SHOOTING

# TARGETS

### 787. GO FOR THE IMMEDIATE STOP.

If you are looking for instant stopping power, aim for his head, specifically the center of the bridge of the nose or the ear for side shots. Here are a few good reasons why you should choose the head as a target: (1) if the adversary is wearing body armor; (2) if the assailant's head is the only available target during the encounter; and (3) if the assailant is high on psychoactive drugs (e.g., PCP). *CAUTION: Beware, however, because the head is a smaller and more difficult target to hit, and in some situations bullets have been known to deflect off the skull.*

### 788. SHOOT CENTER OF MASS.

Although the assailant's head is the most effective target for an immediate stop, the center of his body is probably your best choice. Shooting *center mass* is preferred over the head for the following reasons: (1) the assailant's upper torso is the largest target area and usually the easiest to hit in a stress fire situation, and (2) center mass also contains a large majority of your assailant's vital organs. *REMEMBER: When firing center mass, keep shooting as quickly and as accurately as possible until your assailant ceases to be a threat.*

### 789. SHOOT BELOW THE WAIST.

Body armor will render your center mass shots ineffective. If your assailant is wearing body armor, shoot below his waist. Shooting at the assailant's pelvic area can be fatal and will certainly knock his legs out from under him.

# TACTICS AND TECHNIQUES

### 790. MASTER TRAVERSING SKILLS.

*Traversing* is an essential component of street combat shooting, and it's particularly important when you're confronted with multiple assailants who try to outflank you. Traversing can be employed while standing and kneeling. However, the two key points to traversing while standing are: (1) keeping your knees bent and flexible, and (2) twisting freely at your waist.

### 791. DON'T BECOME DEPENDENT ON YOUR FIREARM.

A firearm is an awesome tool. However, don't make the tragic mistake of assuming that the mere possession of a gun will guarantee your safety. This erroneous assumption forms the common fallacy of dependency. *Dependency* is the sole reliance on a particular weapon for self-defense. Remember, no single weapon is the definitive answer to self-defense. The bottom line is that only you can accept the full responsibility for your protection, and you must have a variety of self-defense measures to meet myriad potential threats. You must be equipped and prepared to rely on all available means, but, most importantly, you must rely on your own intelligence.

### 792. DON'T BLUFF.

Never point a firearm at anyone unless you are technically and psychologically prepared to take a life.

### 793. DOUBLE-TAP.

When firing in self-defense, always assume that your first shot missed and deliver an immediate second round. This is known as the *double-tap* principle. Remember, it is just as easy to squeeze a trigger twice as once. The double-tap principle is important for the following two reasons: (1) it ensures more potential hits and (2) it creates greater wound damage and thus greater stopping potential.

### 794. DON'T MISS.

Accuracy is everything in a gunfight. Remember, it isn't the first loud noise that ends the encounter. It's the first effective round that matters.

### 795. NEVER SURRENDER YOUR WEAPON.

If a friend or loved one is ever held at gunpoint and you are in a standoff, <u>never surrender your firearm</u>. This immediately places the fate of both you and your loved one in the hands of a criminal.

### 796. MAKE IT ACCESSIBLE.

If you own a firearm for home protection, make certain it is easily accessible in an emergency situation. Consider keeping a push-button strong box by your bed, and be capable of opening it quickly in the dark.

### 797. DON'T RUSH THE FIREFIGHT.

During a firefight, don't rush or give up cover. Be patient and systematic. Remember, just one tactical mistake might cost you your life!

### 798. MASTER THE QUICK PEEK.

The *quick-peek* technique is executed from a position of cover by rapidly darting out a small portion of your head and one eye to observe. It's important that you never perform the quick peek twice at the same height. If your assailant sees the first quick peek, he may aim at its last location. Therefore, if your first quick peek is high and a second one is needed, then peek low. *WARNING: Firearm position and foot placement are critical when performing the quick-peek technique. A protruding foot or firearm can give you away to the criminal.*

### 799. BEWARE OF THE "FATAL FUNNEL."

The *fatal funnel* is a danger area that is created by such openings as doorways, windows, hallways, and stairwells. These locations are dangerous because they are "choke points" that constrict your movement, and they usually provide no cover. Two of the safest methods of moving through the fatal funnel are the crisscross and button hook maneuvers.

### 800. CRISSCROSS.

The *crisscross* is an entry maneuver that allows you to travel across a threshold quickly while employing a correct ready-weapon position. To execute the crisscross maneuver, apply the following steps: (1) start with your firearm in the proper ready position - your gun hand should be farther away from the wall with the muzzle pointed at the door and securely tucked back; (2) place the foot that is closer to the wall forward, which permits your rear foot to take the first step across the threshold and places your body at a protective angle in the fatal funnel (or threshold); (3) maintain the correct weapon position and move quickly through the fatal funnel; and (4) clear to the corner of the room and assume a two-hand hold or kneeling position.

### 801. MASTER THE LIMITED PENETRATION.

The *limited penetration* (LP) is a corner-clearing movement performed by positioning your firearm and one eye around the corner. The tactical advantage of the limited penetration is that it offers maximum cover and provides a good observation point. The limited penetration is generally executed after a quick peek has revealed the presence of a threatening assailant around the corner. If you determine that no threat is around the corner, maintain the limited penetration to (1) observe and (2) deny mobility. If a firefight ensues, maintain the limited penetration until your immediate threat is removed.

## 802. MASTER THE SIDE FALL.

The *side fall* is an engagement technique that is executed from a kneeling position behind cover. It requires you to perform a controlled fall, allowing only minimal head and muzzle exposure around a corner. To perform the side fall maneuver, execute the following steps.

(1) Begin on one knee with your downed knee closer to the corner.

(2) Make certain your firearm is positioned on the same side as your downed knee, which permits you to fall correctly.

(3) Always maintain a constant ready-weapon position at the corner in case your assailant should appear.

(4) From the kneeling position, drop to the side of your body, making certain to land in sequence - on your calf, hip, then shoulder blade. Keep your firearm tucked back, and during the fall thrust your arms forward in a two-hand hold. Try to prevent your elbows from hitting the ground, as this will disturb your point of aim.

(5) Engage the enemy with fire.

(6) To recover from the side-fall position, quickly tuck your lower leg under your upper leg, then perform a kicking motion with your upper leg and rock your body back to the original kneeling position. Be certain your weapon is back in the ready position.

## 803. COVER VERSUS CONCEALMENT.

Make certain that you know the difference between cover and concealment. *Cover* is any object that protects you from gunfire. *Concealment* makes you invisible to your adversary and often allows you the element of tactical surprise; however, it does not necessarily protect you from gunfire.

## 804. BE COVER CONSCIOUS.

Always remember that your first move in a firefight is to take cover and maintain it. Cover is simply a feature or location that temporarily protects you from gunfire. Taking cover in a gunfight is important for the following reasons: (1) it protects you from the assailant's gunfire; (2) it buys you some time to identify the location of the gunfire; (3) it allows you to assess the situation from a position of safety; (4) it allows you to return fire from a relatively safe position; and (5) cover can be used to stabilize your weapon when shooting. Some of the best objects of cover include the engine block of a car, a large rock, the corner of a building, a large concrete utility pole, and concrete steps. Remember, always try to question or challenge your adversary from a position of cover. This added security measure can save your life.

## 805. DON'T RELY ON THESE OBJECTS.

When taking cover in a gunfight, avoid the tragic error of choosing the following objects: (1) internal doors, (2) small trees, (3) car doors, (4) glass windows, (5) drywall, (6) tall grass, (7) car trunks, (8) overturned tables, (9) trash cans, (10) shrubbery, and (11) fences.

## 806. WEAPON POSITION IS CRITICAL.

Since many firefights are spontaneous and occur at close range, don't stalk your assailant with your muzzle pointed up

FIREARMS & COMBAT SHOOTING

or down (low point hold). Furthermore, avoid holding your handgun with both of your arms extended out and locked. This positioning leaves you vulnerable to a sudden grab or disarm maneuver from the assailant. Always have your weapon in a ready weapon position that is close to your torso and be prepared for sudden engagement. The ready weapon position will facilitate immediate firing capability, maximize weapon retention, and, most importantly, allow for quick target acquisition.

**807. NEVER SPRAY AND PRAY.**

If you are ever involved in a gunfight and innocent bystanders are present, never fire your weapon unless you are absolutely certain that you will hit your target. Remember, precision with a firearm is critical.

**808. WHAT YOU CAN'T SEE MAY KILL YOU.**

In a gunfight, just because you can't see your assailant doesn't mean that he can't see you. Always remember to find and use good cover. Until you locate your assailant, be reluctant to move.

**809. USE A FLASHLIGHT.**

Utilizing a flashlight in conjunction with your firearm is important for the following reasons: (1) to positively identify your target, (2) to temporarily blind your assailant as you fire at him, (3) to provide a source of illumination to see where you are going in the dark, (4) to illuminate your assailant for accurate shooting, and (5) to use as a makeshift striking weapon when lethal force is not warranted or justified.

**810. BE PREPARED FOR MUZZLE FLASH.**

*Muzzle flash* is an incandescent burst of light that is emitted from the muzzle and cylinder of your handgun. During normal lighting conditions, muzzle flash is hardly noticeable. However, when shooting in the dark or very dim light, muzzle flash can startle you and temporarily inhibit your vision. To minimize the adverse effects of muzzle flash, you'll need to get yourself accustomed to it by regularly engaging in night-firing practice.

### 811. EXPLOIT HIS MUZZLE FLASH.

When confronted by an armed assailant in a dark environment, you can exploit his muzzle flash and use it to your advantage. From behind cover, throw something (e.g., rock, bottle, stick, book, ashtray) away from your position to draw his gunfire. Once your adversary fires his weapon, watch for the muzzle flash that reveals his approximate location. Quickly counter fire where you last saw the assailant's muzzle flash. *REMEMBER: When shooting in the dark or in poor lighting conditions, you'll have a tendency to shoot high, so aim slightly low.*

### 812. DEFEND AGAINST MULTIPLE ARMED ASSAILANTS.

Defending against multiple armed assailants is extremely difficult and very dangerous. Here are some tactics that you should employ to enhance your chances of surviving the encounter.

(1) Seek cover - always try to seek cover immediately (e.g., large concrete utility poles, large rocks, thick trees, an engine block, the corner of a building). This will temporarily protect you from the assailants' gunfire.

(2) Attempt a tactical retreat - scan your environment for any possible escape routes. Look for windows, doors, fire escapes, or any other avenue that will allow you to flee the altercation safely and quickly. *WARNING: Never leave a position of cover to escape unless you absolutely have to and you're certain you can do so safely.*

(3) Shoot the immediate threat - you must determine which assailant is the greatest and most immediate threat to you. Generally, this will be the assailant who is closest to your position of cover.

(4) Shoot sparingly - avoid running out of ammunition. Shoot only when you have to and try to keep an approximate count of the rounds that you have fired. Remember, emptying your entire magazine before you've eliminated your threat can get you killed.

(5) Be prepared to move - always be prepared to move or escape at a second's notice. When moving from a position of cover (especially in the fatal funnel), always move as quickly as possible, with your weapon in the ready weapon position. Be aware of the surface area on which you are standing. You don't want to slip or trip.

## 813. MASTER ONE-HAND RELOADING.

There may come a time when one of your hands becomes wounded in a firefight and you'll have to reload your weapon with one hand. Develop this skill for both an autoloader and a revolver.

Although there are several different methods for reloading an autoloader one-handed, here is one that you should master: (1) drop the empty magazine to the ground; (2) place your autoloader between your knees, and angle the gun so the muzzle is pointed away from you; and (3) insert a fresh magazine with your good hand, grip your firearm, and return to the ready position.

For the revolver, the process is as follows: (1) insert the revolver vertically in your belt, (2) open the cylinder, (3) push out the used cartridges, (4) insert new rounds, (5) remove the weapon from your belt (keep your finger out of the trigger guard), (6) close the cylinder, and (7) resume firing.

### 814. KNOW HOW TO CONTACT SHOOT.

Develop *contact shooting* (touching target) and *close-to-contact* (approximately one inch away from target) skills. However, be careful after executing a contact shot. Blood and human tissue have been known to obstruct the barrel of a firearm. A firearm malfunction can occur, thereby subjecting you to a greater possibility of being disarmed.

### 815. NO WARNING SHOTS.

Don't fire warning shots at your adversary. It's dangerous and risky for the following reasons: (1) firing into the air can injure or kill an innocent bystander; (2) firing into the floor, ground, or ceiling can cause ricochets and over penetration into an adjacent room; (3) warning shots take your sights off your immediate threat (the assailant) and expose you to possible counter fire; and (4) it wastes ammunition. Remember, shoot to kill - not to intimidate.

### 816. TAKE YOUR HAND AWAY.

When cycling your autoloader, be certain to take your hand away from the muzzle. You don't want an accident to occur.

### 817. DOGS ARE NOT WEAPONS.

Never send a dog where you can send a bullet. Don't take chances or expose your four-legged friend in a firefight. In fact, never send him/her out to do your bidding in any emergency self-defense situation. It's cruel, cowardly and immoral.

# FIREARMS & COMBAT SHOOTING

### 818. CREATE THE FATAL FUNNEL.

If you ever have the drop on your assailant, try to take a low position of cover, preferably at the end of a hallway or a narrow staircase. Once your assailant moves forward, he will be at a tremendous disadvantage. His lateral movement will be dramatically limited, and he will be forced into your "kill zone." When this occurs, your assailant will be in your fatal funnel.

### 819. SHOOT TO STOP, NOT TO WOUND.

If you are legally warranted and justified in shooting a criminal assailant, <u>shoot to stop his threatening action</u> and not to wound him. Shooting to wound is risky for the following reasons: (1) wound targets are generally smaller and more difficult to hit in real-life encounters, and (2) wounds will not guarantee that your adversary will stop his attack.

### 820. TIME IS A VITAL FACTOR.

Most people don't realize that time is a vital factor in a gunfight. In many cases, you're more likely to run out of time than ammunition.

### 821. MOVE LATERALLY.

When under gunfire and running for cover, try to run laterally. Also keep in mind that linear movements (advancing or retreating) can be accomplished with broken rhythm, serpentine running patterns.

### 822. MASTER DRAKE SHOOTING.

When your assailant pins you down with suppressive fire and you cannot tell exactly where it's coming from, employ the *drake shooting* tactic. Drake shooting is executed by firing your weapon into places of likely cover and accomplishes the following objectives: (1) it helps identify your assailant's position of cover, (2) it helps flush your adversary out, (3) it aids in suppressing your assailant's gunfire, and (4) it denies mobility to your assailant.

### 823. BE PREPARED FOR THE MEXICAN STANDOFF.

The *Mexican standoff* is a precarious situation where both you and your adversary have the drop on each other. In such a situation, it's important to utilize either a verbal or physical distraction so that you can safely take the initiative by firing first. A verbal distraction might consist of asking your adversary a question such as, "Are you sure you want to do this?" While asking the question, shoot repeatedly at your assailant. A physical distraction might consist of quickly shifting your eyes to the side, changing the expression on your face, or smiling and looking over your assailant's shoulder. Once your assailant is distracted, shoot him repeatedly.

### 824. SHOOT AND SPEAK AT THE SAME TIME.

This tactic is invaluable, especially during a Mexican standoff with a criminal assailant.

### 825. SHOOT, EVALUATE, SHOOT, REEVALUATE.

When firing at your assailant, don't make the tactical error of emptying your entire magazine or cylinder. After firing a few rounds, you will need to see if your shots have been effective. You must evaluate your shots quickly or you will never eliminate the threat. Remember, when evaluating your shooting, do so from a position of tactical cover.

## 826. MOVE AS QUICKLY AS POSSIBLE.

In a gunfight, move from a position of cover to another position of cover as rapidly as possible. Though some situations might justify moving and shooting at the same time, it is best to fire from a stationary position of cover. *CAUTION: Never move without a plan. Moving from a position of cover without first locating another place of cover can get you killed in a firefight. Moving and firing at the same time, called "suppression fire," is only used to keep the bad guy down.*

## 827. KEEP YOUR GUN HAND FREE.

Whenever possible, try to get into the habit of keeping your gun hand free of food, smartphone, books, flashlights, and so on. Practice using your non gun or weak hand for everything.

## 828. EXPECT ANYTHING AND EVERYTHING.

Don't make the fatal error of assuming anything in a gunfight. For example, don't make the false assumption that your assailant is wounded or dead just because there is a temporary pause in gunfire.

## 829. KNOW THE EIGHT FATAL ERRORS.

Avoid the eight fatal errors that have killed many self-defense practitioners: (1) failing to concentrate - if you fail to keep your mind on the task at hand, you will make tactical errors that can cost you and your loved ones your lives; (2) yielding to tombstone courage - if the situation allows, wait for police assistance (only under the most extreme situations should you engage in a gunfight with a criminal assailant); (3) not getting enough rest - to protect yourself effectively, you must be alert (being sleepy in a potentially threatening situation will endanger you); (4) taking a bad position - never let anyone get a better or more secure position than you; (5)

ignoring danger signs - as a trained combatant, you will need to recognize danger signs (e.g., movements, strange cars, or other warnings) that should alert you to watch your step and approach with caution; (6) failure to watch the assailant's hands to see whether he is reaching for a weapon or getting ready to strike you; (7) relaxing too soon - never relax until you are absolutely certain that danger is eliminated; and (8) having a dirty or inoperative weapon. (Is your revolver or autoloader clean? Will it fire effectively in a time of need? How about the ammunition? When was the last time you visited the firing range? Why rely on a firearm that might not work?)

## 830. DON'T INTIMIDATE YOUR ASSAILANT.

A firearm or any self-defense weapon should never be used to intimidate or coerce another person. You should only display your weapon when you reasonably believe that you or another person is in imminent danger of grievous bodily harm or death.

## 831. DON'T DISPLAY YOUR FIREARM IN PUBLIC.

If you do carry a firearm on your person, be extremely careful to avoid any trivial confrontations on the street. When carrying a concealed gun, never let anyone see it until you are about to use it. The privilege to carry a firearm carries the obligation and responsibility to exercise discipline, discretion, restraint, and good judgment.

## 832. DRAW YOUR FIREARM SAFELY.

When drawing a gun from your holster, always keep your finger out of the trigger guard until the weapon clears the holster. You don't want to shoot yourself in the process of drawing your weapon. Practice smooth quick-draw techniques on a regular basis. And never practice with a loaded gun!

## FIREARMS & COMBAT SHOOTING

### 833. REHOLSTER YOUR FIREARM SAFELY.

When reholstering your firearm, remember to keep your finger out of the trigger guard and your thumb behind the hammer. This will help minimize the possibility of an accidental discharge.

### 834. BARE YOUR WEAPON AND THEN DRAW.

When drawing your firearm from concealment (e.g., sports coat, jacket, long shirt, EDC bag, ankle holster), make certain to pull your clothes out of the way with both of your hands and then draw your weapon.

# HOME INVASION

### 835. PREPARE FOR THE INTRUDER.

The serious fighter thinks nothing of spending countless hours preparing for a possible street fight. However, very few practitioners are adequately prepared to handle an intruder in their home. Richard Ramirez, the infamous "Night Stalker" who terrorized Los Angeles residents for nearly a year before being caught and convicted, was notorious for his ability to surreptitiously enter victims' homes, rob them, and, in many cases, kill or rape family members before leaving. The Night Stalker case is just one of many similar cases that occur in American homes each night. According to law enforcement statistics, there is a strong possibility such an occurrence can happen to you and your family. Yet the unfortunate fact is that criminal intrusion is a subject seldom addressed in the martial arts studio.

Ask yourself some important questions. Do you have a tactical plan should someone invade your home? Do you have the knowledge and expertise to keep both you and your family out of harm's way? Do you own a firearm, and are you trained to use it in this type of situation? Do you have a designated "safe room"? If you answered "no" to any of these questions, you and your loved ones may be at great risk.

## 836. ASSESS YOUR HOME.

Now is the time for you and your family to assess your home and design a tactical plan in case you are ever faced with a criminal intruder. Begin by drawing a detailed diagram of your home and discuss your safety options and the various strategies you can employ. Make certain all of your family members are familiar with the layout of your home, including all entrances, escape routes, and possible ambush zones. You must also assess your home for various points of cover in case there is a shoot-out with an intruder.

Discuss what types of makeshift weapons are located throughout the house, and make certain that everyone knows how to use them correctly. If you have a security alarm system in your home, make certain everyone is familiar with its operation and limitations.

## 837. DESIGNATE A SAFE ROOM.

Designate a *safe room* in your house in case you and your family are faced with a criminal intrusion. The safe room is a strategic location in your home where family members can escape from an intruder and wait for the police to arrive. Most people choose a particular bedroom in their house. Be certain there is a charged cell phone in the safe room so you can contact an emergency dispatcher during the encounter.

When you and your family arrive in the safe room, do the following: (1) keep the doors locked, (2) have everyone stay away from the entrance and find cover behind a protective barrier, (3) keep your firearm pointed at the entrances, (4) stay focused and alert with your finger on the trigger, (5) if the intruder attempts to enter the safe room, tell him that you have called the police, that they are on the way, and that you are armed with a gun, and (6) if the criminal assailant still forces entry despite your warnings and he presents a deadly threat to you or your family, then shoot him. *WARNING: Before squeezing the trigger, be certain of your target.*

## 838. HOLD YOUR ADVERSARY AT GUNPOINT.

If you manage to capture and hold a criminal at gunpoint, stay behind cover with your gun in the ready weapon position. Keep your assailant at a safe distance and in an awkward position. You must always be in complete control of the situation! Order the assailant to do the following: (1) put his hands in clear view; (2) turn and face away from you so he cannot see what you are doing; (3) slowly raise his hands straight over his head (be certain you can see his fingertips); (4) slowly drop to his knees, without using his hands; (5) once he's on his knees, cross one leg over the other; (6) have him lie on his stomach with his arms stretched at his sides; and, finally, (7) place his hands flat on the floor with his palms facing up.

Under no circumstances should you allow your assailant to get within grabbing distance of your gun. And do not search him for any weapons. Simply keep him in this awkward position until the police arrive. *WARNING: If you do see a weapon (e.g., knife or gun) on your assailant, do not allow him to touch it or remove it. Warn him that if he makes any slight move in the direction of the weapon, you will shoot him immediately. And don't make the fatal assumption that your assailant only has one weapon. Many criminals have backup guns.*

Keep your words to a minimum. Do not engage in any conversation with your assailant. Bark out commands loudly, firmly, and confidently; let him know that you mean business.

Stay focused and alert at all times. Keep your finger on the trigger and aim your gun at the center of his body. Don't take your eyes off him, and be aware that he might have accomplices nearby. If your assailant attempts to run away, let him go. Finally, if your adversary makes a move that a reasonable person would interpret as life threatening, or if he tries to take your weapon away from you, then shoot him repeatedly or until all hostile action has ceased.

*When holding a criminal at gunpoint, be certain to keep him at a safe distance and in an awkward position.*

## 839. PREPARE FOR HOSTAGE SITUATIONS.

If an intruder grabs a family member and holds him/her hostage using a deadly weapon (e.g., gun, knife, etc.), it is permissible for you to use deadly force to end the confrontation. If such a situation occurs, try employing the following tactics: (1) prevent your hostage taker from leaving the area; (2) keep your assailant contained in one area until help (the police) arrives; (3) if you have a clear shot at your assailant's head, take it (in most cases you will only get one shot); (4) never surrender your weapon to your adversary; (5) if you are unarmed and taken hostage, keep your cool and look for any possible opportunity to escape or disarm the intruder; and (6) don't make the fatal error of believing the hostage taker's assurances that he will release you unharmed if you cooperate. *WARNING: Hostage takers are characteristically unstable, desperate, and untrustworthy.*

## 840. KEEP YOUR FIREARM OUT OF SIGHT.

After a shoot-out with an intruder, be careful not to display your gun. Keep it out of sight when the police arrive. Never approach them with a firearm (or any weapon) in your hand. This is extremely dangerous because the police have no way of knowing who is the law-abiding citizen and who is the criminal.

If you are holding a criminal at gunpoint and the authorities arrive, immediately shout "Don't shoot!" and quickly tell them who you are. If the police command you to drop your weapon, do so immediately. Do not argue with them or offer any type of resistance. Avoid making any sudden moves, and always keep both of your hands in plain view.

## 841. KNOW HOW TO COUNTER GUN GRABS.

There may come a time when your assailant will try to grab your weapon when it's either holstered or in your hand. Here are some life-saving points to remember: (1) you must regain control of your weapon immediately (remember, the longer a struggle lasts with your adversary, the less are your chances of survival); (2) keep in mind that if your handgun is a revolver (in the double-action mode) and your assailant grabs hold of the cylinder, he will prevent it from firing; and (3) if your handgun is an autoloader and your assailant grabs hold of it, it will usually fire once, but you'll have a malfunction after the first shot. So be prepared to clear any malfunctions immediately.

One of the most effective methods of regaining control of

your handgun is to jerk your weapon back toward your abdomen and strike your assailant with your non gun hand. You can finger-jab his eyes, knife- hand-strike his throat, hammer fist strike his nose, or palm heel strike his chin. Once your weapon is free from your assailant's grasp, immediately clear any malfunction (if it's an autoloader) and shoot him until he is no longer a threat.

### 842. YOU ARE YOUR OWN WORST ENEMY.

Your biggest enemy in a gunfight is your mixed-up moral conscience. Being forced to use deadly force can create apprehension during a life-and-death encounter with a criminal assailant. This is because of incorrect perceptions or misinterpretation of many religious or associated beliefs.

Our culture and system of government are both based on the Judeo-Christian ethic. With this in mind, morality issues have been ingrained in us by our parents, teachers, friends, and cultural upbringing. Therefore, such common statements as "pick on someone your own size" or "don't hit a woman" often leave you with the fatal perception that a smaller or female adversary should be treated differently, when, in reality, anyone - regardless of size, age, gender, race, or appearance—has the potential to destroy you.

The Bible can also be easily misinterpreted regarding the use of deadly force. This misinterpretation can be identified in two situations.

(1) Hesitation or failure to act - The commandment *"Thou shalt not kill"* can cause people to hesitate to fire. A more accurate translation of this commandment is *"Thou shalt not murder"* (Exodus 20:13) (murder being the unjustifiable taking of another human life). Some people feel they have no right to kill another human being. When using deadly force, your objective is not to take life from another human being, but to stop your adversary from causing you grievous bodily harm or

possible death. However, the possibility of the adversary dying should be of no consequence to you. The bottom line is when warranted and justified, killing another person is permitted even under God's law.

(2) Guilt - people who justifiably employ deadly force later suffer some degree of guilt over their actions. They often question their right to take another life in defense of their own. They believe that life is sacred and that only God has the right to take it away. However, in the Bible, if someone tries to kill another unjustifiably, he forfeits the sanctity of his life, and he suffers any consequences brought on by his own actions (Exodus 21:12 and 14). God commands us to protect our lives from others who would take it away unjustifiably. At the same time, God removes the sanctity of a person who chooses to attempt to take the life of someone else unjustifiably.
*CAUTION: People must resolve any moral conflicts in their own minds prior to placing themselves and others in a situation where deadly force might be employed.*

# DISARMING TECHNIQUES

### 843. MASTER THE NINE DISARMING PRINCIPLES.

There is always the possibility that you will be at the wrong end of a gun. Therefore, it behooves you to master gun disarming. Successfully disarming a criminal assailant involves the following nine critical principles: (1) become familiar with all types of firearms, (2) try to determine the gunman's intent, (3) determine the proximity and exact positioning of the gun, (4) try to blade your body, (5) use a verbal distraction, (6) quickly get out of the line of fire, (7) redirect and grab the firearm, (8) control the firearm, and (9) neutralize the gunman.

## 844. KNOW YOUR GUNS.

The foundation of learning how to disarm someone with a firearm is familiarizing yourself with the weapon. Now is the time to eliminate the mystery and uncertainty about guns by informing yourself. Try to study the various models that are on the market. The more you know about a particular weapon, the less fear of the unknown you are apt to experience when faced with the real thing. Learn different firearm operations, sounds, ranges, accuracy, ammunition capacities, recoil, and penetration. Most importantly, you must know the general mechanical operation and nomenclature of a particular firearm if you plan to disarm the gunman successfully. Remember, knowledge is power, and power is survival.

## 845. DETERMINE THE GUNMAN'S INTENT.

When you encounter any gunman, assess his demeanor and pay close attention to what he is saying and doing. Find out exactly what it is he wants you to do. For example, does he just want to intimidate you with the weapon? Or is he hell-bent on blowing your brains out? Does he want you to go with him somewhere? Does he want your car or your wallet? If he wants anything material, give it to him. It can always be replaced. Never argue with a gunman or fight for your possessions. However, if you believe that your adversary is going to kill you—and sometimes it's very hard to know—then you have no choice but to attempt a disarm technique. In some situations, you may need to rely on your instincts. Remember, if something doesn't feel right, chances are it isn't.

## 846. PROXIMITY IS VITAL.

Successfully disarming a gunman requires that you determine the proximity of the weapon. You can disarm somebody only if his firearm is within arm's reach. If a criminal assailant is 10 feet away from you, then you can forget disarming him. Instead, you should concentrate on maneuvering yourself or the assailant into disarming range. For example, during the initial seconds of the encounter, try to move slightly closer to the gunman. In most situations, the closer the gun, the better, but sometimes a little distance can be used to your advantage.

### 847. POSITIONING IS CRITICAL.

Successfully disarming a gunman also requires that you determine the positioning of your assailant's firearm. It's essential that you know exactly where the weapon is located. For example, is the gun pointed at your face, your right hip, or your heart? Or is it pressed hard into the center of your back?

In addition to the strategic implications of the gun's position, you need to know your own target vulnerabilities for every particular disarm. For example, when you redirect the firearm, will it travel across such vital targets as your face, throat, or chest, or will the gun pass across your shoulder?

When you are analyzing the gun's positioning, it is critical to understand that your assailant can commit the assault from four sides: (1) frontal assault - the gun is pointing at the front of your head or body, (2) rear assault - the gun is pointing at the rear of your head or body, (3) right assault - the gun is pointed at the right side of your head or body, and (4) left assault - the gun is pointed at the left side of your head or body.

Each assault side can then be broken down into one of three different height classifications: (1) high - the assailant's gun is pointed at either your head, throat, or neck, (2) medium - the assailant's gun is pointed at either your chest, back, stomach, or ribs, (3) low - the assailant's gun is pointed at either your lower back, hips, waist, groin, or legs.

## 848. DISTRACT BEFORE YOU DISARM.

Assume that you have determined that disarming your assailant is your only chance for survival, you are in disarming range, you know where the firearm is located in proximity to your body or head, and you are aware of the target vulnerabilities for the particular disarm you are going to attempt. Now is the time for some type of verbal distraction. Ask the gunman a question that will require a verbal response. For example, you might ask, "Where are you taking me?" or "What do you want from me?" These questions are critical because they will distract your adversary temporarily and give you a split second to act with your disarm maneuver.

## 849. MOVE OUT OF THE LINE OF FIRE.

When utilizing a verbal distraction during a disarming technique, it's also important to make a non telegraphic and lightning-quick movement. Your goal is to reposition your body or head (depending on where the muzzle is pointed) rapidly so that you are out of the line of fire. For example, if the assailant's firearm is pointed at the front of your head, quickly slip your head sideways. Or if the gun is pointed at your torso, quickly turn and twist sideways. *WARNING: When attempting to move out of the line of fire, do not telegraph your intentions. It could cost you your life!*

## 850. REDIRECT AND GRAB THE FIREARM.

At the same time that you move your body and head to get out of the line of fire, you must redirect the assailant's gun or gun hand with your closer hand and move it in a direction opposite your body or head target. Do not glance at the firearm before you attempt to redirect it. This glance will telegraph your intentions. Once you've redirected the firearm, grab hold of the barrel (revolver) or slide (autoloader) and maintain control over the weapon. Don't be afraid to grab the barrel or slide. It is not the gun or any of its parts that will kill you. It's the bullet that comes screaming out of the muzzle!

Once you grab the firearm, immediately reinforce your hold with your other hand. Literally hold on for dear life, and also be certain that all of your body parts stay clear of the muzzle. Reinforcing your grip provides greater control and leverage for the inevitable life-and-death struggle.

## 851. NEUTRALIZE THE GUNMAN.

With the firearm redirected and temporarily under control, attack your assailant with everything you've got. Employ vicious knee strikes to the gunman's thigh or groin. Or you may have to attack with head butts to his nose, bites to his face, or any other offensive action that doesn't diminish your control over the weapon or move you back into the line of fire. Continue with repeated strikes until your assailant releases his grip on the gun, is completely neutralized, or both. If the weapon falls to the ground, then quickly pick it up and use it to keep your adversary sufficiently incapacitated. *CAUTION: Some firearms (especially autoloaders and shotguns) can discharge accidentally if dropped.*

## 852. KNOW WHAT TO DO IF YOU ARE SHOT.

If you are shot, try to stay on your feet, maintain your shooting position, and stay behind a position of cover. Do not look at your wound until your threat has been eliminated. Ignore the pain and keep shooting until your assailant has been neutralized. Mentally tell yourself that you will survive the encounter and fight back no matter what.

Expect the following symptoms: severe pain, burning sensation in the wound, breathlessness, reduced vision, potential lack of mobility, anger, fear response, and a tendency to lose your nerve.

# LEGAL CONSIDERATIONS

### 853. DON'T SHOOT A FLEEING FELON.

Don't shoot a fleeing felon in the back unless he is still armed, dangerous, and an immediate deadly threat to you or others in your immediate surroundings.

### 854. JEOPARDY MUST EXIST.

Legally, in order for you to be justified in using deadly force, *jeopardy* must exist. There are three elements that constitute jeopardy: (1) ability - the assailant must have the ability to cause you or another person grievous bodily harm or death (he must have access to something that he can use to cause grievous bodily harm or death); (2) opportunity - the assailant must have the opportunity to cause you or another person harm or death (usually involving proximity or control of their chosen weapon or both); and (3) intent - the assailant must have shown a manifested intent to cause you or another person grievous bodily harm or death.

### 855. USE A FIREARM ONLY AS A LAST RESORT.

Your firearm should be discharged only as a last resort when you reasonably believe that there is a threat of imminent danger or loss of life or grievous bodily harm to yourself or another person, and then it should be used only to stop the threat. Because a firearm places you in the position of judge, jury, and executioner in seconds, always make certain your actions are legally justified. Remember, once you squeeze the trigger, you can never call the bullet back.

# FIREARMS & COMBAT SHOOTING

# TRAINING

### 856. VISIT THE FIRING RANGE ON A REGULAR BASIS.

Shooting a gun is just like any other physical skill that requires practice to become proficient. The firing range is the best place to learn how to use a firearm effectively in a self-defense situation. If you do own a firearm and plan on using it in an emergency situation, then it's your responsibility to visit the firing range on a consistent basis. This is especially important for law enforcement officers.

### 857. HOLD ONTO YOUR FIREARM.

Make it your business to practice firearm retention skills. This includes both holstered and drawn firearms, for both long and short guns.

### 858. BE INSTINCTIVE.

Take the time to develop and practice instinct shooting, loading, drawing, holstering, traversing, retention, disarming, and malfunction skills. Remember, thinking creates lag time, and lag time means loss of initiative and possibly death. Action will always be faster than reaction.

### 859. PRACTICE WITH YOUR EYES CLOSED.

To acquire a greater understanding of your firearm, practice field-stripping, assembly, loading, and unloading of your weapon with your eyes closed.

## 860. DISARMS IN DIFFERENT ENVIRONMENTS.

Disarming someone with a firearm (long or short) is a very dangerous task performed under very desperate circumstances. Remember, you can't master disarming principles and techniques by reading about them. Practice with qualified instructors who know what they are doing and use mock training pistols with functional triggers. Rehearse in many different environments and conditions. For example, practice in such places as your car, stairwells, elevators, and alleys. Attempt disarming techniques when your hands are slippery and wet or when wearing gloves. Experiment under such adverse conditions as snow, rain, and in darkness or dim light. The more varied the situations and environments, the better prepared you'll be for the actual encounter. Remember, when you're disarming someone with a firearm, there are no second chances!

## 861. PREPARE FOR THE 12 ASSAULT POSITIONS.

When studying how to disarm someone with a firearm, you must be prepared to defend against the following 12 general assault positions: (1) frontal assault high, (2) frontal assault medium, (3) frontal assault low, (4) rear assault high, (5) rear assault medium, (6) rear assault low, (7) right assault high, (8) right assault medium, (9) right assault low, (10) left assault high, (11) left assault medium, and (12) left assault low.

## 862. VISUALIZE FIREARM-RELATED SCENARIOS.

Practice visualizing various firearm-related skills and scenarios. For example, visualize the appropriate use of cover and concealment, immediate action drills, disarming maneuvers, holding a criminal at gunpoint, malfunction remedies, one hand reloading skills, muzzle flash exploitation, correct shooting positions, and various other scenarios.

## FIREARMS & COMBAT SHOOTING

### 863. PRACTICE SPEED-LOADING DRILLS.

Reloading speed and technical fluidity are essential. Practice reloading skills from out-of-battery and in-battery positions. When reloading, always keep your finger out of the trigger guard, keep your gun on target, cant the weapon slightly, and bring your magazine to the firearm. And remember to avoid instilling bad habits (e.g., leaving empty cartridge cases or dropping empty magazines on the floor).

### 864. RELOAD BY FEEL.

Learn and practice reloading your firearm by feel. Reloading by feel and not sight is important for two reasons: (1) it allows you to keep your eyes on the assailant's location, and (2) it allows your weapon to be aimed in the correct direction. Remember, when practicing reloading skills with your firearm, always use dummy cartridges.

### 865. PRACTICE IMMEDIATE ACTION DRILLS.

Here are three immediate action drills (IADs) that you should practice on a regular basis: (1) if the assailant has the initiative (gunfire), seek cover; (2) if neither you nor the assailant has the initiative, act first (take the initiative) and fire; (3) if you have the initiative over your assailant, then fire. *REMEMBER, ALL IADs MUST BE INSTINCTIVE.*

### 866. PRACTICE WEAK HAND SHOOTING.

Ambidexterity with firearms is an invaluable skill that will set you apart from shooters who can use only one hand. Here are just a few reasons why this is critical: (1) there is a possibility that your strong gun hand may be injured in a firefight, (2) weak-hand shooting will enhance your combat confidence, and (3) your environment or position of cover may require you to shoot with your weak hand.

## 867. GET QUALIFIED TRAINING.

No matter what type of gun you own, it isn't going to help you unless you know what you are doing. Get trained by a qualified instructor in the following topics: (1) the fundamentals of safe gun handling, (2) basic operation and maintenance, (3) basic marksmanship skills, and (4) combat shooting skills and tactics. Ideally, if a firearm is to be kept in your home, family members should be trained as well. *BEWARE: Don't be duped by martial art instructors claiming to be firearms instructors. Most martial art instructors are completely ignorant on the subject of firearms. Always check out the instructor's qualifications thoroughly before signing up.*

# CHAPTER NINE
## Philosophy

*"The most difficult task in the world is to think clearly."*

# AXIOMS & APHORISMS

What follows are over one-hundred axioms and aphorisms which I have developed over the past thirty-five years. They have stood the test of time because they were inspired in the heat of conflict and formulated in the coolness of reflection.

They are here because they speak the time-tested truth of human competition and confrontation. Moreover, they both inspire and instruct and will no doubt be used and re-used by those who have heard them. I modestly hope that they will also lead you through the trials and tribulations of your own struggles and incumbent triumphs.

**868. WHEN DANGER IS IMMINENT, STRIKE FIRST, STRIKE FAST, STRIKE WITH AUTHORITY, AND KEEP THE PRESSURE ON.**

**869. VENGEANCE CAN BE AN HONORABLE TRAIT.**

**870. VIOLENCE CAN BE VIRTUOUS.**

**871. IT'S BETTER TO DIE WITH DIGNITY THAN TO LIVE WITH DISHONOR.**

**872. HUMANKIND IS AN OXYMORON.**

873. THERE ARE NO REAL SECRETS IN LIFE, JUST FACTS HIDDEN BY IGNORANCE.

874. COMBAT IS ATTRACTIVE TO THOSE WHO HAVEN'T EXPERIENCED IT.

875. IT'S OKAY TO BE DANGEROUS.

876. TO MASTER THE ESSENCE OF COMBAT, YOU MUST STUDY IT AS A SCIENCE AND EXPRESS IT AS AN ART.

877. APPROACH COMBAT IN TERMS OF BLACK AND WHITE, BUT BE PREPARED FOR GRAY.

878. NEVER UNDERESTIMATE THE VICIOUS CAPABILITY OF A HUMAN BEING.

879. IT'S NEVER A GOOD DAY TO DIE.

880. IT IS BETTER TO BE TRIED BY TWELVE THAN CARRIED BY SIX.

881. EVERY FIGHT MUST BE WON FAST.

882. EMBRACE YOUR MASCULINITY.

883. ACQUIRE AN INSATIABLE HUNGER FOR KNOWLEDGE.

884. VIOLENCE BEGINS WHERE DIPLOMACY ENDS.

885. TREAT BOOKS WITH RESPECT AND VENERATION.

886. ADHERENCE TO TRADITIONAL PERSPECTIVES WILL ALMOST GUARANTEE YOU DEATH IN COMBAT.

## PHILOSOPHY

887. COMBATIVE COMPETENCY DOESN'T OCCUR THROUGH SOME MYSTICAL TRANSFORMATION. IT'S ACQUIRED THROUGH DEDICATION AND LOTS OF HARD WORK.

888. BEWARE OF THE EGO. HE IS A DARK BEAST DESIROUS OF DESTRUCTION.

889. IF ANY STYLE OR SYSTEM OF COMBAT WILL NOT ALLOW FOR CHANGE, THEN IT WILL SURELY DIE.

890. NEVER SHOW AN ACT OF DEFIANCE THAT YOU ARE NOT PREPARED TO DEFEND.

891. A GREAT FIGHTER WILL ALWAYS ACT SWIFTLY AND DECISIVELY; HE DOESN'T KNOW THE MEANING OF APPREHENSION.

892. A TRUE WARRIOR IS ALWAYS ALONE.

893. SUPPORT CAPITAL PUNISHMENT.

894. NEVER TEACH SELF-DEFENSE TO ANYONE ON THE WRONG SIDE OF THE LAW.

895. FRUSTRATION AND TIME ARE THE GATEKEEPERS THAT SEPARATE THE AMATEUR FROM THE EXPERT.

896. PERCEPTION IS REALITY.

897. THE BETTER PREPARED YOU ARE, THE LESS LUCK YOU'LL NEED.

898. DESPAIR IS OFTEN ONE STEP AWAY FROM DEATH.

899. THERE ARE NO ABSOLUTES IN COMBAT.

900. A STUPID PERSON DIES A STUPID DEATH.

901. TRAIN FOR THE EXCEPTION AND THE RULE.

902. BEWARE OF THE TRADITIONAL MARTIAL ARTS. THEY WILL TEACH YOU JUST ENOUGH TO GET YOURSELF KILLED IN A REAL FIGHT.

903. BLOOD ISN'T THICKER THAN WATER.

904. ORDER AND JUSTICE CAN ONLY BE EXECUTED THROUGH A HAND OF MIGHT.

905. CHI IS A FOOLISH MYTH.

906. TRADITIONAL MARTIAL ARTS ARE NOTHING MORE THAN SOCIALLY ACCEPTED CULTS.

907. A KARATE OR KUNG-FU INSTRUCTOR IS NO MORE QUALIFIED TO TEACH SELF-DEFENSE THAN A FITNESS INSTRUCTOR AND NOT NEARLY AS QUALIFIED AS A HIGH SCHOOL COACH.

908. NOT ALL FIGHTING STYLES ARE CREATED EQUAL. THERE ARE SUPERIOR SYSTEMS OUT THERE.

909. QUESTION AUTHORITY; JUST DO IT RESPECTFULLY.

910. YOU WILL ALWAYS HAVE MORE TO LOSE THAN YOUR ADVERSARY.

911. NEVER BETRAY A FRIEND.

912. THERE IS NO HONOR IN DEFEAT.

PHILOSOPHY

913. NEVER REJECT A FIGHTING TECHNIQUE SIMPLY BECAUSE YOU DISLIKE ITS SOURCE.

914. KEEP YOUR SECRETS TO YOURSELF. A CLOSE FRIEND TODAY COULD BE YOUR ENEMY TOMORROW.

915. HELP THE MISGUIDED BY DEMYTHOLOGIZING THE MARTIAL ARTS.

916. COMBATIVE TRUTH ISN'T RELATIVE.

917. FOR EVERY ATTACK, THERE'S A LOGICAL COUNTER.

918. ALWAYS KEEP A MINDFUL EYE ON YOUR OWN ATTITUDE. IT IS USUALLY THE FIRST THING THAT WILL GET YOU INTO A FIGHT.

919. HUMANKIND IS GETTING MORE VIOLENT WITH THE TIMES.

920. SILENCE IS OFTEN AS BAD AS A LIE.

921. LOGIC CHANGES.

922. A WELL-SEASONED FIGHTER IS AN EXCELLENT PREDICTOR OF MOVES.

923. DON'T RESPECT PACIFISTS OR FIGHT FOR THEM.

924. WHAT YOU DON'T KNOW CAN GET YOU KILLED.

925. YOU'LL NEVER KNOW THE MEANING OF TRUE LOYALTY UNTIL YOU OWN AND LOVE A DOG.

926. NEVER "BEND THE KNEE" TO ANOTHER HUMAN.

927. WHAT YOU ALLOW, WILL CONTINUE.

928. YOUR FUTURE ENEMY TRAINED TODAY. DID YOU?

929. YOU'RE RESPONSIBLE FOR WHAT YOU DON'T KNOW.

930. DELAYED GRATIFICATION OPENS THE WIDOW TO SUCCESS.

931. THE MORE YOU KNOW, THE LESS YOU WILL FEAR.

932. SUCCESS AND FAILURE TRANSLATE TO LIFE AND DEATH IN COMBAT.

933. BLIND BELIEF AND ADHERENCE TO UNPROVEN PRINCIPLES IS PURE AND SIMPLE SUICIDE.

934. TO ABANDON STRUCTURE IS TO ABANDON THE FUNDAMENTALS OF COMBAT.

935. CONCEPTUALIZATION SHAPES AND MOLDS COMBAT CHARACTERISTICS, BUT IT BECOMES USELESS IF IT IS NOT SOLIDLY AND SAFELY ACTUALIZED.

936. DEFEND THE WEAK.

937. CONCRETE SYSTEMS AND STRATEGIES PROVIDE EFFICIENCY AND OVERALL COMBAT DIRECTION.

938. A FORMIDABLE FIGHTER IS A COLD AND VICIOUS ANIMAL, ALBEIT AN INTELLIGENT ONE.

939. A FUNCTIONAL SELF-DEFENSE SYSTEM IS ALWAYS IN A STATE OF GENESIS.

940. TOXIC MASCULINITY IS A TERM CREATED BY PEOPLE WHO SECRETLY WISH THEY WERE MEN.

941. SELF-MASTERY SEPARATES THE TRUE EXPERT FROM THE ETERNAL NOVICE.

942. BEWARE OF THE CALL OF VIOLENCE AND BE EVER VIGILANT OF THE EGO'S CHARMS.

943. COMBAT FORMLESSNESS IS THE FETUS OF DEATH.

944. A FIGHTER MUST POLICE HIS SKILLS WITH A MORAL FABRIC CALLED HONOR.

945. FEAR IS ESTABLISHED WHEN IGNORANCE IS ACTUALIZED.

946. EVERY MAN IS AFRAID OF SOMETHING.

947. ACQUIRE THE COURAGE AND INSIGHT TO QUESTION AND CHANGE COMBAT PARADIGMS.

948. EXPERIMENTATION IN THE FACE OF DANGER IS AN INVITATION TO DISASTER.

949. THERE IS ELEGANCE IN SIMPLICITY.

950. IT TAKES A LIFETIME TO MASTER A CREDIBLE SYSTEM OF COMBAT.

951. WHAT'S PRACTICAL ISN'T ALWAYS POPULAR, AND WHAT'S POPULAR ISN'T ALWAYS PRACTICAL.

952. THOSE WHO INSTRUCT LEARN.

953. LIFE BETRAYS EVERYONE.

954. TACTICS CAN BE STUDIED AND TECHNIQUES CAN BE LEARNED, BUT FIGHTING MUST BE EXPERIENCED.

955. IN COMBAT, EVERYONE LOSES IN THE GAME OF CONCEPTUAL ABSTRACTION.

956. VIOLENCE IS A DARK CLOAK THAT YOU MUST WEAR EVEN IF YOU DON'T LIKE THE WAY IT FITS.

957. AS LONG AS HUMANKIND WALKS THE EARTH, THERE WILL ALWAYS BE A TIME, NEED, AND PLACE FOR COMBAT.

958. NEVER TEACH SOMEONE ALL THAT YOU KNOW ABOUT FIGHTING.

959. IF LUCK FACTORS INTO YOUR SELF-DEFENSE FORMULA, THEN YOU'RE STILL NOT PREPARED FOR COMBAT.

960. EVERY PROBLEM HAS A SOLUTION.

961. IN COMBAT, ANYTHING THAT CAN GO WRONG MIGHT GO WRONG.

962. THE FIRST CASUALTY OF FIGHTING IS THE EGO.

PHILOSOPHY

963. NEVER, EVER FORGIVE EVIL.

964. THOSE WHO SPEAK THE TRUTH ARE NEVER LIKED.

965. FEAR KILLS A MAN TWICE.

966. COWARDS MAKE THE BEST BULLIES.

967. IT IS FAR BETTER TO DIE BY YOUR OWN THEORY THAN TO DIE BY SOMEONE ELSE'S.

968. LEAVE NOTHING TO CHANCE.

969. THERE ARE TWO TYPES OF PEOPLE IN THIS WORLD: VICTIMS AND VICTORS. WHICH ONE ARE YOU?

970. A TRUE INNOVATOR CREATES FOR HIMSELF AND NO ONE ELSE.

971. THE ONLY THING THAT STANDS BETWEEN YOU AND DEATH IS YOUR ABILITY TO FIGHT.

972. YOU WILL NEVER KNOW ALL THERE IS TO KNOW, BUT TRY ANYWAY.

973. EVERYONE THINKS THEY'RE A BADASS UNTIL THEY TASTE THEIR OWN BLOOD.

974. A PACIFIST IS A MAN WHO IS TOO COWARDLY TO FIGHT AND TOO FAT TO RUN.

975. GREAT FIGHTERS ARE SLAVES TO PERFECTION.

976. KNOW THE LAWS AND RULES OF COMBAT BEFORE YOU ATTEMPT TO CRITICIZE THEM.

977. DON'T LIVE AN UNEXAMINED LIFE.

978. SELF-DEFENSE IS NOT JUST A RIGHT; IT'S A RESPONSIBILITY.

979. ACTION BEATS REACTION, EVERY TIME.

980. RESPECT RANK!

981. TRUST IN GOD, BUT ALWAYS LOCK YOUR DOOR.

982. DON'T UNDERVALUE WHAT YOU HAVE. BELIEVE IN IT!

983. THE LONGER A FIGHT LASTS, THE GREATER YOUR CHANCES OF INJURY OR DEATH.

984. ATTACK EVEN WHEN YOU RETREAT.

985. SELF-DISCIPLINE IS THE TICKET TO SUCCESS. WITH IT YOU CAN ACCOMPLISH JUST ABOUT EVERYTHING.

986. IF YOUR WORKOUT IS "FUN", YOU'RE DOING IT WRONG.

987. TRUTH GIVES YOU THE POWER TO MAKE THINGS BETTER.

988. ALTHOUGH COMBAT PREPAREDNESS IS CRITICAL TO YOUR SURVIVAL, NEVER FORGET THE IMPORTANCE OF LOVE, LIFE, AND LAUGHTER.

989. STRIVE FOR THE LIFE YOU WANT, NOT THE LIFE YOU HAVE.

PHILOSOPHY

990. TRUST YOUR INSTINCTS BEFORE YOUR HEART AND YOUR HEART BEFORE YOUR MIND.

991. THE GREATNESS OF A MAN IS MEASURED BY HIS CHARACTER, NOT HIS FISTS.

992. FOCUS ON THE OPPORTUNITY, NOT THE PROBLEM.

993. TRUST YOURSELF, ALWAYS.

994. UNBRIDLED EMOTION IS A PREREQUISITE FOR FAILURE.

995. IT'S FAR BETTER TO BE A GOOD SOLDIER THAN A POOR GENERAL.

996. WE ARE OFTEN BETRAYED BY THE ONES WE TRUST THE MOST.

997. YOU WILL NEVER BE HERE AGAIN, BUILD YOUR LEGACY NOW.

998. SURVIVING THROUGH HARDSHIPS WILL STRENGTHEN YOU FOR ALL THE DAYS OF YOUR LIFE.

999. RESPECT THE PATRIARCHY. IF IT WASN'T FOR THEM, YOU AND I WOULDN'T BE HERE.

1,000. BELIEVE IN THE GOD OF YOUR UNDERSTANDING, NOT SOMEONE ELSES.

1,001. ?

# GLOSSARY

Many of the terms in this book may be strange to the first time reader. This is because most of the lexicon in this text are unique only to Contemporary Fighting Arts. What follows are some important terms often used in my CFA system.

## A

**Accuracy** - The precise or exact projection of force. Accuracy is also defined as the ability to execute a combative movement with precision and exactness.

**Action** - A series of moving parts that permit a firearm to be loaded, unloaded and fired.

**Adaptability** - The ability to physically and psychologically adjust to new or different conditions or circumstances of combat.

**Aerobic Exercise** - "With air." Exercise that elevates the heart rate to a training level for a prolonged period of time, usually 30 minutes.

**Affective Domain** - This includes the attitudes, philosophies, ethics, values, discretionary use-of-force, and the spirit (killer instinct) required to use your combative tool or technique appropriately.

**Affective Preparedness** - Being emotionally and spiritually prepared for the demands and strains of combat.

**Aggression** - Hostile and injurious behavior directed toward a person.

**Aggressive Hand Positioning** - Placement of hands so as to imply aggressive or hostile intentions.

**Aggressive Stance** - (See Fighting Stance.)

**Aggressor** - One who commits an act of aggression.

**Agility** - An attribute of combat. One's ability to move his or her body quickly and gracefully.

**Amalgamation** - A scientific process of uniting or merging.

**Ambidextrous** - The ability to perform with equal facility on both the right and left sides of the body.

**Ambush** - To lie in wait and attack by surprise.

**Ambush Zones** - Strategic locations (in everyday environments) from which assailants launch surprise attacks.

**American Stick Strangle** - A stick strangle used with a hammer grip.

**Analysis and Integration** - One of the five elements of CFA's mental component. This is the painstaking process of breaking down various elements, concepts, sciences, and disciplines into their atomic parts, and then methodically and strategically analyzing, experimenting, and drastically modifying the information so that it fulfills three combative requirements: efficiency, effectiveness and safety. Only then is it finally integrated into the CFA system.

**Anatomical Handles** - Various body parts (i.e., appendages, joints, and in some cases, organs) that can be grabbed, held, pulled or otherwise manipulated during a ground fight.

**Anatomical Power Generators** - Three points on the human body that help torque your body to generate impact power. Anatomical Power Generators include: (1) Feet; (2) Hips; (3) Shoulders.

**Anatomical Striking Targets** - The various anatomical body targets that can be struck and which are especially vulnerable to potential harm. They include: the eyes, temple, nose, chin, back of neck, front of neck, solar plexus, ribs, groin, thighs, knees, shins, and instep.

**Arm Lock** - A joint lock applied to the arm.

**Assailant** - A person who threatens or attacks another.

# GLOSSARY

**Assault** - The willful attempt or threat to inflict injury upon the person of another.

**Assault and Battery** - The unlawful touching of another person without justification.

**Assert** - One of the five possible tactical responses to a threatening situation. To stand up for your rights (see Comply, Escape, De-Escalate, and Fight Back).

**Assessment** - The process of rapidly gathering, analyzing, and accurately evaluating information in terms of threat and danger. You can assess people, places, actions, and objects.

**Attachment** - The touching of the arms or legs prior to executing a trapping technique.

**Attack** - Offensive action designed to physically control, injure, or kill another person.

**Attack By Draw** - One of the five conventional methods of attack. A method of attack whereby the fighter offers his assailant an intentional opening designed to lure an attack.

**Attributes of Combat** - The physical, mental, and spiritual qualities that enhance combat skills and tactics.

**Attribute Uniformity** - Various combative attributes (i.e., speed, power, accuracy, balance, etc.) which are executed the same way every time.

**Autoloader** - A handgun that operates by mechanical spring pressure and recoil force that ejects the spent cartridge case and automatically feeds a fresh round from the magazine. (Also known as a Semiautomatic).

**Awareness** - Perception or knowledge of people, places, actions, and objects. (In CFA there are three categories of tactical awareness: Criminal Awareness, Situational Awareness, and Self-Awareness.)

**Axiom** - A truth that is self-evident.

# B

**Back Position** - One of the ground fighting positions. The back position is assumed when your chest is on top of your assailant's back.

**Back fist** - A punch made with the back of the knuckles.

**Back strap** - The rear, vertical portion of the pistol frame.

**Balance** - One's ability to maintain equilibrium while stationary or moving.

**Barrier** - Any large object that can be used to obstruct an attacker's path or angle of attack.

**Blading the Body** - Strategically positioning your body at a 45-degree angle.

**Block** - A defensive tool designed to intercept the assailant's attack by placing a non-vital target between the assailant's strike and your vital body target.

**Bludgeon** - Any club like weapon used for offensive and defensive purposes (e.g., baseball bat, club, pipe, crowbar, heavy tree branch, etc.) Bludgeons are usually heavier and thicker than sticks.

**Body Composition** - The ratio of fat to lean body tissue.

**Body Language** - Nonverbal communication through posture, gestures, and facial expressions.

**Body Mechanics** - Technically precise body movement during the execution of a body weapon, defensive technique, or other fighting maneuver.

**Body Weapon** - One of the various body parts that can be used to strike or otherwise injure or kill a criminal assailant. (Also known as Tool).

**Bore** - The inside of the barrel of a firearm.

**Boxing** - (See Western Boxing).

**Break fall** - A method of safely falling to the ground.

# GLOSSARY

**Burn Out** - A negative emotional state acquired by physically over training. Some symptoms of burn-out include: physical illness, boredom, anxiety, disinterest in training, and general sluggish behavior.

**Bushido** - The ancient and honorable code of the samurai or warrior.

# C

**Cadence** - Coordinating tempo and rhythm to establish a timing pattern of movement.

**Caliber** - The diameter of a projectile.

**Cardiorespiratory Conditioning** - A component of physical fitness that deals with the heart, lungs, and circulatory system.

**Carriage** - The way you carry yourself.

**Cartridge** - A cylindrical case containing components of a round of ammunition: case, primer, powder charge, and bullet.

**Center-Fire** - A type of firearm cartridge that has its primer located in the center of the case bottom.

**Centerline** - An imaginary vertical line that divides your body in half and which contains many of your vital anatomical targets.

**Center Mass** - The center portion of the torso.

**Chamber** - 1) The part of a firearm in which a cartridge is contained at the instant of firing. 2) The raising of the knee to execute a kick.

**Choice Words** - (See Selective Semantics.)

**Choke** - A close quarter (grappling range) technique that requires one to apply pressure to either the trachea of carotid arteries.

**Circular Movement** - Movements that follow the direction of a curve.

**Close Quarter Combat** - One of the three ranges of knife and bludgeon combat. At this distance, you can strike, slash, or stab your assailant with a variety of close-quarter techniques.

**Close to Contact Shooting** - Discharging a firearm with the muzzle approximately one inch distance from the target.

**Cognitive Development** - One of the five elements of CFA's mental component. The process of developing and enhancing your fighting skills through specific mental exercises and techniques. (see Analysis and Integration, Killer Instinct, Philosophy and Strategic/Tactical Development.)

**Cognitive Domain** - This encompasses the specific concepts, principles and knowledge required to use your combative tools or techniques effectively.

**Cognitive Exercises** - Various mental exercises used to enhance fighting skills and tactics.

**Combat Arts** - The various arts of war. (See Martial Arts.) Combative Attributes - (See Attributes.)

**Combative Fitness** - A state characterized by cardiorespiratory and muscular/ skeletal conditioning, as well as proper body composition.

**Combative Mentality** - A combative state of mind necessary for fighting. Also known as the Killer Instinct. (see Killer Instinct.)

**Combat Ranges** - The various ranges of armed and unarmed combat.

**Combative Power** - The ability of capacity to perform or act effectively in combat.

**Combative Truth** - A combative element that conforms to fact or actuality and which is proven to be true.

**Combative Utility** - The quality of condition of being combatively useful. Combination(s) - (See Compound Attack.)

**Come-Along** - A series of holds or joint locks that force

# GLOSSARY

your adversary to move in any direction you desire.

**Coming to a Base** - The process of getting up to your hands and knees from the prone position.

**Common Peroneal Nerve** - A pressure point area located approximately four to six inches above the knee on the midline of the outside of the thigh.

**Completion Phase** - One of the three stages of a stick or bludgeon strike. The completion phase is the completion point of a swing.

**Comply** - One of the five tactical responses to a threatening situation. To obey an assailant's demands. (see Assert, De-Escalate, Escape, and Fight Back.)

**Composure** - A combative attribute. Composure is a quiet and focused mind set that enables you to acquire your combative agenda.

**Compound Attack** - One of the five conventional methods of attack. Two or more body weapons launched in strategic succession whereby the fighter overwhelms his assailant with a flurry of full speed, full force blows. (see Indirect Attack, Immobilization Attack, Attack By Draw, and Single Attack.)

**Concealment** - Not being visible to your adversary.

**Conditioning Training** - A CFA training methodology requiring the practitioner to deliver a variety of offensive and defensive combinations for a four minute period (see Proficiency Training and Street Training.)

**Confrontation Evasion** - Strategically manipulating the distance or environment to avoid a possible confrontation.

**Congruency** - The state of harmoniously orchestrating the verbal and non verbal de-escalation principles.

**Contact Evasion** - Physically moving or manipulating your body targets to avoid being struck (i.e., slipping your head to the side or side stepping from a charging assailant).

**Contact Shooting** - Discharging a firearm with the muzzle touching the target.

**Contemporary Fighting Arts® (CFA)** - A modern martial art and self-defense system made up of three parts: physical, mental, and spiritual.

**Conventional Ground Fighting Tools** - Specific ground fighting techniques designed to control, restrain and temporarily incapacitate your adversary. Some conventional ground fighting tactics include: submission holds, locks, certain choking techniques, and specific striking techniques.

**Cool-down** - A series of light exercises and movements that immediately follow a workout. The purpose of the cool-down is to hasten the removal of metabolic wastes and gradually return the heart to its resting rate.

**Coordination** - A physical attribute characterized by the ability to perform a technique or movement with efficiency, balance, and accuracy.

**Counterattack** - Offensive action made to counter an assailant's initial attack.

**Courage** - A combative attribute. The state of mind and spirit that enables a fighter to face danger and vicissitudes with confidence, resolution, and bravery.

**Courageousness** - (See Courage).

**Cover** - Any object that protects you from gunfire.

**Criminal Awareness** - One of the three categories of CFA awareness. It involves a general understanding and knowledge of the nature and dynamics of a criminal's motivations, mentalities, methods, and capabilities to perpetrate violent crime. (see Situational Awareness and Self-Awareness.)

**Criminal Justice** - The study of criminal law and the procedures associated with its enforcement.

**Criminology** - The scientific study of crime and criminals.

**Criss Cross** - An entry maneuver which allows you to

travel across a threshold quickly while employing a correct ready weapon position.

**Cross Stepping** - The process of crossing one foot in front or behind the other when moving.

**Crushing Tactics** - Nuclear grappling range techniques designed to crush the assailant's anatomical targets.

**Cutting Accuracy** - The ability to cut your assailant with precision and exactness.

**Cutting Makeshift Weapon** - One of the four types of CFA makeshift weapons. Any object or implement that can be used to effectively stab or slash an assailant. (see also Distracting Makeshift Weapon, Shielding Makeshift Weapon, and Striking Makeshift Weapon.)

**Cylinder** - The part of a revolver that holds cartridges in individual chambers.

# D

**Deadly Force** - Weapons or techniques that may result in imminent, unconsciousness, permanent disfigurement, or death.

**Deadly Weapon** - An instrument designed to inflict serious bodily injury or death (e.g., firearms, impact tools, edged weapons).

**Deception** - A combative attribute. A stratagem whereby you delude your assailant.

**Decisiveness** - A combative attribute. The ability to follow a tactical course of action that is unwavering and focused.

**De-escalation** - One of the five possible tactical responses to a threatening situation. The science and art of diffusing a hostile individual without resorting to physical force. (see Assert, Comply, Escape and Fight Back).

**De-escalation Stance** - One of the many strategic stances used in the CFA system. A strategic and non aggressive stance used when diffusing a hostile individual.

**Defense** - The ability to strategically thwart an assailant's attack (armed or unarmed).

**Defensive Flow** - A progression of continuous defensive responses. Defensive Mentality - A defensive mind-set.

**Defensive Range Manipulation (DRM)** - The strategic manipulation of ranges (armed or unarmed) for defensive purposes.

**Defensive Reaction Time** - The elapsed time between an assailant's physical attack and your defensive response to that attack (see Offensive Reaction Time).

**Demeanor** - One of the essential factors to consider when assessing a threatening individual. A person's outward behavior.

**Dependency** - The dangerous phenomenon of solely relying on a particular person, agency, instrument, device, tool, animal, or weapon for self-defense and personal protection.

**Destructions** - A technique that strikes the assailant's attacking limb. Diet - A life-style of healthy eating.

**Distance Gap** - The spatial gap between the different ranges of armed and unarmed combat.

**Distancing** - The ability to quickly understand spatial relationships and how they relate to combat.

**Distracting Makeshift Weapon** - One of the four types of CFA makeshift weapons. An object that can be thrown into an assailant's face, body, or legs to distract him temporarily (see Cutting Makeshift Weapon, Striking Makeshift Weapon, and Shielding Makeshift Weapon.)

**Distraction Tactic**s - Various verbal and physical tactics designed to distract your adversary.

**Dojo** - The Japanese term for "training hall."

**Dominant Eye** - The eye which is primarily used for aiming a firearm. The dominant eye is the one which is stronger and does more work.

**Double-Action** - A type of pistol action in which squeezing the trigger will both cock and release the hammer.

**Drake Shooting** - Shooting into places of likely cover.

**Dry Firing** - The process of shooting an unloaded firearm.

**Duck** - A defensive technique that permits you to evade your assailant's strike. Ducking is performed by dropping your body down and forward to avoid the assailant's blow.

# E

**Ectomorph** - A body type classified by a high degree of slenderness, angularity, and fragility (see Endomorph and Mesomorph).

**Effectiveness** - One of the three criteria for a CFA body weapon, technique, tactic or maneuver. It means the ability to produce a desired effect (see Efficiency and Safety).

**Efficiency** - One of the three criteria for a CFA body weapon, technique, tactic or maneuver. It means the ability to reach an objective quickly and economically (see Effectiveness and Safety).

**Ejector** - The part of a pistol which ejects empty cartridge cases.

**Embracing the Range** - A ground fighting tactic whereby you pull or embrace your assailant.

**Emotional Control** - One of the nonverbal principles of strategic de-escalation. The ability to remain calm when faced with a hostile or threatening person.

**Emotionless** - A combative attribute. Being temporarily devoid of human feeling.

**Endomorph** - A body type classified by a high degree of roundness, softness, and body fat (see Ectomorph and Mesomorph).

**Entry Method** - A method that permits you to safely enter a combat range. **Entry Technique** - A technique that permits you to safely enter a combat range.

**Entry Tool** - A tool that permits you to safely enter a combat range.

**Escape** - Also known as tactical retreat. One of the five possible tactical responses to a threatening situation. To flee rapidly from the threat or danger. (See Comply, De-Escalate, Assert and Fight Back).

**Escape Routes** - Various avenues or exits that permit you to escape from a threatening individual or situation.

**Evasion** - A defensive maneuver that allows you to strategically maneuver your body away from the assailant's strike.

**Evasive Sidestepping** - Evasive footwork where the practitioner moves to either the right or left side.

**Evasiveness** - A combative attribute. The ability of avoid threat or danger. Evolution - A gradual process of change.

**Excessive Force** - An amount of force that exceeds the need for a particular event and is unjustified in the eyes of the law.

**Experimentation** - The painstaking process of testing a combative hypothesis or theory.

**Explosiveness** - A combative attribute that is characterized by a sudden outburst of violent energy.

# F

**Fake** - Body movements that disguise your attack. This includes movements of the eyes, head, shoulders, knees, feet and in some cases the voice.

**Fatal Funnel** - A danger area that is created by openings such as doorways, windows, hallways, stairwells, etc.

**Feed** - (See Attachment.)

GLOSSARY

**Fear** - A strong and unpleasant emotion caused by the anticipation or awareness of threat or danger. There are three stages of fear in order of intensity: Fright, Panic, and Terror. (see Fright, Panic, Terror).

**Feeler** - A tool that tests the assailant's reaction time and overall abilities.

**Feint** - A tool that draws an offensive reaction from the assailant, thereby opening him up for a real strike. Feints are different from fakes because they are performed through the movement of an actual limb.

**Femoral Nerve** - A pressure point area located approximately six inches above the knee on the inside of the thigh.

**Fight Back** - One of the five possible tactical responses to a threatening situation. To use various physical and psychological tactics to either incapacitate or terminate a criminal assailant. (See Comply, Escape, Assert and De-Escalate.)

**Fighting Stance** - One of the different types of stances used in CFA's system. A strategic posture you can assume when face-to-face with an unarmed assailant (s). (See De-escalation Stance, Knife Defense Stance, Knife Fighting Stance, Firearms Stance, Natural Stance, Stick Fighting Stance).

**Fight-or-Flight Syndrome** - A response of the sympathetic nervous system to a fearful and threatening situation, during which it prepares your body to either fight or flee from the perceived danger.

**Finesse** - A combative attribute. The ability to skillfully execute a movement or a series of movements with grace and refinement.

**Firearm Follow Through** - Continuing to employ the shooting fundaments throughout the delivery of your shot.

**First Strike Principle (FSP)** - A CFA principle which states that when physical danger is imminent and you have no other tactical option but to fight back, you should strike first, strike fast, and strike with authority.

**Flexibility** - The muscles' ability to move through maximum natural ranges (see Muscular/Skeletal Conditioning).

**Follow** - A defensive technique used in the mid to long range of knife combat.

**Forms** - Traditional martial arts training methodology whereby the practitioner performs a series of prearranged movements that are based upon a response to imaginary opponents (see Kata).

**Formlessness** - A principle that rejects the essence of structure or system.

**Footwork** - Quick, economical steps performed on the balls of the feet while you are relaxed, alert, and balanced. Footwork is structured around four general movements: forward, backward, right, and left.

**Fractal Cognizance** -Being knowledgeable and aware of the fractal ranges and tools of combat.

**Fright** - The first stage of fear; quick and sudden fear (see Panic and Terror).

# G

**Gi** - A traditional martial art uniform constructed of heavy cotton canvas material. The gi is commonly worn by practitioners of karate, judo, aikido, and jujitsu.

**Grappling Range** - One of the three ranges of unarmed combat. Grappling range is the closest distance of unarmed combat from which you can employ a wide variety of close-quarter tools and techniques. The grappling range of unarmed combat is also divided into two different planes: vertical (standing) and horizontal (ground fighting). (see Kicking Range and Punching Range)

**Grappling Range Tools** - The various body tools and techniques that are employed in the grappling range of unarmed combat, including head butts; biting, tearing, clawing, crushing, and gouging tactics; foot stomps, horizontal, vertical, and diagonal elbow strikes, vertical and diagonal knee strikes, chokes, strangles, joint locks, and holds. (see and Kicking Range Tools).

**Grapevine** - A stabilizing technique used during a ground fight. The grapevine can be applied when you have either one (single leg grapevine) or both (double leg grapevine) of your feet hooked around the assailant's legs.

**Ground Fighting** - Fighting that takes place on the ground. (Also known as horizontal grappling plane).

**Guard** - 1) A fighter's hand positioning. 2) One of the positions used in ground fighting. The guard is a scissors hold applied with the legs.

# H

**Hammer** - The moving part of a gun causes the firing pin to strike the cartridge primer.

**Hammer Grip** - A hand grip used to hold an edged weapon, bludgeon and some makeshift weapons; assumed when the top of the bludgeon or the tip of the edged weapon is pointing upwards.

**Handgun** - A firearm that can be held and discharged with one hand. Hand Positioning - (See Guard.)

**Hang fire** - A perceptible delay in the ignition of a cartridge after the primer has been struck.

**Head-Hunter** - A fighter who primarily attacks the head.

**High-Line Kick** - One of the two different classifications of a kick. A kick that is directed to targets above an assailant's waist level. (See Low-Line Kick.)

**Histrionics** - The field of theatrics or acting.

**Homicide** - The death of another person without legal justification of excuse.

**Hook Kick** - A circular kick that can be delivered in both kicking and punching ranges.

**Hook Punch** - A circular punch that can be delivered in both the punching and grappling ranges.

**Hold** - A specific manner of grasping or holding an assailant.

**Human Shield** - Using your assailant's body as a shield or obstacle in combat.

# I

**Ice Pick Grip** - A hand grip used to hold an edged weapon, bludgeon and some makeshift weapons; assumed when the tip of the edged weapon or the top of the bludgeon is pointing downward.

**Ice Pick Stick Strangle** - A stick strangle used with an ice pick grip.

**Immobilization Attack** - One of the five conventional methods of attack. A highly complex system of moves and countermoves that allows you to temporarily control and manipulate the assailant's limbs (usually his arms and hands) in order to create an opening of attack.

**Impact Power** - Destructive force generated by mass and velocity.

**Impact Training** - A training exercise that develops pain tolerance.

**Incapacitate** - To disable an assailant by rendering him unconscious or damaging his bones, joints or organs.

**Indirect Attack** - One of the five conventional methods of attack. A progressive method of attack whereby the initial tool or technique is designed to set the assailant up for follow-up blows.

**Initiation Phase** - One of the three stages of a stick or bludgeon strike. The initiation phase is initiation point of a swing.

**Insertion Points** - Specific anatomical targets you can stab with a knife and some makeshift weapons.

**Inside Position** - The area between both of your assailant's arms where he has the greatest amount of control.

**Intent** - One of the essential factors to consider when assessing a threatening individual. The assailant's purpose or motive (see Demeanor, Positioning, Range, and Weapon Capability).

**Intuition** - The innate ability to know or sense something without the use of rational thought.

**Intuitive Tool Response (ITR)** - Spontaneously reacting with the appropriate combative tool.

# J

**Jab** - A quick, probing punch designed to create openings in the assailant's defense.

**Jeet Kune Do** - "Way of Intercepting Fist." Bruce Lee's approach to the martial arts, which includes his innovative concepts, theories, methodologies, and philosophies of unarmed combat.

**Joint Lock** - A grappling range technique that immobilizes the assailant's joint.

**Judo** - "Gentle Way." A Japanese grappling art (founded by Jigoro Kano in 1882) which is used as a sport. Judo utilizes shoulder and hip throws, foot sweeps, chokes, and pins.

**Jujitsu** - "Gentleness" or "suppleness." A system of self-defense that is the parent of both Judo and Aikido. Jujitsu specializes in grappling range but is known to employ a few striking techniques.

# K

**Karate** - "Empty hand" or "China hand," a traditional martial art that originated in Okinawa and later spread to Japan and Korea (see Kung-Fu).

**Kata** - "Pattern" or "Form". A traditional training methodology whereby the practitioner practices a series of prearranged movements.

**Kick** - 1) A sudden, forceful strike with the foot (see High-Line Kick and Low- Line Kick); 2) The recoil of a firearm.

**Kick boxing** - A popular combat sport that employs full-contact tools.

**Kicking Range** - One of the three ranges of unarmed combat. Kicking range is the furthest distance of unarmed combat wherein you use your legs to strike an assailant. (see Grappling Range and Punching Range).

**Kicking Range Tools** - The various body weapons employed in the kicking range of unarmed combat, including side kicks, push kicks, hook kicks, and vertical kicks.

**Killer Instinct** - A cold, primal mentality that surges to your consciousness and turns you into a vicious fighter.

**Kinesics** - The study of nonlinguistic body movement communications (i.e., eye movement, shrugs, facial gestures, etc.).

**Kinesiology** - The study of principles and mechanics of human movement.

**Kinesthetic Perception** - The ability to accurately feel your body during the execution of a particular movement.

**Kneeling Firearm Stance** - A strategic stance you assume when kneeling down with a handgun.

**Knife-Defense Stance** - One of the many stances used in CFA's system. A strategic stance you assume when face-to-face with an knife or edged weapon attacker. (See De-escalation Stance, Fighting Stance, Knife Fighting Stance, Firearms Stance, Natural Stance, Stick Fighting Stance).

**Kung-Fu** - "Accomplished task or effort," a term used erroneously to identify the traditional Chinese martial arts (see Karate).

# L

**Lead Side** - The side of the body that faces an assailant.

**Leg Block** - A blocking technique used with the legs. The leg block can be angled in three different directions: forward, right and left.

**Limited Penetration** - The (LP) is a corner clearing movement performed by positioning your firearm and one eye around the corner.

**Linear Movement** - Movements that follow the path of a straight line.

**Long Range Combat** - The furthest distance of knife and bludgeon combat. At this distance you can only strike or slash your assailant's hand.

**Low Maintenance Tool** - Offensive and defensive tools that require the least amount of training and practice to maintain proficiency. Low maintenance tools generally don't require preliminary stretching.

**Low-Line Kick** - One of the two different classifications of a kick. A kick that is directed to targets below the assailant's waist level. (See High-Line Kick.)

**Lock** - (see Joint Lock).

**Loyalty** - The state of being faithful to a person, cause, or ideal.

# M

**Makeshift Weapon** - A common everyday object that can be converted into either an offensive or defensive weapon. There are four Makeshift Weapon classifications in the CFA system: Cutting Makeshift Weapons, Shielding Makeshift Weapons, Distracting Makeshift Weapons, and Striking Makeshift Weapons.

**Maneuver** - To manipulate into a strategically desired position.

**Manipulation Accuracy** - The ability to manipulate your assailant's limbs and joints with precision and exactness.

**Martial Artist** - One who studies and practices the martial arts.

**Martial Arts** - The traditional "arts of war" (see Karate and Kung-Fu).

**Martial Truth** - (See Combative Truth.)

**Mechanics** - (See Body Mechanics.)

**Medicine Ball** - A large, heavy ball used to strengthen and condition a fighter's stomach muscles.

**Meet** - A defensive technique that intercepts your assailant's line of attack with a slash.

**Mental Attributes** - The various cognitive qualities that enhance your fighting skills.

**Mental Component** - One of the three vital components of the CFA system. The mental component includes the cerebral aspects of fighting including the Killer Instinct, Strategic & Tactical Development, Analysis & Integration, Philosophy and Cognitive Development (see Physical Component and Spiritual Component).

**Mesomorph** - A body type classified by a high degree of muscularity and strength. (see Endomorph and Ectomorph).

**Methods of Attack** - The five conventionally recognized

methods of attacking. They include: single attack, indirect attack, attack by draw, immobilization attack, and compound attack.

**Mexican Standoff** - A precarious situation where both you and your adversary have the drop on one another.

**Mid Phase** - One of the three stages of a stick swing. The mid phase is the contact or impact point of the swing.

**Mid Range Combat** - One of the three ranges of knife and bludgeon combat. At this distance you can strike, slash or stab your assailant's head, arms and body with your weapon.

**Misfire** - A failure of a cartridge to fire after the primer has been struck.

**Mobility** - A combative attribute. The ability to move your body quickly and freely while balanced. (see Footwork).

**Modern Martial Art** - A pragmatic combat art that has evolved to meet the demands and characteristics of the present time.

**Modernist** - One who subscribes to the philosophy of the modern martial arts.

**Modification** - To make fundamental changes to serve a new end.

**Mounted Position** - One of the five general ground fighting positions. The mounted position is where the practitioner sits on top of his assailant's torso or chest.

**Mouthpiece** - A rubber protector used to cover your teeth when sparring. There are two types of mouthpiece: single and double.

**Muscular Endurance** - The muscles' ability to perform the same motion or task repeatedly for a prolonged period of time.

**Muscular Flexibility** - The muscles' ability to move through maximum natural ranges.

**Muscular Strength** - The maximum force that can be

exerted by a particular muscle or muscle group against resistance.

**Muscular/Skeletal Conditioning** - An element of physical fitness that entails muscular strength, endurance, and flexibility.

**Muzzle** - The front end of the barrel.

**Muzzle Flash** - An incandescent burst of light which is emitted from the muzzle and cylinder of a handgun.

# N

**Natural Stance** - One of the many stances used in CFA's system. A strategic stance you assume when approached by a suspicious person who appears non threatening. (See De-escalation Stance, Fighting Stance, Knife Fighting Stance, Firearms Stance, Knife-Defense Stance, and Stick Fighting Stance).

**Neutralize** - (See Incapacitate.)

**Neutral Zone** - The distance outside of the kicking range from which neither the practitioner nor the assailant can touch the other.

**Nomenclature Awareness** - The ability to understand and recognize the system of names used in combat.

**Non aggressive Physiology** - Strategic body language used to de-escalate a potentially violent individual.

**Non telegraphic Movement** - Body mechanics or movements that do not inform an assailant of your intentions.

**Nuclear Ground Fighting Tools** - Specific grappling range tools designed to inflict immediate and irreversible damage. Some nuclear tools and tactics include: (1) Biting tactics; (2) Tearing tactics; (3) Crushing tactics; (4) Continuous Choking tactics; (5) Gouging techniques; (6) Raking tactics; (7) And all striking techniques.

## O

**OC (Oleoresin Capsicum, also known as pepper gas)** - A natural mixture of oil and cayenne pepper used as a self-defense spray. OC is an inflammatory agent that affects the assailant's mucus membranes (i.e. eyes, nose, throat, lungs).

**Offense** - The armed and unarmed means and methods of attacking a criminal assailant.

**Offensive Flow** - A progression of continuous offensive movements or actions designed to neutralize or terminate your adversary. (see Compound Attack).

**Offensive Range Manipulation (ORM)** - The strategic manipulation of ranges (armed or unarmed) for offensive purposes.

**Offensive Reaction Time (ORT)** - The elapsed time between target selection and target impaction.

**One-Hand Reloading** - The process of reloading a firearm with only one hand.

**One-Mindedness** - A state of deep concentration wherein you are free from all distractions (internal and external).

**Opposite Poles** - One of the ground fighting positions. The opposite pole position is assumed when both you and your assailant are facing opposite directions. This often occurs when sprawling against your adversary.

**Ornamental Techniques** - Techniques that are characterized as complex, inefficient, and or impractical for real combat situations.

## P

**Pain Tolerance** - Your ability to physically and psychologically withstand pain. 490

**Palming** - The strategic concealment of a knife or edged weapon behind the forearm. Also known as Knife Palming.

**Panic** - The second stage of fear; overpowering fear (see

Fright and Terror).

**Parry** - A defensive technique; a quick, forceful slap that redirects an assailant's linear attack.

**Pass** - A defensive technique used in knife fighting.

**Patience** - A combative attribute. The ability to endure and tolerate difficulty.

**Perception** - Interpretation of vital information acquired from your senses when faced with a potentially threatening situation.

**Perpendicular Mount** - One of the five general ground fighting positions. The perpendicular mount is established when you are lying on top of your adversary and both of your legs are on one side of his body.

**Philosophical Resolution** - The act of analyzing and answering various questions concerning the use of violence in defense of yourself and others.

**Philosophy** - One of the five aspects of CFA's mental component. A deep state of introspection whereby you methodically resolve critical questions concerning the use of force in defense of yourself or others.

**Physical Attributes** - The numerous physical qualities that enhance your combative skills and abilities.

**Physical Component** - One of the three vital components of the CFA system. The physical component includes the physical aspects of fighting including Physical Fitness, Weapon/Technique Mastery, and Combative Attributes (see Mental Component and Spiritual Component).

**Physical Conditioning** - (See Combative Fitness).

**Pistol** - A gun with a short barrel that can be held, aimed, and fired with one hand.

**Power** - A physical attribute of armed and unarmed combat. The amount of force you can generate when striking an anatomical target.

# GLOSSARY

**Physical Fitness** - (See Combative Fitness).

**Pitch** - One of the four components of the human voice. The relative highness or lowness of the voice.

**Poker Face** - A neutral and attentive facial expression that is used when de- escalating a hostile individual. The poker face prevents a hostile person from reading your intentions or feelings.

**Positioning** - The spatial relationship of the assailant to the assailed person in terms of target exposure, escape, angle of attack, and various other strategic considerations.

**Positions of Concealment** - Various objects or locations that permit you to temporarily hide from your adversary. Positions of Concealment are most commonly used to evade engagement with your assailant(s) and they permit you to attack with the element of surprise. Positions of Concealment include: trees, shrubbery, behind doors, the dark, walls, stairwells, under cars, large and tall objects, etc.

**Positions of Cover** - Any object or location that temporarily protects you from the assailant's gun fire. Some Positions of Cover include: large concrete utility poles, large rocks, thick trees, an engine block, corner of a building, concrete steps, etc.

**Post Traumatic Syndrome (PTS)** - A group of symptoms that may occur in the aftermath of a violent confrontation with a criminal assailant. Common symptoms of Post Traumatic Syndrome include denial, shock, fear, anger, severe depression, sleeping and eating disorders, societal withdrawal, and paranoia.

**Power Generator** - (See Anatomical Power Generators)

**Premise** - An axiom, concept, rule or any other valid reason to modify or go beyond that which has been established.

**Pressure Point** - A point on the body where a nerve lies

close to its surface and it is supported by bone or muscle mass.

**Probable Reaction Dynamics (PRD)** - the opponent's anticipated or predicted movements or actions during both armed and unarmed combat.

**Probe** -A offensive tool that tests the assailant's combative abilities.

**Proficiency Training** - A CFA training methodology requiring the practitioner to execute a specific body weapon, technique, maneuver or tactic over and over for a prescribed number or repetitions (see Conditioning Training and Street Training).

**Progressive Indirect Attack** -(see Indirect Attack).

**Proxemics** - The study of the nature and effect of man's personal space.

**Proximity** - The ability to maintain a strategically safe distance from a threatening individual.

**Pseudospeciation** - A combative attribute. The tendency to assign subhuman and inferior qualities to a threatening assailant.

**Psychological Conditioning** - The process of conditioning the mind for the horrors and rigors of real combat.

**Psycho/Emotional Training** - Combative training conducted when you're experiencing different types of emotional states.

**Psychomotor Domain** - This includes the physical skills and attributes necessary to execute a combative tool, technique or maneuver.

**Psychopath** - A person with an antisocial personality disorder, especially one manifested in aggressive, perverted, criminal, or amoral behavior.

**Pummel** - A flurry of full-speed, full-force strikes delivered from the mounted position.

GLOSSARY

**Punch** - A quick, forceful strike of the fists.

**Punching Range** - One of the three ranges of unarmed combat. Punching range is the mid range of unarmed combat from which the fighter uses his hands to strike his assailant. (see Kicking Range and Grappling Range)

**Punching Range Tools** - The various body weapons that are employed in the punching range of unarmed combat, including finger jabs, palm heel strikes, rear cross, knife hand strikes, horizontal and shovel hooks, uppercuts, and hammer fist strikes. (see Grappling Range Tools and Kicking Range Tools).

# Q

**Qualities of Combat** - (see Attributes of Combat).

**Quick Peek** - A technique which is executed from a position of cover by rapidly darting out a small portion of your head and one eye to quickly observe.

# R

**Range** - The spatial relationship between a fighter and a threatening assailant.

**Range Deficiency** - The inability to effectively fight and defend in all ranges (armed and unarmed) of combat.

**Range Manipulation** - A combative attribute. The strategic manipulation of combat ranges.

**Range Proficiency** - A combative attribute. The ability to effectively fight and defend in all ranges (armed and unarmed) of combat.

**Ranges of Armed Combat** - The various distances a fighter might physically engage with an assailant while involved in armed combat: including knives, bludgeons, projectiles, make-shift weapons, and firearms.)

**Ranges of Engagement** - (See Combat Ranges).

**Ranges of Unarmed Combat** - The three distances a fighter might physically engage with an assailant while involved in unarmed combat: kicking range, punching range, and grappling range.

**Reaction Dynamics** - The assailant's physical response to a particular tool, technique, or weapon after initial contact is made.

**Reaction Time** - The elapsed time between a stimulus and the response to that particular stimulus (see Offensive Reaction Time and Defensive Reaction Time).

**Rear Cross** - A straight punch delivered from the rear hand that crosses from right to left (if in a left stance) or left to right (if in a right stance).

**Rear Side** - The side of the body furthest from the assailant (see Lead Side).

**Reasonable Force** - That degree of force which is not excessive for a particular event and which is appropriate in protecting yourself or others.

**Refinement** - The strategic and methodical process of improving or perfecting.

**Repetition** - Performing a single movement, exercise, strike or action continuously for a specific period.

**Research** - A scientific investigation or inquiry.

**Rest Position** - A relaxed posture you assume (when holding a stick or bludgeon) during idle periods in class (i.e., talking to another students, receiving instructions, etc.).

**Reverberation Path** - The path at which your stick or bludgeon can bounce back at you.

**Revolver** - A handgun consisting of a cylinder that brings several chambers successively into line with the barrel of the gun.

**Rhythm** - Movements characterized by the natural ebb and flow of related elements.

**Right to Bear Arms** - A provision of the Second Amendment to the United States Constitution that prohibits our government from interfering with the right of the people to arm themselves.

**Rimfire** - A firearm cartridge which has its primer located around the rim of the case bottom.

**Round** - 1) A period of time. 2) A single unit of ammunition (see Cartridge).

# S

**Safe Room** - A strategic location in your residence where you and family members can escape from an intruder who has entered your home.

**Safety** - One of the three criteria for a CFA body weapon, technique, maneuver or tactic. It means the that the tool, technique, maneuver or tactic provides the least amount of danger and risk for the practitioner (see Efficiency and Effectiveness).

**Scissors Hold** - (see Guard).

**Secondary Hand** - A close quarter technique used in both knife and bludgeon fighting whereby you temporarily hold your assailant's weapon hand in place after you have employed a defensive maneuver.

**Secondary Weapons** - Various natural body weapons that are applied during armed combat.

**Selective Semantics** - The selection and utilization of strategic words to de-escalate a hostile person. Also known as Choice Words.

**Self-Awareness** - One of the three categories of CFA awareness. Knowing and understanding yourself. This includes aspects of yourself which may provoke criminal violence and which will promote a proper and strong reaction to an attack. (see Criminal Awareness and Situational Awareness.)

**Self-Confidence** - Having trust and faith in yourself.

**Self-Defense** - The act of defending yourself or one's family (also called Personal Protection or Self-Protection).

**Self-Enlightenment** - The state of knowing your capabilities, limitations, character traits, feelings, general attributes, and motivations (see Self- Awareness.)

**Semiautomatic Handgun** - (see Autoloader).

**Sensei** - Teacher.

**Set** - A term used to describe a grouping of repetitions.

**Setup Tool** - A tool used to throw the assailant off balance and/or open his defenses.

**Shadow Fighting** - A CFA training exercise used to develop and refine your tools, techniques, and attributes of armed and unarmed combat.

**Shielding Makeshift Weapon** - One of the four types of CFA makeshift weapons. Any object that can be used to effectively shield oneself from an assailant's attack (see also Distracting Makeshift Weapon, Cutting Makeshift Weapon, and Striking Makeshift Weapon.)

**Shooting Accuracy** - The ability to shoot a firearm with precision and exactness.

**Shot** - A package or wad of metal balls that vary in size and spread out as they travel away from the muzzle of a shot gun.

**Shotgun** - A single-or double-barreled, smooth-bore firearm used for firing shot or slugs at a relatively close distance.

**Shoulder Roll** - A defensive technique that rocks your body away from a punch in order to nullify its force.

# GLOSSARY

**Side Fall** - A firearm engagement technique which is executed from a kneeling position behind cover.

**Sifu** - (See Sensei.)

**Sight Alignment** - A component of marksmanship whereby you correctly align your dominant eye with both the front and rear sights of your firearm.

**Sights** - Various electronic, optical, and mechanical devices used to aim a firearm.

**Single Action** - A type of pistol action in which pulling the trigger will release the hammer.

**Single Attack** - One of the five conventional methods of attack. A method of attack whereby you deliver a solitary offensive strike. It may involve a series of discreet probes or one swift, powerful strike aimed at terminating the encounter. (See Compound Attack, Indirect Attack, Immobilization Attack, and Attack By Draw).

**Situational Awareness** - One of the three categories of CFA awareness. A state of being totally alert to your immediate surroundings, including people, places, objects, and actions. (see Criminal Awareness and Self-Awareness.)

**Skeletal Alignmen**t - The proper alignment or arrangement of your body. Skeletal Alignment maximizes the structural integrity of striking tools.

**Slash** - One of the two ways to cut someone with a knife or edged weapon. A quick, sweeping stroke of a knife (see Stab.)

**Slipping** - A defensive maneuver that permits you to avoid an assailant's linear blow without stepping out of range. Slipping can be accomplished by quickly snapping the head and upper torso sideways (right or left) to avoid the blow.

**Snap Back** - A defensive maneuver that permits you to avoid an assailant's linear and circular blow without stepping out of range. The snap back can be accomplished by quickly snapping the head backwards to avoid the assailant's blow.

**Somatotyping** - A method of classifying human body types or builds into three different categories: ectomorph, mesomorph, and endomorph.

**Speed** - A physical attribute of armed and unarmed combat. The rate or a measure of the rapid rate of motion.

**Spinning Kicks** - Kicks delivered with a spin of the body.

**Spinning Punches** - Punches delivered with a spin of the body.

**Spiritual Component** - One of the three vital components of the CFA system. The spiritual component includes the metaphysical issues and aspects of existence (see Physical Component and Mental Component).

**Sprawling** - A defensive technique in grappling range. The sprawl technique is accomplished by lowering your hips to the ground while simultaneously shooting both of your legs back.

**Square-Off** - To be face-to-face with a hostile or threatening assailant who is about to attack you.

**Squib Load** - A cartridge which develops less than normal velocity after the ignition of a cartridge.

**Stab** - One of the two ways to cut someone with a knife or edged weapon. A quick thrust made with a pointed weapon or implement, usually a knife. (see Slash.)

**Stable Terrain** - Terrain which is principally characterized as stationary, compact, dense, hard, flat, dry, or solid.

**Stance** - One of the many strategic postures that you assume prior to or during armed or unarmed combat.

**Stance Selection** - A combative attribute. The ability to instinctively select a stance appropriate for a particular combat situation.

**Standing Firearm Stance** - A strategic stance you assume when standing with a handgun.

**Step and Drag** - Strategic footwork used when standing on

# GLOSSARY

unstable terrain. **Stick Block** - A defensive technique that stops your assailant's stick strike.

**Stick Deflection** - A defensive technique that deflects and redirects your assailant's stick strike.

**Stick Twirl** - A dexterity exercise performed with either one or two sticks. **Stop-Hit** - A method of hitting the assailant before his tool reaches full extension.

**Stopping Power** - A firearm's ability to stop the assailant from continuing any further action.

**Strategic Leaning** - A defensive maneuver which permits you to evade a knife slash while remaining in range to counter.

**Strategic Positioning** - Tactically positioning yourself to either escape, move behind a barrier, or use a makeshift weapon.

**Strategy** - A carefully planned method of achieving your goal of engaging an assailant under advantageous conditions.

**Street Fight** - A spontaneous and violent confrontation between two or more individuals wherein no rules apply.

**Street Fighter** - An unorthodox combatant who has no formal training. His combative skills and tactics are usually developed in the street by the process of trial and error.

**Street Smarts** - Having the knowledge, skills and attitude necessary to avoid, defuse, confront, and neutralize both armed and unarmed assailants.

**Street Training** - A CFA training methodology requiring the practitioner to deliver explosive compound attacks for ten to twenty seconds (see Conditioning Training and Proficiency Training).

**Strength Training** - The process of developing muscular strength through systematic application of progressive resistance.

**Striking Accuracy** - The ability to strike your assailant with precision and exactness (this includes natural body weapons, bludgeons and some makeshift weapons).

**Striking Art** - A combat art that relies predominantly on striking techniques to neutralize or terminate a criminal attacker.

**Striking Tool** - 1) A natural body weapon that impacts with the assailant's anatomical target. 2) A hand-held implement that impacts with the assailant's anatomical target.

**Striking Makeshift Weapon** - One of the four types of CFA makeshift weapons. Any object that can be used to effectively strike a criminal assailant (see also Distracting Makeshift Weapon, Cutting Makeshift Weapon, and Shielding Makeshift Weapon.)

**Strong Side** - The strongest and most coordinated side of your body. Structure - A definite and organized pattern.

**Style** - The distinct manner in which a fighter executes or performs his combat skills.

**Stylistic Integration** - The purposeful and scientific collection of tools and techniques from various disciplines, which are strategically integrated and dramatically altered to meet three essential criteria: efficiency, effectiveness, and combative safety.

**System** - The unification of principles, philosophies, rules, strategies, methodologies, tools, and techniques or a particular method of combat.

# T

**Tactical Calming** - (See De-Escalation.)

**Tactic** - The skill of using the available means to achieve an end.

**Tactical Option Selection** - A combative attribute. The ability to select the appropriate tactical option for any particular self-defense situation.

**Tactile Sight** - A combative attribute. The ability to "see" through tactile contact with your assailant.

# GLOSSARY

**Takedowns** - Various grappling maneuvers designed to take your assailant down to the ground.

**Target Exploitation** - A combative attribute. The strategic maximization of your assailant's reaction dynamics during a fight. Target Exploitation can be applied in both armed and unarmed encounters.

**Target Impaction** - The successful striking of the appropriate anatomical target.

**Target Orientation** - A combative attribute. Having a workable knowledge of the assailant's anatomical targets. Target orientation is divided into five different categories: (1) Impact Targets - anatomical targets that can be struck with your natural body weapons; (2) Non-Impact Targets - anatomical targets that can be strangled, twisted, torn, crushed, clawed, gouged, broken, dislocated, or strategically manipulated; (3) Edged Weapon Targets - anatomical targets that can be punctured or slashed with a knife or edged weapon; (4) Bludgeon Targets - anatomical targets that can be struck with a stick or bludgeon; (5) Ballistic Targets - anatomical targets that can be shot by a firearm.

**Target Recognition** - The ability to immediately recognize appropriate anatomical targets during an emergency self-defense situation.

**Target Selection** - The process of mentally selecting the appropriate anatomical target for your self-defense situation. This is predicated on certain factors, including proper force response, assailant's positioning and range.

**Target Stare** - A form of telegraphing whereby you stare at the anatomical target you intend to strike.

**Target Zones** - The three areas which an assailant's anatomical targets are located. (See Zone One, Zone Two and Zone Three.)

**Technique** - A systematic procedure by which a task is accomplished.

**Telegraphic Cognizance** - A combative attribute. The ability to recognize both verbal and non-verbal signs of aggression or assault.

**Telegraphing** - Unintentionally making your intentions known to your adversary. Tempo - The speed or rate at which you speak.

**Terrain** - The type of surface that you are standing on. There are two classifications of terrain: stable and unstable. (See Stable Terrain and Unstable Terrain)

**Terrain Orientation** - A combative attribute. Having a working knowledge of the various types of environmental terrains and their advantages, dangers, and strategic limitations.

**Terror** - The third stage of fear; defined as overpowering fear (see Fright and Panic).

**Throw** - Grappling techniques designed to unbalance your assailant and lift him off the floor.

**Timing** - A physical and mental attribute or armed and unarmed combat. Your ability to execute a movement at the optimum moment.

**Tone** - The overall quality or character of your voice.

**Tool** - (See Body Weapon.)

**Traditional Style/System** - (See Traditional Martial Art.)

**Traditionalism** - The beliefs and principles of a traditional or classical martial art.

**Traditionalist** - One who subscribes to the principles and practices of traditional martial arts.

**Traditional Martial Arts** - Any martial art that fails to evolve and meet the demands and characteristics of the present time (see Karate and Kung-Fu).

**Training Drills** - The various exercises and drills aimed at perfecting combat skills, attributes, and tactics.

# GLOSSARY

**Training Methodologies** - Training procedures utilized in the CFA system.

**Training Zone** - The training zone (or target heart rate) is a safe and effective level of physical activity that produces cardiorespiratory fitness.

**Trapping** - Momentarily immobilizing or manipulating the assailant's limb or limbs in order to create an opening to attack.

**Trapping Range** - The distance between punching and grappling range in which trapping techniques are attempted.

**Traversing Skills** - Pivoting and twisting laterally. Traversing skills can be used for both armed and unarmed combat.

**Trigger Squeeze** - A component of marksmanship. Trigger Squeeze is achieved by squeezing the trigger of your firearm straight to the rear in a smooth and fluid manner without disturbing the sight alignment.

**Trouble Shooting Skills** - A combative attribute. The ability to immediately diagnose and solve problems when engaged with the adversary.

# U

**Unified Mind** - A mind which is free and clear of distractions and focused on the combative situation.

**Uniform Crime Report (UCR)** - A nationwide cooperative statistical compilation of the efforts and reports of 16,000 state and local law enforcement agencies that voluntarily report data on crime.

**Unstable Terrain** - Terrain which is characterized as mobile, uneven, flexible, slippery, wet, or rocky. (See Stable Terrain).

**Unstructured Modernist** - A martial artist who adheres to the abstract principles of combative formlessness.

**Use of Force Response** - A combative attribute. Selecting the appropriate level of force for a particular emergency self-defense situation.

# V

**V-Grip** - A strategically defensive grip used to defend against an edged weapon attack.

**Vertical Trapping** - Trapping techniques that are applied while standing face to face with your adversary. (See Immobilization Attack).

**Viciousness** - A combative attribute. Dangerously aggressive behavior. Victim - Any person who is the object of a particular crime.

**Visualization** - The purposeful formation of mental images and scenarios in the mind's eye.

**Visual Monitoring Points** - Specific points or locations on your assailant that you should look at during an emergency self-defense situation.

# W

**Warm-up** - A series of mild exercises, stretches, and movement designed to prepare you for more intense exercise.

**Weak Side** - The weakest and most uncoordinated side of your body.

**Weapon and Technique Mastery** - A component of CFA's physical component. The kinesthetic and psychomotor development of a weapon or combative technique.

**Weapon Capability** - An assailant's ability to use and attack with a particular weapon.

**Weapon Hierarchy Mastery** - Possessing the knowledge, skills and attitude necessary to master the complete hierarchy of combat weapons.

**Weapon Uniformity** - Gripping and/or drawing your hand-held weapon the same way every time.

# GLOSSARY

**Webbing** - The first phase of the Widow Maker Program. Webbing is a two hand strike delivered to the assailant's chin. It is called Webbing because your hands resemble a large web that wraps around the enemy's face.

**Western Boxing** - A Western combat sport that only employs punching-range tools.

**Widow Maker Program** – A CFA program specifically designed to teach the law abiding citizen how to use extreme force when faced with immediate threat of unlawful deadly criminal attack. The Widow Maker program is divided into two phases or methodologies: Webbing and Razing.

# Y

**Yell** - A loud and aggressive scream or shout used for various strategic reasons.

# Z

**Zero Beat** – One of the four beat classifications of the Widow Maker, Feral Fighting and Savage Street Fighting Programs. Zero beat strikes are full pressure techniques applied to a specific target until ruptures. They include gouging, crushing, biting, and choking techniques.

**Zone One** - Anatomical targets related to your senses, including the eyes, temple, nose, chin, and back of neck.

**Zone Three** - Anatomical targets related to your mobility, including thighs, knees, shins, and instep.

**Zone Two** - Anatomical targets related to your breathing, including front of neck, solar plexus, ribs, and groin.

**Zoning** - A defensive maneuver designed to negate your assailant's stick strike through strategic movement and precise timing. Zoning can be accomplished by either moving into the direction of your assailant's strike (before it generates significant force) or by moving completely out of his stick's arc.

# Suggested Reading & Viewing

**SUGGESTED READING (BOOKS):**

• Boxing Domination: A 21-Day Program to Psych-Out, Confuse, Frustrate, and Beat Your Opponent in Boxing and MMA

• Power Boxing Workout Secrets

• Speed Boxing Secrets: A 21-Day Program to Hitting Faster and Reacting Quicker in Boxing and Martial Arts

• Knife Fighting: A Step-by-Step Guide to Practical Knife Fighting for Self-Defense

• The 10 Best Knife Fighting Techniques

• The 10 Best Power Punches: For Boxing, Martial Arts, MMA and Self-Defense

• The 10 Best Mental Toughness Exercises

• The 10 Best Ways to Defeat Multiple Attackers

• The 10 Best Ways to Develop Your Killer Instinct:

• The 10 Best Bar Fighting Moves: Down and Dirty Fighting Techniques to Save Your Ass When Things Get Ugly

• The 10 Best Sucker Punch Tricks

• Survival Weapons: A User's Guide to the Best Self-Defense Weapons for Any Dangerous Situation

• Knockout: The Ultimate Guide to Sucker Punching

• The 10 Best Kicking Techniques

• The 10 Best Stick Fighting Techniques

• Cane Fighting: The Authoritative Guide to Using the Cane or Walking Stick for Self-Defense

• The Heavy Bag Bible: 3 Best-Selling Heavy Bag Books In One Massive Collection

• Double End Bag Workout

• The 10 Best Things To Do When Held At Gunpoint

• The 10 Best Ways To Defeat Multiple Attackers

• The 10 Best Things To Do During a Mass Shooting

# 1001 STREET FIGHTING SECRETS

- The 10 Best Stick Fighting Techniques
- Bruce Lee's 5 Methods of Attack
- The Widow Maker Compendium (Books 1-3)
- Heavy Bag Workout
- Heavy Bag Combinations
- Invincible: Mental Toughness Techniques for the Street, Battlefield and Playing Field
- Unleash Hell
- Feral Fighting
- Savage Street Fighting
- Stand and Deliver
- The Widow Maker Program
- Maximum Damage
- Kubotan Power
- The Complete Body Opponent Bag Book
- Self-Defense Tips & Tricks
- Heavy Bag Training: Boxing, Mixed Martial Arts & Self-Defense
- Out of the Cage: A Complete Guide to Beating a Mixed Martial Artist on the Street
- Gun Safety: For Home Defense and Concealed Carry
- Warrior Wisdom: Inspiring Ideas from the World's Greatest Warriors
- Ground War: How to Destroy a Grappler in a Street Fight
- War Craft: Street Fighting Tactics of the War Machine
- War Machine: How to Transform Yourself into a Vicious and Deadly Street Fighter
- The Bigger They Are, The Harder They Fall: How to Defeat a Larger & Stronger Adversary in a Street Fight
- First Strike: Mastering the Preemptive Strike for Street Combat
- When Seconds Count: Everyone Guide to Self Defense
- Killer Instinct: Unarmed Combat for Street Survival
- Street Lethal: Unarmed Urban Combat

**SUGGESTED VIEWING (VIDEOS):**

- Combat Energy Drills
- Punching Mitts: Drills & Workout Routines
- Judge, Jury & Executioner
- Pepper Spray: A Video Guide to Using Pepper Spray for Self Defense
- Pressure Points: The Science of Striking Vital Targets
- Sparring: Tips: Tips, Tactics & Techniques to Dominate Your Opponent
- Kubotans & Yawaras: A Quick & Dirty Guide
- Submission Fighting for the Street (Volume 1)
- Submission Fighting for the Street (Volume 2)
- Submission Fighting for the Street (Volume 3)
- Medicine Ball Workout (Volume 1)
- Medicine Ball Workout (Volume 2)
- Double End Bag Training
- Heavy Bag Training
- Power Punching
- Speed Training for Street Fighting (Volume 1): Visual Reflexes
- Speed Training for Street Fighting (Volume 2): Tactile Reflexes
- Speed Training for Street Fighting (Volume 3): Recognition & Auditory Reflexes
- Speed Training for Street Fighting (Volume 4): Movement Speed
- Wrist Locks For The Street (Volume 1)
- Wrist Locks For The Street (Volume 2)
- Choke Out
- Body Opponent Bag Training
- War Machine II
- Sneak Peek
- Armed to the Teeth (Volume 1)
- Armed to the Teeth (Volume 2)

# 1001 STREET FIGHTING SECRETS

- Defend or Die
- Escape Master
- In Your Face
- Engage With Rage
- First Strike
- Ground Fighting in The Streets
- Batter Up
- Under The Gun
- Street Stick Fighting
- Use It or Lose It
- Rat Packed
- ,Ground Pounders
- Control & Conquer (Volume 1)
- Control & Conquer (Volume 2)
- Savage Street Fighting: Tactical Savagery As A Last Resort
- The WidowMaker Program: Maximum Punishment for Extreme Situations
- Feral Fighting Program: Level 2 WidowMaker
- War Blade Program: A Complete Guide to Tactical Knife Fighting

# About Sammy Franco

With over 35 years of experience, Sammy Franco is one of the world's foremost authorities on armed and unarmed self-defense. Highly regarded as a leading innovator in combat sciences, Mr. Franco was one of the premier pioneers in the field of "reality-based" self-defense and martial arts instruction.

Sammy Franco is perhaps best known as the founder and creator of Contemporary Fighting Arts (CFA), a state-of-the-art offensive- based combat system that is specifically designed for real-world self-defense. CFA is a sophisticated and practical system of self-defense, designed specifically to provide efficient and effective methods to avoid, defuse, confront, and neutralize both armed and unarmed attackers.

Sammy Franco has frequently been featured in martial art magazines, newspapers, and appeared on numerous radio and television programs. Mr. Franco has also authored numerous books, magazine articles, and editorials, and has developed a popular library of instructional videos.

Sammy Franco's experience and credibility in the combat sciences is unequaled. One of his many accomplishments in this field includes the fact that he has earned the ranking of a Law Enforcement Master Instructor, and has designed, implemented, and taught officer survival training to the United States Border Patrol (USBP). He has instructed members of the US Secret Service, Military Special Forces, Washington DC Police Department, Montgomery County, Maryland Deputy Sheriffs, and the US Library of Congress Police. Sammy Franco is also a member of the prestigious International Law

Enforcement Educators and Trainers Association (ILEETA) as well as the American Society of Law Enforcement Trainers (ASLET) and he is listed in the "Who's Who Director of Law Enforcement Instructors."

Sammy Franco is a nationally certified Law Enforcement Instructor in the following curricula: PR-24 Side-Handle Baton, Police Arrest and Control Procedures, Police Personal Weapons Tactics, Police Power Handcuffing Methods, Police Oleoresin Capsicum Aerosol Training (OCAT), Police Weapon Retention and Disarming Methods, Police Edged Weapon Countermeasures and "Use of Force" Assessment and Response Methods.

Mr. Franco holds a Bachelor of Arts degree in Criminal Justice from the University of Maryland. He is a regularly featured speaker at a number of professional conferences and conducts dynamic and enlightening seminars on numerous aspects of self-defense and combat training.

On a personal level, Sammy Franco is an animal lover, who will go to great lengths to assist and rescue animals. Throughout the years, he's rescued everything from turkey vultures to goats. However, his most treasured moments are always spent with his beloved German Shepherd dogs.

For more information about Mr. Franco, you can visit his website at: ContemporaryFightingArts.com

www.ingramcontent.com/pod-product-compliance
Lightning Source LLC
Chambersburg PA
CBHW071644160426
43195CB00012B/1350